Medieval Midrash

The Brill Reference Library of Judaism

VOLUME 52

The titles published in this series are listed at *brill.com/brlj*

Medieval Midrash

The House for Inspired Innovation

By

Bernard H. Mehlman
Seth M. Limmer

BRILL

LEIDEN | BOSTON

Cover Illustration: King Solomon, famed for his justice and wisdom is depicted seating on a throne shaped like the roof of a building. At his feet there are several animals, most likely hinting at his ability to converse with the animal kingdom. Coburg, Germany, c. 1396 (British Library Add MS 19776, f. 54v). Public Domain as stated 6 April 2016: http://britishlibrary.typepad.co.uk/asian-and-african/2014/11/digital-hebrew-trea-sures-from-the-british-library-collections.html.

Library of Congress Cataloging-in-Publication Data

Names: Mehlman, Bernard H., 1937– author. | Limmer, Seth M., author.
Title: Medieval Midrash : the house for inspired innovation / by Bernard H. Mehlman, Seth M. Limmer.
Description: Leiden ; Boston : Brill, [2017] | Series: The Brill reference library of Judaism, ISSN 1571-5000 ; volume 52 | Includes bibliographical references and index.
Identifiers: LCCN 2016032416 (print) | LCCN 2016033052 (ebook) | ISBN 9789004331327 (hardback : alk. paper) | ISBN 9789004331334 (E-book)
Subjects: LCSH: Midrash—History and criticism.
Classification: LCC BM514 .M44 2017 (print) | LCC BM514 (ebook) | DDC 296.1/406—dc23
LC record available at https://lccn.loc.gov/2016032416

Typeface for the Latin, Greek, and Cyrillic scripts: "Brill". See and download: brill.com/brill-typeface.

ISSN 1571-5000
ISBN 978-90-04-33132-7 (hardback)
ISBN 978-90-04-33133-4 (e-book)

Copyright 2017 by Koninklijke Brill NV, Leiden, The Netherlands.
Koninklijke Brill NV incorporates the imprints Brill, Brill Hes & De Graaf, Brill Nijhoff, Brill Rodopi and Hotei Publishing.
This book is printed on acid-free paper and produced in a sustainable manner.

והיינו דאמר רבי:
הרבה תורה למדתי מרבותי, ומחביריי יותר מהם, ומתלמידי יותר מכולן.

This is what Rabbi Judah the Nasi Said:
Much Torah have I learned from my teachers,
from my *chevruta* more than them,
and from my students most of all.
—Babylonian Talmud, *Makkot* 10a

in memory of
Fay Barban Mehlman
and in honor of her future
Sarah, Jillian, Aliza Fay, Ari, Jules, Theo and Henry

in love
Molly Morse Limmer
Rosey Esther and Lily Benjamin Limmer

∴

Contents

Preface

What We Don't Know about Minor Midrash

Going to School: Hebrew Union College-Jewish Institute of Religion

For many years, we simply accepted the appellation "Minor Midrash," although we knew the cheaply-reprinted pages filled with miniscule type belied the presence of literary masterpieces. Together—first as professor and student, and later as Ḥevruta—we sat and studied stories about the eagle and the raven in *The Alphabet of Ben Sira* and about the valor of Judith in *Ma'aseh Yehudit.* We were impressed at how the interpretive devices of classical Midrash combined with the style of the medieval *novellae* to create remarkable Jewish narratives. Even while we enjoyed encountering these pieces, we remained frustrated by the scarcity of information available about many of these texts: outside of a few German sentences in Adolph Jellinek's introductions, or some sparse Hebrew from J. D. Eisenstein, almost nothing seemed to be known about the origins of these Jewish treasures.[1]

Regardless, we continued to study. What began as an elective course at HUC-JIR transcended those boundaries. Texts like *Ma'aseh Avraham Avinu, Midrash Petirat Aharon*, and *Midrash Jonah* became staples of adult education classes. In the thirty idle minutes before Shabbat services, a volume of *Beit Midrasch* would be brought off the shelf, and the craftsmanship of any tale would be a delight in preparation for Shabbat. A few years ago, we moved more formally from classroom discussions to the work of analysis; between early morning Midrash classes and afternoon Homiletics sessions, we bunkered down in the library and immersed ourselves in the study of these smaller midrashim. We originally set out to create a critical translation of all the pieces connected to holidays, hoping together they might prove to be a helpful volume. Then, when a tour through Purim material introduced us to *Abba Gurion*, we encountered extended pieces about King Solomon.

Solomon, the paradigmatic figure of wisdom for the Bible and the Rabbis alike, proved illuminating to us as well in this field of later Midrashim.

---

1 We should note that further, albeit limited, writing about the field is found in *The Jewish Encyclopedia* of 1901 as well as, *Introduction to the Talmud and Midrash* by H. L. Strack and Günter Stemberger, [1996]. More recent scholarship is scattered in: *The Hebrew Story in the Middle Ages* by Joseph Dan, [1974], *Rabbinic Fantasies* by David Stern & Mark Mirsky, [1990], *The Hebrew Folktale* by Eli Yassif, [1999], *Folktales of the Jews*, 3 vols., edited by Daniel Ben Amos [Philadelphia, Jewish Publication Society of America], 2006.

Translating the tales of Solomon began to open up new horizons regarding these so-called Minor Midrashim; questions we long held—and those students asked year after year—finally found some answers. Many of those questions, because of the paucity of research in the field, had long been unanswerable, even though they were the classical journalistic ones: **Who** crafted these? **What** exactly are they? **When** were they written? **Where** do these legends originate? **Why** did anyone create these tales? **How** did they come to be part of the genre we call "Midrash"? Sitting in the library between classes, we began to realize that—yet again—King Solomon was the key figure opening up a new generation to a long-hidden series of truths.

Finding Sage Questions Wise Answers

Throughout Jewish tradition—and extending beyond it as well—King Solomon is the paradigm of wisdom. His mastery of Jewish tradition and worldly ways allowed him to answer almost every inquiry. Witness this remarkable exchange from *Midrash on Proverbs*, a relatively late text that comes from the close of the Rabbinic Period:[2]

> Another interpretation: *But where can wisdom be found?* (Job 28:12)—this refers to the Queen of Sheba, who heard of King Solomon's wisdom. She said, "I'll go see whether or not he is wise." Whence [do we learn] that she had heard of Solomon's wisdom? From the verse, *The queen of Sheba heard of Solomon's fame, through the name of the Lord, and she came to test him with hard questions* (1 Kings 10:1). What are *hard questions*? Rabbi Jeremiah said, "Parables."
>
> She asked him: "Are you the Solomon, about whom and whose wisdom I have heard?"
>
> He answered, "Yes."
>
> She said, " If I ask you something will you answer me?"
>
> He answered, *For the Lord grants wisdom; Knowledge and discernment are by His decree* (Prov 2:6).
>
> She said, "Seven leave and nine enter, two pour and one drinks?"
>
> He said, "Surely [this means] seven days of menstrual [unfitness] leave, then nine months of pregnancy enter; two breasts pour [forth milk] and the infant drinks."

---

2 Burton L. Visotsky sets forth the dating parameters for *Midrash Mishle*. He argues for a date of redaction in the 9th century CE and "...the latest possible date of compilation—the beginning of the eleventh century." Burton L. Visotsky, *The Midrash on Proverbs*, (New Haven and London: Yale University Press), 1992, pp. 9–10.

She said, "You are a great sage, but if I ask you another question will you answer me?"

He replied: *For the Lord grants wisdom* (Prov 2:6).

She said, "Who is the woman who says to her son, 'Your father is my father, your grandfather is my husband, you are my son and I am your sister?'"

He replied: "Surely [these are the] daughters of Lot who say to their sons, 'Your father is my father, your grandfather is my husband, you are my son and I am your sister.'"

She gave him another test. She brought in girls and boys, all the same appearance, all of the same height, all clothed the same. Then she said to him, "Distinguish the boys from the girls."

He immediately motioned to his eunuchs, to fetch some parched grain and nuts and began passing them out. The boys unashamedly stuffed their tunics full, but the girls, being modest, [only] filled their kerchiefs. He then told the queen, "These are the boys, and those are the girls." She said, "My son, you are a great sage."

Then she gave him one more test. She brought circumcised and uncircumcised men before him, all of them of the same appearance, all of the same height, all clothed the same. Then she said to him, "Distinguish between the circumcised and the uncircumcised."

He motioned immediately to the High Priest to open the Ark of the Covenant. The circumcised among them bowed from their waist, and their faces were filled with the radiance of the Shekinah, while the uncircumcised among them fell on their faces. Solomon said to her, "These are the circumcised, and those are the uncircumcised."

"How did you know?" she asked.

He explained: "From [the case of] Balaam for it is written: *Who beholds visions from the Almighty, [prostrate, but with eyes unveiled]* [Numbers 24:4]? Had he not fallen, he would not have seen anything.

If you do not want to learn from Balaam, come and learn from [the case of] Job. When his three friends came to comfort him, he said to them, *But I, like you have a mind. I fall not beneath you.* [Job 12:3]—[what is meant is] "I do not fall down like you do."[3]

3   Ibid. pp. 18–19. See also, Solomon Buber, ed., *Midrash Mishle*, 1. Additional riddles posed by the Queen of Sheba to King Solomon are to be found in the *Targum* literature, in *Targum Sheni* to Esth. 1:3; and in the late midrash: *Midrash Ḥefez*, published by Solomon Schechter, *The Folk-Lore Journal*, 1890,1, (London: Whiting and Co.), 349–358. These legends, in compact

The riddles of the Queen of Sheba delight Solomon and the reader. Solomon attributes his wisdom in discovering their solutions to God; however, only half of the riddles are unraveled through Scripture, while the other two are solved through savvy and smarts. Furthermore, even those answers based on the Bible have nothing to do with the Bible: this extended passage comes not to explicate a verse about Solomon or the section relating his relationship with the Queen of Sheba.[4] Instead, Solomon literally comes to embody the sixth verse of the second chapter of Proverbs: he is the one who proves God grants enlightenment.

Light is, in some ways, the perfect metaphor to illustrate our conjecture. Before we study the history of Jewish literature, let us look at the world of pictorial art. From 1892–94, Claude Monet painted 30 canvases studying the effect of light on the façade of the Cathedral at Rouen. In his lifetime, these impressionist works caused outrage in the art world schooled on classic forms: *Why*? Seventy years later, of course, this series was rightly understood as a masterpiece. In 1969, Roy Lichtenstein created a triptych, *Rouen Cathedral Set V*, during the beginnings of the "Pop" art movement in America: he rendered Monet's famous façade in the Ben-Day dots with which he would forever be associated. Monet studied light, which led him to a sort of mass-production of the outside of a Cathedral; Lichtenstein studied mass production, and relied on Monet's canvasses of Rouen as his object. Both artists, each with his own impetus and objective, created visual pieces that in part represent a building in Northern France. While one could argue they are both "artists" who are creating "paintings," Monet is clearly an Impressionist while Lichtenstein embodies the approach of Pop Art. They share a common field of technique and practice, but are distinguished by both method and their distinct cultural *sitz-im-leben*. Each employed the visual arts to shine a light on a particular aspect of their contemporary reality.

The making of Midrash has likewise been a practice that is rooted in its past while building a new arc of artistry to the future. Just as *Leviticus Rabbah* differs from the earlier *Genesis Rabbah* in certain styles and structures, so to—it seems—does every age that innovates through Midrash adapt inherited forms to address current cultural issues. Thus we see above, in *Midrash on Proverbs*, Solomon has an answer to every question: some come from Scripture, some

---

form, were also collected by Louis Ginzberg, *The Legends of the Jews* (Philadelphia: The Jewish Publication Society of America) 1947, vol. IV, 142–149.

4   See 1 Kings 10, which this Midrash does not deem it necessary to cite. It is important to note here that the Rabbis of the Talmud claim no such Queen of Sheba ever existed. See, *BT, Baba Batra* 15b.

come from the application of his own intelligence. What a perfect creative parallel, it seems, to this category we used to call "Minor Midrash": much of it seems based on Rabbinic Midrash, yet the genre so obviously overflows those literary banks as it floods into new literary territory. In the course of our studies, King Solomon (and the authors who fashioned new narratives around his inherited figure) helped us find answers to the many questions we had about the identity, form, function, and creation of this remarkable literary grouping. We hope you find his lessons illuminating as well.

The Little We Do Know about Minor Midrash

The genre often called "Minor Midrash" is one of the less explored territories of the vast landscape of Jewish Literature. This material attracts little attention in either the academic or the popular press, and has remained relatively unexamined in the fields of both literary history and rabbinic thought. The great *Jewish Encyclopedia* of 1904, in its article, "Midrashim, Smaller," begins with the vague description, "A number of midrashim exist which are smaller in size and generally later in date."[5] The article provides brief narrative outlines [and limited manuscript information copied directly from original publications] regarding eighteen of the larger texts; however little is said about the entirety of the genre. In fact, the article ends with the following summation:

> The more recent collections of small midrashim mentioned in this article and in MIDRASH HAGGADAH are the following: [a bibliographical list ensues]. In these collections, especially in Jellinek's "Bet ha-Midrash," there are many small midrashim, either edited there for the first time or reprinted, as well as a number of works under other names, a discussion of which belongs rather to an article on mystic literature.[6]

Outside of providing abstracts of a limited set of these "Midrashim, Smaller," the *Jewish Encyclopedia* is silent when it comes to any descriptive details of the genre (saving, perhaps, the insight they might not even belong to any genre called "midrash"). This relative silence is hardly outperformed by the *Encyclopaedia Judaica* of 1971, which relegates its words on "Smaller Midrashim" to a supplementary volume. Twentieth Century academia basically avoided any

---

5   Isidore Singer, ed., The *Jewish Encyclopedia*, (New York: Funk and Wagnall) 1904, Hereafter, *JE*.
    J. Theodor, "Midrashim, Smaller," vol., VIII: 572.

6   *JE.*, VIII: 575–6.

evaluation of this area as a cohesive field of study, and opted rather to opine upon or illuminate particular works from the catalogue. However, because these analyses were often done in a vacuum, they often came to conclusions that would have been—to anyone who read the texts themselves—difficult to obtain. Witness this example from Meyer Waxman's four-volume *History of Jewish Literature*:

> The Jews, like the Arabs and all the people of the East, loved the pointed proverb, the apothegm, which is the best vehicle of wisdom, and not only delights but instructs as well. "The Proverbs of Solomon," and other wisdom books are the best examples of such predilection for this form of literature.[7]

First and foremost, the reader of "The Proverbs of Solomon"—which we will examine in full herein—would immediately know that while that work might delight certain audiences, it hardly seems to provide any sort of instruction. However, it is not only of issue that Waxman, in his 1930 opus, misrepresents the contents of one "minor midrash". It is also important that this text, and the entire genre of which it is a part, receives no attention in the section of Waxman's work dedicated to Midrash. Instead, Waxman only makes mention of "The Proverbs of Solomon" in his section on the literature of Jews in Arab lands: to him, these "minor midrashim" seem not to qualify as midrash at all.

One year after Waxman published his thorough, if faulted, *History of Jewish Literature*, Hermann Strack brought to light his masterpiece of academia, *Introduction to the Talmud and Midrash*. However, despite the great erudition and thorough scholarship of Strack's work, he has nothing at all to say about "Minor Midrash". His twenty-third chapter, "Midrash Collections," only lists the anthologies of Jellinek, Horowitz, Wertheimer, Grünhut and Eisenstein, yet makes no commentary on the material therein. In fact, it took a biblical generation until the academy paid specific attention to this genre, when John T. Townsend published his article "Minor Midrashim" in 1976.[8] In his introductory material, however, Townsend plays down any opportunity to see these works as cohesive: he opens with the disclaimer, "[these] midrashic collections form a labyrinth which few can navigate. Even those relatively familiar with the literature sometimes have trouble." Ultimately, Townsend concludes

---

7   Meyer Waxman, *History of Jewish Literature* (New York: Bloch Publishing Co.), *1930*, I:*459*.

8   John T. Townsend, "Minor Midrashim" in Lawrence V. Berman, et.al., *Bibliographic Essays in Medieval Jewish Studies: The Study of Judaism Vol. II.*, (New York: Anti-Defamation League of B'nai Brith by KTAV Publishing Co. Inc.), 1976.

that, "The midrashim called 'minor' or 'small' do not comprise any particular genre of midrash although the vast majority of them are haggadic . . . the term *midrashim*, when used of these collections, is applied very broadly."[9] After arriving at this conclusion, Townsend provides a familiar bibliography of the extant collections. The real novelty of Townsend's contribution is an alphabet-ized "index of titles" of all the texts he knows from the aforementioned col-lections. However, even this relatively complete index offers no information about content, form, origin, date, or any other such helpful information regard-ing any of the Midrashic texts themselves.

By the second printing of Günter Stemberger's continuation of Hermann Strack's groundbreaking *Introduction to the Talmud and Midrash*[10] in 1932, we see the addition of a helpful new chapter. Part Three: Midrashim, VIII "Compilations; Commentaries known as 'Midrash'" ends with section (11) "Other Midrashim and related works". Here, Stemberger lists the same five major collections as Strack and Townsend before him, and adds to the list a few Yemenite Midrashim, as well as *Torah Shelemah* and A. B. Hyman's indexi-cal *Torah Haketubah Vehamessurah*. When it comes to evaluating these "other midrashim and related works," however, Stemberger offers no comment; he only adds the reference, "For additional bibliography, see J. T. Townsend in *The Study of Judaism* . . .".

This brings to date the complete story of the incomplete story the academy has been able to tell about the field of Jewish literature often called "Minor Midrash".

However, there is much more to learn about these remarkable texts enclosed within the covers of those volumes Stemberger describes as "Other Midrashim and related works". While each of those individual texts likely merits its own assessment—and noting that many of the more substantive pieces have, in fact, received such thorough individuated examination—it is our conjecture that more can be said about this category of Jewish literature often labeled "minor midrash". Moving towards a more thorough understanding of this little-explored genre is the goal of our current work.

The specifics and limitations of our understandings of "minor midrash" will be explored in the subsequent study. In the first section we will evaluate, the question of the Canon of this genre, and then move on to an examination of the historical *sitz im leben* in which these Midrashim were created. We will

9   Ibid., p. 333.

10   Hermann L. Strack, *Introduction to the Talmud and the Midrash*, (Philadelphia: Jewish Publications Society), 1931. We note especially that this is an earlier version of the work before G. Stemberger entered the editorial process.

discover how the canon was formed through the far-flung scholarly endeavors of the *Wissenschaft des Judentums* period, and arrive at a more precise name for the genre, Medieval Midrash, when we conclude these texts were written in the days following the close of the rabbinic period and prior to the dawn of the Enlightenment. Furthermore, we will see how Jewish life astride the great medieval empires of Byzantine and Roman Catholic Christianity and Islam helped feed the formation of this emerging Jewish literary style.

Our second section consists of annotated translation of the six Medieval Midrashim whose literary focus is the figure of King Solomon. We will move from the relatively rabbinic *Midrash Al Yithallel* through to the thoroughly imperial, "The Throne and Hippodrome of King Solomon, Peace be upon Him!" in order both to know Medieval Midrash through closer contact with six individual texts, and also to evaluate the evolution of this genre through the similarities and differences through which those same six texts address the figure of Solomon. By the end of our second major section, we will have seen how Medieval Midrash builds upon Rabbinic traditions and Midrashic styles, yet pushes those past old boundaries by absorbing literary tropes and motifs of the Medieval world, from historical realia through folktales to the traditions of neighboring religions.

Our final section attempts to state what we can know, and what remains elusive, about the field of Medieval Midrash. In addition to a full conclusion, we will conjecture that, in the main, these Medieval Midrashim were written by Jews of the assimilated, educated, and cosmopolitan mercantile class. We will even allow ourselves the supposition that a desire to connect their ancient Jewish traditions and forms to the popular culture of their day was, in large part, the motivation for creating this new literary arena we call Medieval Midrash.

Acknowledgements

This book could not have come into being had it not been for the Hebrew Union College-Jewish Institute of Religion. Not only were we both trained and ordained by this College-Institute, but the programs of our Seminary were seminal in almost every phase of our relationship. We first came to know each other during the Corkin-Smith Summer Internship Program, which brought Seth to work with Bernard in Boston. Soon after, Bernard began teaching his "Minor Midrash" elective on the New York campus of HUC-JIR, and Seth was a student the first semester it was offered. Bernard's continued tenure on the New York faculty allowed the two of us Thursday mornings to study together amidst the wisdom collected in the people and volumes of the Klau Library. There, we were greeted every week by the interest, attention, and support of the chief librarian, Dr. Yoram Bitton. Dr. Bitton went beyond providing us with the space and materials necessary for our project; he was often a third mind at the brainstorming table, and an intrepid tracker of arcane data. Our work is immeasurably more valuable because of his input.

This book was born in New York City, but it came to life in three other locations as well: Armonk, New York; Boston, Massachusetts; and Chicago, Illinois. In each of these places, our congregations granted us support to pursue our scholarly passions. We are indebted to them: Temple Israel of Boston, Congregation B'nai Yisrael of Armonk, and Chicago Sinai Congregation. In particular, the people who helped plan out meetings, explain our absences, help us with photocopies, and provide other needed assistance deserve special mention: Susan Misselbeck, Alicia Allison and DeeDee Dukes.

As we explain later, we would never have imagined the midrashim about King Solomon to have been deserving of book-length treatment. We owe a sincere debt of gratitude to Dr. Alan Avery-Peck of The College of the Holy Cross, Worcester, Massachusetts, for his constant encouragement and confidence that our work was worthy of a more expansive treatment. His personal interest in the project and his realization that the world needed to learn the story of Medieval Midrashim helped us transform a series of translations into what we hope will serve as an introduction to this long-overlooked subject.

Many of our friends have also provided critical assistance along our way. Dr. Gabriel E. Padawer provided us with a needed translation of Barukh Asher Perles' early article when we lacked time to render its German into readable English. We are proud to feature his worthy translation as an appendix to this volume. Dr. Edmond Murad served as our resident Arabic expert, to whom we turned for matters of culture and translation, great and small. Dr. Murad also served as one of the readers of our manuscript, and provided innumerable illustrating comments along the way. Ms. Ann Abrams, Librarian at Temple Israel of Boston, assisted us with the acquisition of printed resources for our work and aided us in locating several sources for our work; Dr. James Rosenbloom, Judaica Librarian, Brandeis University, Waltham, MA, provided us with his wise counsel and help; Rabbi Liz P. G. Hirsch, in the waning hours preceding her ordination, did a great deal of work for us on the textual history of our Solomon Midrashim, and in particular tried to help us identify the elusive Rabbi Joel. Furthermore, while all mistakes in this volume are our own, we are thankful to have had so many able and acute minds help us in the work of proofreading: Rabbi Seth Bernstein, Rabbi Gustav Buchdahl, Beverly Huckins, Rabbi Elizabeth Miller, and Patrick Morse. Stephen G. Limmer, with whom we disagree about the usage of the "Oxford comma," is nonetheless to be commended for reading each draft with an eye as exacting as his heart is filled with love and pride.

Lastly, a word about the family to whom we dedicate this volume:

Seth Limmer: Ever since Molly Morse Limmer said, "I Do," under the chuppah—with Bernard officiating, of course!—she has likewise provided me indescribable support in every way possible, including these scholarly endeavors that not only brought me into Manhattan on a weekly basis or to Boston for the occasional retreat, but also required many hours of sequestered work around the home. Molly, I hope you know you are as admired and appreciated as you are loved. As for Lily Benjamin and Rosey Esther [the younger one has to come first sometime!], I love you both for who you are. But it doesn't hurt that you both love the reading, imagination, humor, intelligence and wordplay that I find so delightful in the art of Midrash.

Bernard Mehlman: This book is a culmination of decades of study of the midrashic genre we name Medieval Midrash in this volume. In 1977, I translated and annotated *Midrash Jonah*. Metaphorically, I crossed the sea in that, my first journey into the world of Medieval Midrash. I visited many ports, explored many cultural byways, and learned the breadth of the scope of the world of the midrashim I studied. This journey would never have commenced without the early encouragement of my mother, Fay Barban Mehlman, who implanted within me a sense of self-worth; my late wife, Emily whose love nourished me; and our grandchildren who are the hope for our future.

PART 1

The World of Medieval Midrash

∴

Canon: The House of Midrash

Adolph Jellinek: *Beit HaMidrash*

The story of Minor Midrashim begins in Moravia. On June 26, 1821, in the little town of Drslavice (that today covers little more than three miles square), Adolph Jellinek was born into a traditional Jewish home. As he grew he began to learn in the yeshiva of Moshe Katz in Prossnitz, and by 1838 travelled 287 kilometers to study in Prague. Not long after his 21st birthday, Jellinek stepped fully outside the walls of the yeshiva when he enrolled at the University of Leipzig and registered in courses in philology and philosophy. While the former fed his scholarly pursuits, the latter became of more immediate importance when in 1845 he was appointed preacher in the New Synagogue in Leipzig (that had been established under the guidance of Zacharias Frankel). It was in this role that Jellinek first found fame as a leading preacher of his day.

Midrash was key to Jellinek's success: aggadah was integrated into his sermons, which often synthesized midrashic literature with contemporary matters. Adolph Kurrein, a Bohemian Rabbi from Teplitz, described Jellinek as "the greatest, most gifted Jewish preacher that modern Judaism has produced." He continues his praise, "[Jellinek's] thorough knowledge of the Midrash, and the startling uses he made of it in his sermons, distinguish him especially from his contemporaries and predecessors."[11] Jellinek's pursuit of material exceeded the normal canon of Rabbinic aggadah: by 1853 he had collected no fewer than 60 midrashic texts, many previously unknown, some taken from manuscripts and others from existing printed editions. These he published in four volumes under the Hebrew title, בית המדרש, a pun on the traditional name for the yeshiva that could be rendered "The House of Midrash".[12] Placing these texts in a literal "House of Midrash" was a clear indicator of their genre: on the frontispiece of the volume, Jellinek described the narratives within as "different Minor Midrashim and various precious statements" of the Jewish people.[13] And the foundation Jellinek laid in Leipzig was just a beginning: even being called to Vienna to be the preacher at the *Leopoldstädter Tempel* (and later the *Steinstettengasse Tempel*) didn't quench Jellinek's thirst for more midrashic material: by 1878 the fifth and sixth volumes of the *Beit HaMidrasch*

---

11   *Jewish Encyclopedia*, vol. VII, 93.

12   Ironically, when Jellinek founded an academy in Vienna in 1862, he called it—what else?—*Beit HaMidrasch*.

13   Here we translate קטנים as "minor", as opposed the literal "smaller".

were printed.[14] In the end, the complete volumes amass 99 texts Jellinek calls "midrashim", many of which were unknown to the masses in his day, and perhaps in previous generations as well.

Adolph Jellinek's life work and publications earned him the deepest respect of those who likewise plowed the fields of midrash: Judah David Eisenstein claimed, "Jellinek built the foundation of the study of Minor Midrashim."[15] There is little doubt that without Jellinek, a proper house for the study of Minor Midrashim might not have been built (or at least would not have stood so soundly for over 150 years.) If Jellinek is the primary architect of this work, he nonetheless was born into a European climate perfectly suited for such academic pursuits. And while a thorough intellectual history of the 19th century lies outside the scope of the present work, it is nonetheless necessary to undertake a partial investigation of that epoch in order to trace the origins and development of Minor Midrashim as a genre, and then later a canon.

The *Bibliotheca Hebraica*: Cataloguing Hebrew Literature

Johann Christoph Wolf, a Christian professor of Oriental languages and literature, is perhaps an unlikely catalyst for the study of Minor Midrashim. However, when in 1712 he was appointed to become professor at the Hamburg gymnasium, his interests in Jewish literature serendipitously led him into contact with the Oppenheimer collection of manuscripts: the sum of those addends was the publication—in four volumes between the years 1715 to 1733—of his Latin *Bibliotheca Hebraica*. This far-reaching study contained a wide variety of subjects: a chronology of biblical history according to the Hebrew dating and Gregorian calendars [1:27ff.]; a catalogue of biblical Hebrew names with their Latinate equivalents [1:30ff.]; a lengthy listing of Hebrew authors and sages [1:41–1161]; and an entire second volume dealing with subject matter such as Bible, Kabbalah, Talmud and "anonymous scriptural texts" [11]. The impact of Wolf's scholarship (and thousands of pages of print) was so significant that Joseph Jacobs, president of the Jewish Historical Society of England, once claimed "the knowledge of Christendom about the Talmud was for nearly a

---

14   Adolph Jellinek, *Sammlung Kleiner Midraschim u. vermischter Abhandlungen aus der älteren jüdischen Literatur, Nach Handschriften u. Drückwerken gesammelt u. nebst Einleitungen herausgegeben*, I–IV, Leipzig 1853–57, V, VI, Vienna 1872, 1877.

15   Julius D. Eisenstein, "Introduction," *Oẓar Midrashim: A Library of Two Hundred Minor Midrashim*, 2 vols., [Eisenstein: New York], 1915.

century and a half derived from Wolf's statements."[16] *Bibliotheca Hebraica*, however, altered the lives of two men in particular who would help shape the study of Minor Midrashim. The second of those, whom we will encounter again, is Moritz Steinschneider, who catalogued the Hebrew manuscripts of Oxford's Bodleian Library with nearly constant reference to Wolf. More importantly, Wolf's work helped shape the life and direction of Leopold Zunz.

Leopold Zunz: Creating a Scientific Study of Judaism

Leopold Zunz, known in Yiddish as Yom Tov Lipmann, was born in Detmold, Germany, in 1794 to Talmudic scholar Immanuel Menachem Zunz and Hendel Behrens (daughter of Dov Beer, the famed crafter of parables known as the Maggid of Mezeritch). Despite a frail constitution, young Leopold survived the infant death of his twin sister, and likewise outlived all his other brothers and sisters. Being the only child left to his parents, he began to study Talmud with his father even before he turned five. His father's death that same year led Leopold packing for the Samson School and Wolfenbüttel, where he immediately attracted the attention of his instructors due to his remarkable aptitude in both mathematics and trouble-making. Before becoming bar mitzvah, Zunz demonstrated his affection for creative Hebrew literature, when he authored in the Holy Tongue a scathing satire sparing neither students nor teachers. That work was soon sacrificed in flames as part of the author's forced "atonement" for his misdeeds.

At the same tender age that Leopold Zunz was experimenting with writing, he also began to immerse himself in reading. Learning to integrate the annals of Jewish history with the chronicles of Christendom, Zunz, in the summer of 1811, read David Gans' 1592 masterpiece, *Tzemach David*. More importantly for our undertaking, it was during that same season that Zunz first read Wolf's *Bibliotheca Hebraica*. We can only imagine how profound an impact these two books made on Zunz' obviously curious and cataloguing mind. But in the following six years, likely pursuing a passion ignited by Wolf's work, Zunz undertook the arduous work of copying manuscripts (such as *Sefer HaMa'alot* of Shem Tob ibn Falaquera), and studying Turkish and Palestinian manuscripts shared with him by the Polish Jew, David ben Aaron. In December 1817, Zunz set to writing an essay about what he had learned to that point in the course of his studies.

---

16   *JE*, vol. XII, 549.

*"Etwas über die Rabbinische Literatur; Nebst Nachrichten über ein Altes bis
Jetzt Ungedrücktes Hebräisches Werk,"* today known as *On Rabbinic Literature,*
was published in 1818.[17] No lesser sage than Emil G. Hirsch remarked that "this
little book marks an epoch in the history of modern Jewish scholarship."[18] *On
Rabbinic Literature* bears the obvious influence of *Bibliotheca Hebraica*'s com-
mensurate catalogue: only one exposed to the wide array of Jewish authors
and subjects as captured by Wolf could argue—as Zunz does—that Jewish
literature must be understood more widely than according to the traditional
strictures of the biblical and Rabbinic canon. But Gans' guidance is also present in *On Rabbinic Literature*: Zunz asserts that the widest-ranging knowledge
of Jewish literature leads us to understand how Jewish history is an inseparable
part of the history of human culture in general, and the humanities in particular. Zunz's genius was evident, however, in how he synthesized the teachings of
these two authors (and perhaps the various academic tendencies of his time)
into a clearly-stated plan of work and outlined program for the "scientific"
study of Judaism. *Wissenschaft,* German for "science", appears in the first sentence of his essay; by its third paragraph, Zunz is lamenting the richness and
wonder absent from any understanding of "later productions of the Hebrew
nation" because no *Wissenchaft* has been applied to their examination. By the
end of the work, Zunz calls for a complete scientific examination of Jewish
texts and traditions, a *Wissenschaft des Judentums*:

> In accord with the rigor with which we recommend that science be
> treated generally, we have in the present case attempted to set the task
> which this work is to fulfill: to present in this critique not only the theo-
> retical skeleton but also to impart all in pleasing form such that nothing,
> not even what is veiled, is overlooked. But beyond this desired complete-
> ness we hope that our effort will beckon others, more worthy of the sub-
> ject and closer to the goal, to follow in our footsteps.[19]

---

17   Leopold Zunz, "Etwas über die Rabbinische Literatur," *Gesammelte Schriften* (Berlin,
      1875), vol. 1, 1–31. Translated by A. Schwartz, in Paul Mendes-Flohr, *The Jew in the Modern
      World: A Documentary History (Second Edition)*, (New York, Oxford University Press), 1995,
      221–230.
         It should be noted that the shorter translated title fails to capture the original impor-
      tance attached to the lessons learned from "newly recovered Hebrew manuscripts and
      works".

18   *JE,* vol. XII, 700.

19   Zunz, *On Rabbinic Literature,* 228.

A formal society, a generation, and a movement did follow in Zunz's footsteps. The scientific study of Judaism caught hold of the hearts and minds of a wide circle of thinkers in Germany and beyond. The opportunity to unite the age-old teachings of Jewish tradition with the spirit and method of the modern academy led to a tremendous outpouring of scholarly activity. Especially as the Enlightenment began to shine its light on the Jews of Western Europe, a Jewish elite emerged that sought to study its particular past through the "universal" tools provided by universities. This circle of scholars influenced not only the Jewish community of their time, but also has continued to shape European and American Judaism up to the present day. Perhaps the greatest testament to the enduring legacy of Zunz's 1818 essay is this encomium, written over a century later by Isaac Elbogen, professor at the *Hochschule fur die Wissenschaft des Judentums* in Berlin:

> Despite the ardent study of Talmud in the 18th century, the whole sub-ject matter fell into such disrepute that Zunz in 1818 considered Jewish Literature as having come to a full stop. He even wanted to record it as dead. To him be the credit due that now after a lapse of a hundred years, it has entered on an undreamed of expansion and deepening, and has become a source of power in the life of Jewry at large. In his small work "Etwas zur Rabbinischen Literatur", Zunz, for the first time, disclosed the many-sidedness of its contents and directed the attention of the student to the manifoldness and valuableness of its contents. He demonstrated its importance for world culture. The investigation of Jewish literature, has, by its zealous work of half a century, revived the dead.[20]

Leopold Zunz's first publication altered the course of the history of Jewish culture. *On Rabbinic Literature* also altered our understanding of Jewish lit-erature. Zunz proposed a powerful question, which Jellinek and his cohorts lined up to answer through their very efforts: "Proceeding now to the literary products of the Jewish people, the first question to be asked is: What do they include?"[21] Zunz answered that question later in his life as he travelled to the British Museum, the Bodleian Library at Oxford, the Palintina Library in Parma to see the De Rossi collection, and Paris to examine nearly 500 manuscripts and 100 rare books: he made it clear that Jewish Literature included stories,

---

20   Isaac Elbogen, "Destruction or Construction," *Hebrew Union College Annual* I, 1924, 634.
21   Zunz, *On Rabbinic Literature*, 223. Here we should note that Jellinek used the phrase "*ältern jüdischen Literatur*" in his German subtitle of *Beit HaMidrasch*.

legends, poetry and philosophy written in the Hebrew tongue.[22] Despite the
prodigious scholarship he undertook in his 92 years of living, he was never able
to finish the task he set forth in 1818: a survey and analysis of the large stock of
Jewish writings hidden away in the world's libraries and rare book collections.
In his own words, "much, however, yet remains to be done."[23]

Moritz Steinschneider: Defining Jewish Literature

There is not a straight line from Zunz to Jellinek that tells the complete story of
Minor Midrashim. There was a wide circle of scholars engaged, not just in the
general project of *Wissenschaft des Judentums*, but also in the specific arena of
midrashic literature. While we will not capture the scope of that entire circle,
certain key figures in the field whose contributions—both before and after
Jellinek published *Bet HaMidrasch*—are worthy of note.

The first of these scholars was five years older than Jellinek and traveled
a remarkably similar path: the Moravian Moritz Steinschneider was born
in Prossnitz, studied there at Yeshiva (although at the one led by Nehemia
Trebitsch), and later went to Prague and then Leipzig for university education. It was in Leipzig that Steinschneider met Zunz, who provided encouragement and direction to the young student. Zunz called for "completeness", and
Steinschneider seems to have complied: in his bibliography, over 1400 items
bear his name and testify to his remarkable literary output. His predominant
interest was in the relationship between the Jewish world and other cultures;
Steinschneider realized early on that a preliminary requirement of any such
work was a thorough and academic catalogue of all its extant manuscripts and
printed materials. Early in his career, Steinschneider was called by the chief
librarian of the Bodleian Library to catalogue all of its printed Hebrew books
published before 1732;[24] after the eight years of the continued publication of

---

22   *JE*, vol. XII, 704.

23   Zunz, *On Rabbinic Literature*, 227.

24   Here the full story, with all its serendipity, seems worth telling:

     During his early years in Berlin, Steinschneider's friendly relations with the book
dealer, A. Asher, for whom he had prepared a catalogue during his student days, proved to
be of great benefit to Asher. In 1847, upon the death of the great book collector Heimann
J. Michael, Asher acquired the valuable Hebrew library brought together by that well-to-
do scholarly Hamburg merchant. After the greater part of the catalogue of the famous
collection had been printed, Asher asked Steinschneider to go to Hamburg in order to
compare the Michael manuscripts with the printed list. In ten or eleven days he went
through the more than eight hundred manuscripts, checked them with the catalogue and

the *Catalogus Librorum Hebraeorum in Bibliotheca Bodleiana*, Steinschneider had catalogued the *entire* collection (including many manuscripts), arranged them according to author (when known), and provided a scholarly apparatus of references to other work and citations in secondary sources.[25] The work garnered such distinction that its author was soon called upon to catalogue libraries in Leiden (1858), Munich (1875), Hamburg (1878) and Berlin (1878). The *Catalogus* is so impressive it continues to be reprinted, with the latest edition being published in 1998.[26]

The *Catalogus* as a response to Zunz is of immense importance to the study of Minor Midrashim: we see the emergence of an inclination to uncover a complete collection. Steinschneider was perhaps the preeminent—but certainly not the only—scholar to travel all over the continent scouring shelves and analyzing manuscripts to be able to define this emerging field of *Rabbinische Literatur*. The excitement aroused by *Wissenschaft des Judentums* led to a vast reclamation of Jewish literature: no longer were the Geonim of the Academies or the Rabbis of the Yeshivot the ones who determined the set list of proper Jewish texts. Sensing that the literature of the Jews was as scattered as that people had been throughout history, scholars initiated a veritable age of exploration to discover not far-away lands to colonize, but long-forgotten texts to reclaim as Jewish tradition. Steinschneider himself seems to have blazed this trail: he not only convinced chief librarian, Badinel, to include Oxford manuscripts in the *Catalogus*, he also convinced Badinel to augment the library's collection and advised him on the purchase prices for newly discovered manuscripts. In searching far and wide for anything that might be considered

---

collected the material for his index of authors which was added to it. In this supplement he incorporated innumerable corrections and amplifications. In order to gain some valuable material for his scholarly plans, he worked through several nights, after an exhausting day's work, making the best of this opportunity in every way. He had to devote the last few days of his stay in Hamburg to a quick checking of the printed books. It was perhaps this experience that showed Asher the energy and unusual capacity for work of the young scholar and caused him to recommend Steinschneider to Dr. Badinel, the chief librarian of the great Bodleian Library at Oxford, for the preparation of a new catalogue of the printed Hebrew books of this, then the greatest existing, collection of Hebraica.
Alexander Marx, "Morris Steinschneider," *Essays in Jewish Biography* (Philadelphia: Jewish Publication Society) 1947, 132–133.

25   Including, as we saw above, the work of Johann Christoph Wolf.

26   In addition to the wonderful extended biography of Steinschneider in Marx, *Essays in Jewish Biography*, information about Steinschneider comes from Menahem Schmelzer and Pelger, Gregor, "Steinschneider, Moritz," *Encyclopaedia Judaica*, ed. Michael Berenbaum and Skolnik, Fred, Second Edition, Vol. 19 (Detroit: Macmillan Reference USA), 2007, 197–199.

Rabbinische Literatur, Steinschneider set the precedent for leaving no stone unturned in uncovering lost Jewish manuscripts.

It was not only the texts themselves that were determining what was up for consideration as "Jewish Literature": secondary literature was of equal importance. Here, too, Steinschneider played a leading role. From his early days in Berlin, Steinschneider was interested in what he called (and later submitted to the University as a proposed course of study) "Jewish Contributions to the Literary History of the Middle Ages."[27] He studied philology (German, Sanskrit, and the classical languages); the history of Greek, Oriental and Ethiopic literature; and the works of the Church Fathers as well.[28] In 1845 he was provided with a unique opportunity: he was asked to write the definitive article on "Jewish Literature" for the *General Encyclopedia of the Sciences and Arts*.[29] Steinschneider couldn't refuse the chance to show the whole magnificent development of Jewish literature, and define the field according to *Wissenschaft* principles. The article, originally meant to cover two pages, took three years to write and was published in full despite growing to seven times its planned size. Subsequently, Steinschneider continued to expand his work, ultimately publishing in 1857 (in English) *Jewish Literature from the Eighth to the Eighteenth Century: with an Introduction on Talmud and Midrash*. In one title—and the *magnum opus* subsumed by it—Steinschneider rejected the traditional focus of Jewish Literature by relegating the Talmud to a mere introduction. For Steinschneider, classical Rabbinics were but a prelude to the great literary flowering of the Jewish imagination.

Solomon Buber: Bringing Old Texts to Light

To many, Solomon Buber is best known as the paternal grandfather to the preeminent philosopher Martin Buber.[30] But in the field of Midrash, the elder takes senior standing: over the course of his career, Solomon Buber published

---

27   Marx, "Steinschneider", 147.

28   Ibid., 120.

29   Ibid., 147. Ultimately, over the course of 80 years, 167 large quarto volumes of this *Encyclopedia* were printed, without finishing the alphabet. It is also worth noting that Steinschneider was only approached to author this essay after Zunz turned down the undertaking.

30   The spelling of Solomon Buber's name varies. It appears as both Solomon and Salomon. The JE, vol. III, 409 entry, lists him as Solomon, however, the photograph of Buber with a space for his signature, which appears on p. 410 of the same volume, shows that he used Salomon as the spelling of his name. The spelling, Solomon, appears throughout this text.

sixteen significant critical editions of midrashic work that were previously outside the standard Rabbinic canon. Such a career of academia was unlikely for Buber, born in 1827 into a well-known and relatively well-off family in Lemberg. His father Isaiah Abraham not only taught him Jewish philosophy, but was able to handpick tutors to educate Solomon at the highest level in the fields of Bible and Talmud. Despite his high level of learning and interest in independent research, Buber pursued a commercial career and rose to high levels in the banking world.

Buber became a man of means, which served not to interrupt but rather to feed his scholarly ambitions.[31] His first publication in 1868 was a previously unpublished (and widely unknown) collection of sermons for special Sabbaths and festivals that was attributed to Rav Kahana. Buber based his work on a manuscript first discovered by Zunz, and purportedly dated to Egypt in 1565. *Pesiqta deRav Kahana* is remarkable not just for the commitment to publish a rare manuscript for a new audience; in the edition, Buber in part created and certainly set the standard for a "critical edition", an academic evaluation of a text along the lines called for by *Wissenschaft des Judentums*. In this work, his very first publication,

> He adopted a certain system to which he has consistently adhered. For a determination of the meaning of the text he avails himself of all accessible manuscripts and printed works—and everything is accessible to him, as he spares no expense in obtaining copies of manuscripts and the rarest printed editions; he conscientiously records the various readings in foot-notes, and he bestows special care, chiefly in the older Midrashim, on the correction and explanation of words in the text borrowed from the Greek and the Latin. In the introductions, which almost assume the proportions of independent works (the introduction to the Tanhuma embraces 212 pages octavo), everything that bears upon the history of the work under consideration is discussed, and a compilation is given of the authors or works cited by the Midrash or serving as sources for it, and those which in turn have drawn upon the Midrash. His work is distinguished by thoroughness, and reveals his synthetic ability as well as the vast extent of his reading.[32]

---

31   His financial position allowed him not only to publish his own works, but also to send
     people to libraries to copy manuscripts for his critical editions.
32   H. Brody, "Buber, Solomon," in *JE*, vol. III, 410.

Solomon Buber distinguished himself in the field of Midrash solely with his continued commitment to creating a critical apparatus for understanding individual works. Of equal, if not greater importance, to our current study are the individual works on which Buber chose to focus. Some of his works, like the *Midrasch Tanḥuma* of 1885, were critical editions of texts that had already been in print for centuries.[33] In that same decade, however, Buber brought to light in a new fashion manuscripts never before printed. In 1883 and 1885 he printed two volumes entitled *Liqqutim*, or "collections". The first of these, *Liqqutim mi-Midrash Abkir*, was Buber's attempt to reconstruct a text known in the 16th century (and then lost) from excerpts of the *Yalqut* and manuscript fragments.[34] The second was another so-called "collection", this time an attempt to reconstruct a smaller midrashic collection on Deuteronomy, published under the title *Liqqutim mi-Midrash Devarim Zuta*. As we will soon see, Buber was beginning a trend of collecting tales and texts under the title *Liqqutim*.

First, however, we must note Buber's singular publication of 1886, the *Sammlung agadischer Commentare zum Buche Ester.*[35] This work gathered existing midrashic traditions about the Book of Esther that seemed related in style and content, and combined them into a single text, with full commentary and critical apparatus regarding textual origins and variants. Beyond the magnitude of this accomplishment, the story of the texts Buber gathered is especially salient. He relied on four major sources: his own *Midrash Leqaḥ Tov*, *Midrash Panim Aḥerim A* and *B*, and *Midrash Abba Gorion*. The last two of these texts Buber discovered in an important place: Jellinek's *Beit HaMidrasch*. Combining that printed material with an Oxford Manuscript (*Midrash Panim Aḥerim A*) and his own previous publication, Buber was bringing not only dusty old manuscripts to life, but combining them with the academic advances of his peers to create new territory in the field of Midrash. Importantly, Buber saw Jellinek's work not as an end-in-itself, but as a *beginning* of the important *Wissenschaft* process of reclaiming the full texts of Jewish Literature. Through his *Liqqutim*, Solomon Buber followed in the footsteps not just of the grand

---

33   The text of *Tanḥuma* was first printed in Constantinople in 1520/22; Buber's two-volume edition was a critical edition that focused on a series of manuscripts from the Bodleian collection, primarily Neubauer 154. Strack/Stemberger, *Introduction*, p. 303. Likewise, *Aggadat Bereshit, Midrash Tehillim, Midrash Mishle, Leqaḥ Tov*, and *Midrash Samuel* were critical editions Buber prepared of texts published in the 16th century. Strack/Stemberger, *Introduction*, 312, 323, 324, 356, 358.

34   Strack/Stemberger, *Introduction*, 313.

35   Salomon Buber, *Sammlung agadischer Commentare zum Buche Ester*, (Vilna: Wittwe et Gebrüder Romm), 1886. It should be noted that *Sammlung* is German for the Hebrew *Liqqut*, or "collection".

project called for by Zunz, but also walked down the particular path blazed by Jellinek of reclaiming Minor Midrashim.

Solomon Buber was hardly alone in continuing the project that truly commenced with Jellinek's publication of *Beit HaMidrasch*. In 1881, Chaim M. Horowitz continued the trend with the publication of his own anthology of aggadah, called *Agadat Aggadot, o Qovets Midrashim Qetanim*.[36] Solomon Aaron Wertheimer, who made his way from Bratslav to Jerusalem, collected Hebrew books and manuscripts with a particular focus on Sephardic material and Geniza fragments. Between the years 1893–1897, Wertheimer created four volumes, or houses, that held his collection including 25 midrashim published for the first time: *Battei Midrashot*.[37] The following year, Wertheimer demonstrated his dedication to bringing rare manuscripts to life with his critical edition of *Midrash Ḥaserot wi-Yetirot*,[38] which collated three Egyptian manuscripts with a primary text from Parma. That same year, 1898, Hungarian rabbi Eleazar Grünhut published his own collection, choosing the "collection" nomenclature of Buber over the "house" metaphor of Jellinek: Grünhut's *Sefer HaLiqqutim* gathered a wide array of midrashic material in six volumes.[39] Not to be outdone, Wertheimer continued to publish, this time choosing the language of the "collections", as his *Leket Midrashim* appeared in 1903. He ultimately published a "treasury" of this material, *Otzar Midrashim*, in two parts in the years 1913–1914.

Nearly thirty years passed between Jellinek's first volume of *Beit HaMidrasch* and the initial publications of Buber's "collections". The subsequent three decades, as we have seen, were not nearly as quiet. Buber, Horowitz, Grünhut and Wertheimer continued to expand the field of Minor Midrashim both in terms of discovering new material and in the arena of printing newer versions (sometimes with criticism and commentary) of known material. Furthermore, August Karl Wünsche demonstrated his commitment to the growing area of academic focus by translating five volumes of these Minor Midrashim into

---

36   Chaim M. Horowitz, Sammlung Kleiner Midraschim, I, (Berlin: Druck von Itzkowski), 1881. Also Bibliotheca Haggadica, 2 fascicles, (Berlin: Slobotski Publishing House), 1881; Sammlung zehn kleiner, nach Zahlen geordneter Midraschim, (Frankfurt am Main: Slobotski Publishing House), 1888.

37   S. A. Wertheimer, *Kleinere Midraschim*, Jerusalem, 4 fascicles, (to) 1897. Also *Leket Midrashim*, Jerusalem, 1903, *Otzar Midrashim*, 2 fascicles, Jerusalem 1913, 14.

38   *Midrash Ḥaserot wi-Yetirot*, "... deals with the words of the Bible that are written with or without *mater lectionis*." Strack/Stemberger, 343.

39   Eleazar Grünhut, *Sammlung alterer Midraschim u. wissenschaftlicher Abhandlungen*, 6 fascicles, Jerusalem 1898–1903.

German for his 1907 *Aus Israels Lehrhallen*.[40] It is important to note not only the increase in the interest surrounding Minor Midrashim, but also the influence of Jellinek on this next generation of scholars.[41] That all of them were familiar with *Beit haMidrasch* is evident from their reprinting at least one of Jellinek's texts (although perhaps in a different recension), as can be seen in the following table:

TABLE 1

Text	Jellinek	Buber	Horowitz	Wertheimer	Grünhut
Aggadat Bereshit	Beit Hamidrasch 4	Aggadat Bereshit			
Megillat Antiochus	Beit Hamidrasch 6			Battei Midrash 1	
Midrash Al Yithallel	Beit Hamidrasch 6				Liqqutim 1
Midrash Eser Galuyot	Beit Hamidrasch 4				Liqqutim 3
Midrash Jonah	Beit Hamidrasch 1		Qovets		
Midrash Maaseh Torah	Beit Hamidrasch 2			Battei Midrash 2	Liqqutim 3
Midrash Petirat Moshe	Beit Hamidrasch 6			Battei Midrash 1	
Midrash Psalms	Beit Hamidrasch 5	Midrash Psalms			
Midrash Temurah	Beit Hamidrasch 1			Battei Midrash 2	
Otiot Rabbi Aqiba	Beit Hamidrasch 3			Battei Midrash 2	
Sefer Zerubbabel	Beit Hamidrasch 2			Battei Midrash 2	

---

40   See, John T. Townsend, for this bibliographic material.

41   It should also be noted that Buber was influential as well: Wertheimer published *Midrash Tanhuma* in *Battei Midrash* vol. 1, and Buber provided commentary and notes to certain editions of Grünhut's *Likkutim*.

The fifty years of scholarly activity that followed the publication of *Beit HaMidrasch* testify to the amazing influence of Adolph Jellinek on both his contemporaries and the burgeoning field of Minor Midrashim.

Judah David Eisenstein: Creation of a Canon

It is strange that a successful coat manufacturer seems to have brought the productive era of the publication and dispersal of Minor Midrashim to its conclusion. It was most assuredly *not* the intent of Judah David Eisenstein to end such a productive era; it is only in hindsight that we can see the capstone he provided to the project initiated by Jellinek. Eisenstein was born in Mezirech one year after the first volumes of *Beit HaMidrasch* were published. By 1872 he had immigrated to the United States, where he met with success (like many of his coreligionists) in the garment industry. He retained his love for the Hebrew language and Jewish traditions, and in 1880 founded *Shoḥarei Sefat Ever*, [Lovers of the Hebrew Language], a society—the first in America—dedicated to Hebrew literature. In 1891, he brought together his Polish roots with his religious convictions and newfound patriotism with a Yiddish and Hebrew translation of the United States Constitution.

Yet it is for his prodigious anthologies that Eisenstein remains a well-known figure to this day. He published eleven collections—most of them multivolume sets—each of which bore the title, *Oẓar*, or "Treasury". His *Oẓar Dinim u-Minhagim*, a 1917 compendium of laws and customs, continues to be printed as a valuable resource for rulings on real-life religious concerns. *Oẓar Yisrael*, an encyclopedia in ten volumes published between 1907 and 1913, remains perhaps Eisenstein's most ambitious work. In other treasuries Eisenstein amassed sermons, travel literature, aphorisms, disputations, and moral teachings.

The two volumes of *Otzar Midrashim*, published in 1915, however, are the most significant contribution Eisenstein made to the study of Minor Midrashim. Eisenstein makes clear in the first line of his introduction the impetus for the books, "I thought it was an urgent matter to gather all the Minor Midrashim scattered throughout our literature into a single edition."[42] The reasons for such a gathering are evident in the "Bibliography" that precedes the introduction: a list of "different midrashic collections and studies regarding midrash" that librarian Zalman Kotler counted in his collection in Odessa included 56 separate works. Not surprisingly, the authors we encountered earlier are responsible for most of the books included in this bibliography. And

---

42   Eisenstein, *Oẓar Midrashim*, x. Our translation from the Hebrew.

Eisenstein is clear about the intellectual history he inherits. "The first to begin to write about these midrashim in a scientific fashion was Yom Tov Lippman Zunz," Eisenstein explains as he sets out to illustrate the establishment of this field of study.

"The preacher, Dr. Aaron [sic] Jellinek, who loved all that was good and beautiful in our literature, strove to gather many midrashim—from different printings and from manuscripts—into six rooms of his *House of Midrash . . .* after him came Rabbi Eleazer Grünhut and Rabbi Solomon Aaron Wertheimer and others in *Liqqutim* along these lines."[43] Once he explains the contributions of his predecessors, Eisenstein moves on to his critique of their efforts:

> A noticeable void in their books is that, because they took what they had at hand and printed them without any order, through this path the different midrashim that spoke to a single topic were scattered; for we find a midrash about Abraham *Avinu* or King Solomon, or about Heaven and Hell, in one volume, and a different recension in a second volume, and a third recension in a third volume, even when they are in the same book! And it isn't necessary to mention that they are scattered throughout various collections, and it is difficult to find a sought after matter because there is no chronology in their books, and neither do we find order or chronology.
>
> In this book there is a correct and straightforward order for we have gathered and edited all the midrashim in alphabetical order according to their title or subject matter, whichever is more determining of their primary content. Furthermore, all the different recensions or topics belonging to a particular specialty will here appear together.[44]

Otzar Midrashim is a pinnacle work of *Wissenschaft des Judentums*. In it, Eisenstein makes a scientific study of the myriad midrashic texts uncovered during the previous generation of scientific discovery. In all, two hundred named Midrashim appear in this incredibly well-indexed *Treasury*. In addition to the bibliography and helpful introduction, Eisenstein also provides an accessible essay on "Preachers and Preaching," [perhaps here better rendered "Midrash-making and Midrash-makers".] In the back there are some helpful notes about odd terms and other parochial matters. In the main text itself, Eisenstein

---

43   Ibid., pp. x–xi. It should also be noted that on the frontispiece of the book, Eisenstein clearly states that in his volumes are amassed "all the midrashim published" in Jellinek's six volumes, along with texts "from other collections".

44   Ibid., xi.

follows Buber slightly more than Jellinek: while Eisenstein's critical apparatus is far from the most developed, he nonetheless provides a helpful—yet
brief—introduction to most of the selections, and commentary to many of
them as well. The stated goal was thoroughness, and the two volumes seem to
meet Zunz's prescribed goal of "desired completeness".

If *Oẓar Midrashim* is the fulfillment of *Wissenschaft* hopes for the study of
minor midrash, we must accept that term in both of its meanings: amongst all
the various collections, it is no doubt the apogee of completeness and order;
simultaneously, and perhaps ineluctably, it is also the true end of the scientific
search for Minor Midrashim. In this fashion, Eisenstein's work is the realization of the goal of *Rabbinische Literatur*: it is the complete collection, the clear
canon. This is an important moment, one which perhaps Eisenstein understood he was making. *Oẓar Midrashim* has not one, but three titles, in three different languages. If in the Hebrew, Eisenstein kept with his continued habit of
naming his books treasuries, he took a different tack with the Latin and English
names he gave to his collection: *Bibliotheca Midraschica* and "A Library of Two
Hundred Minor Midrashim," respectively. This was no "collection" or "house"
he was putting together: Eisenstein was establishing a library.

Coda: The Closing of the *Wissenschaft* Circle

Eisenstein labeled his work a library, and the self-awareness here is critical.
Eisenstein seems not just aware, but actually hopeful, that he is defining once
and for all what belongs in the canon of Minor Midrashim. Finding fault with
previous anthologizers, he not only improves upon their scattershot methods,
but intentionally selects a different name for his work. Eisenstein is trying to be
different, to add something new to the study of Minor Midrashim. We call this
transformational moment "canonization":

> In this sense, canonization is defined in terms of the element added to
> the text—sacredness, authority, value, prestige, and so on. However,
> canonization should be viewed not only as the addition of status to an
> accepted meaning but as a transformation of meaning itself.[45]

The publication of *Oẓar Midrashim* in effect made the library of Minor
Midrashim a sealed canon. For previous scholars, the canon of Minor

---

45   Moshe Halberthal, *People of the Book: Canon, Meaning, and Authority*, (Cambridge:
      Harvard University Press), 1997, 11.

Midrashim was an open canon: providing ample and agreed-upon room to argue for the inclusion of new texts and discoveries into the burgeoning collections of this field. While it might be going too far to say that Eisenstein sought to seal the canon of Minor Midrashim—to eliminate the possibility of any new discoveries, additions, or subtractions—his publication more or less had that immediate effect. Insomuch as "canonization affects not only the status of a text but the way it is perceived and read,"[46] *Oẓar Midrashim* predominantly became the last and most authoritative word on the official list of this genre: to be in Eisenstein's pages was to be a legitimate, accepted, minor midrash.

It is a matter of speculation as to why, effectively for an entire century, *Otzar Midrashim* remains the official *Bibliotheca Midraschica*. But it is clearly the case that Eisenstein's work still remains the last real word on the subject. The authoritative guide to Rabbinic literature of Hermann L. Strack and Günter Stemberger ends its section on "Compilations; Commentaries known as 'Midrash,'" with a list of the collections where they can be found. Temporally, Eisenstein is last on this list.[47] John T. Townsend's authoritative list, "Minor Midrashim," is preceded by a short essay, which likewise lists Eisenstein as the last of the anthologizers.[48] The closest potential parallels are in Moses Gaster's 1924 publication of his Hebrew and English *The Exempla of the Rabbis: Being a collection of Exempla, Apologues and Tales culled from Hebrew Manuscripts and Rare Hebrew Books*.[49] Aside from the obvious fact this collection makes no claim to be part of the canon of Minor Midrashim, it also—due to an admitted eclecticism (and unconfessed scholarly shortcomings) on Gaster's part—never found widespread academic acceptance.[50]

2006 saw the publication of *The Literature of the Sages*, a tome edited by Shmuel Safrai and others that continues the academic history of discussing Zunz's question regarding *Rabbinische Literatur*. In this massive volume, Myron B. Lerner laments the lack of serious work in this field over the prior hundred years. In the years that followed the publication of *Oẓar Midrashim*, Lerner claims, "No other successful scholarly endeavor in this field has been

---

46   Ibid., 11.

47   Strack/Stemberger, *Introduction*, p. 359. Of course, our other scholars are present there. The only work included here later than Eisenstein is Aaron Hyman's *Torah Hakethubah Vehamessorah*, which is a kind of concordance to midrashic material organized according to biblical verses.

48   Townsend, 333.

49   Moses Gaster, *The Exempla of the Rabbis*, (K'tav: New York), 1924.

50   In his introduction, Gaster uses phrases like "rough chronological order" and admits that completeness is "unattainable". Ibid., xlii.

undertaken in the 20th century."[51] He speculates that this might be about the difficulty and diversity of the field; as are we, Lerner is limited to conjecture. What is clear, however, is a single fact: with Eisenstein we have a complete library of accepted Minor Midrashim, a sealed canon built out of the work of assiduous scholarship of the preceding generation.

The story of Minor Midrashim began in Moravia, and ended in America. In the decades that separated *Rabbinische Literatur* from *Oẓar Midrashim*, we see how Zunz's clarion call for re-defining and re-claiming Jewish literature played out in the work of collectors, cataloguers, and critical readers. Minor Midrashim hidden in rare books or singular manuscripts were given wider audience through publication and scientific study. A frenzied thirty-year period of academic activity produced an essential, if sprawling, literature in various "collections" and "houses". The great advances in the name of the scientific study of Judaism culminated in the effective sealing of the canon of Minor Midrashim with Eisenstein's epochal publication. The created canon of Minor Midrashim was a product of *Wissenschaft des Judentums*.

---

51   Myron Lerner, "The Works of Aggadic Midrash," in Shmuel Safrai, et al., Ed., *The Literature of the Sages, Second Part*, (Minneapolis: Fortress Press), 2006, 131.

Dating: Medieval Midrash

Between Two Epochs: Medieval Midrash

The canon of Minor Midrashim was debated, defined and finalized in the rough century separating Zunz from Eisenstein, and this teaches an important lesson about the larger question regarding the dating of this collection of texts. First, it is clear that with a sealed canon, we are studying a fixed group of texts; the era of *Wissenchaft*, quite obviously then, marks the latest possible terminus of the period of the production of Minor Midrashim. However, even given the difficulties of proper dating of manuscripts and publications that we will discuss below, it is clear that all the works collected into the varied volumes of Minor Midrashim from Jellinek onward were written *before* Zunz proclaimed his clarion call for a new examination of *Rabbinische Literatur*. The advent of *Wissenschaft des Judentums* marks the latest possible date of anything that might be part of the canon of Minor Midrashim; all of the works that fall into this category were clearly produced before this modern era.

Just as the dawn of the Jewish Enlightenment marks the *terminus ad quem* for Minor Midrashim, so does the closing of the classical Rabbinic period mark the *terminus post quem* for this literature. Scholarly debates continue about the proper dating for the finalization of the Babylonian Talmud, and the academy doesn't specifically agree about the precise origins or particular terminology concerning the midrashic collections of that time, but there is general agreement that the Mishnah, Tosefta, Palestinian and Babylonian Talmuds, along with certain works of Midrash, belong specifically to the Rabbinic period.[52] Furthermore, while many of the so-called "Minor Midrashim" have their roots in Rabbinic texts, the scholars who collected and published them, as we have seen, were intentionally trying to bring to light a *Rabbinische Literatur* that—contrary to its name—was created *after* the classical period of Rabbinic-Talmudic creativity.

It is for these reasons that the proper terminology for these aggadic works seems to be Medieval Midrash. First, let us address the continued usage of the appellation "midrash". To begin with, many of these texts self-identify as midrash, either through their titles, or through their texts that, in some fashion,

---

52   Strack/Stemberger is of particular help: its chapters on "The Halakhic Midrashim" and "The Oldest Exegetical Midrashim" indicate the collections nearly universally considered to be part of the rabbinic canon; the subsequent chapter, "Homiletical Midrashim" introduces difficulties of assigning certain texts to set periods.

© KONINKLIJKE BRILL NV, LEIDEN, 2017 | DOI 10.1163/9789004331334_003

explicate particular biblical passages. Many of the works of literature printed in *Oẓar Midrashim* do not parallel classical Rabbinic models at all; certainly these works expand the definition of midrash beyond the previous boundaries of the term. With the possible exception of a few texts,[53] however, that pay scant or no attention to biblical citations, we will continue the tradition started by Jellinek and continued consistently to consider the works of this "library" to be midrash.

Even as we carry forward the title of "midrash" Jellinek and others applied to these works, we part ways when it comes to their labeling these works "small" or "minor". It is not just that "minor" seems to be a judgmental phrase, while "small" is sometimes a contraindication of the length of certain works: neither translation of the Hebrew, מדרשים קטנים says anything relevant about the texts themselves. It might have been helpful in the early days of *Wissenschaft* to indicate that these newly-discovered texts were minor, or of abbreviated length, but their clear status as a canon today demands a term for this genre that grows out of its own self-definition. What distinguishes these texts from other midrashic literature is that they were created *between* two epochs: the sun setting on the Rabbinic Period, and the dawn of the Enlightenment. Thus our terminology for this literature henceforth will be Medieval Midrash.

Scholarly Certainty: The Difficulty of Establishing Precise Dates

The Medieval Period is a lengthy span, especially as we define it above. While it would be helpful to date this midrashic material more precisely, tremendous obstacles block any such path. Some of these difficulties are endemic to the general study of Jewish literature during this time, as Eli Yasif indicates when he explains that "the vast majority of Hebrew narrative composition of the Middle Ages were anonymous," and that while we might be able to identify folk traditions, a more complex task faces us when evaluating how these oral tales became written literature:

> The folk traditions are identifiable, but the compositions themselves must be treated with different tools. We should distinguish between the folktales that constituted the basis or the raw materials for the narrative

---

53   Even here we follow the lead of both Jellinek and Eisenstein. The former explicitly stated that his *Beit HaMidrasch* contained "Different Minor Midrashim and varied precious sayings of the Jewish People," and the latter called his book a collection of "Two hundred Minor Midrashim and Aggadot and Exempla." [Each from the frontispiece of the book].

compositions of the Middle Ages, and the cultural process that turned these folk traditions into literature.[54]

Yasif does not specify the tools needed to work out the difficulties of understanding how traditions turned into literature; his focus (fortunately for him) is on the folk traditions only. The difficulty of dating literary material, so much of it anonymous, remains. Our six Medieval Midrashim about King Solomon illustrate more fully the difficulty in establishing proper dates not just for the genre of Medieval Midrash, but for individual texts as well: the history of the texts and manuscripts is unclear; cultural clues can only provide an uncertain specificity as to timeframe; and internal evidence is remarkably unreliable.

The Parables of King Solomon demonstrates the limitations of the inherited textual history of our Medieval Midrashim. Jellinek, in his introduction to the Parables, notes that one tale is related to "references in Sefer Hasidim and by the Saadja Gaon," while another is connected to Tosafot to Menahot.[55] He adds that "these tales are included in the Const. Sammlung, as well as my Salonicher." Jellinek is masterful at explaining how this text is connected to others, and reprinted elsewhere; but he gives us no evidence as to whether the Parables he prints are from a manuscript, found in a rare, early book, or are of some other origin. In reprinting this text nearly verbatim from Jellinek, Eisenstein himself has little else to offer other than additional compilations which also tell these tales:

> The Parables of King Solomon, stories and episodes of his, are found in a Kushta collection and a Thessalonian collection, and also amongst other midrashim, as in the episode of the three sons in the matter of the theft that is found in Midrash Aseret HaDibrot in the eighth dibbur; the first story here is found in Sefer Hasidim (and see as well Tosefot to Menahot 36). These Parables were printed by Jellinek in Beit HaMidrasch 4:145.[56]

We see in The Parables that we inherit from the age of Wissenschaft a full midrashic text—complete with title and theme—that seems both to have been printed elsewhere and to be connected to some discoverable previous

---

54   Yasif, The Hebrew Folktale, 246–7.

55   Jellinek, Beit HaMidrasch, "Gleichnisse des Königs Salomo" vol. 4, xiv. Our translation. There Jellinek notes that the reference is to BT Menahot 36a, which is a typo: the connection is to 37a.

56   Eisenstein, Ozar Midrash, 526. Interestingly, he makes the same mis-citation of b. Menahot that is found in Jellinek.

tales. The actual origin of the text remains unknown: there is not even an extant manuscript about which to speculate.[57] An absence of information likewise plagues the textual history of *An Episode Concerning King Solomon*.[58] Eisenstein merely reprints Jellinek's text without any comment; Jellinek tells us where he found the tale, but can only conjecture as to the tale's true origins:

> The Orient makes Solomon the focus of how this legend was formed. The wise king is depicted in the form of a penitent wanderer, also as an artistic chef, and as a hero of a romantic novel. Our legend is taken from the book *Emeq HaMelech* 14d–15a, and is connected to the report concerning Solomon and Ashmedai, Lord of the Demons, in *Gittin* 7.[59]

We seek not to blame or insult the early pioneers who collected Medieval Midrashim when we assert the truth: the textual history of many of the 200 midrashim ultimately printed by Eisenstein is undiscoverable. For many of these texts, as with *The Parables of King Solomon* and *An Episode Concerning King Solomon*, all we can say with certainty is that these texts were printed as midrash in the 19th Century and later.

Cultural clues can provide context in the absence of a solid manuscript history. *The Episode of the Ant* is particularly helpful here: while Jellinek does tell us of the original manuscript in which he discovered the text, he dedicates far more energy to exploring the origins of these tales from their cultural *sitz im leben*.[60] He speculates that "the general characteristics of this legend indicate that it did not originate from the more modest Hebrew spirit." More likely, it was derived from the more "fantasy-rich Arab spirit, even though its wording is not a word-for-word translation from the Arabic."[61] Jellinek continues to list a wide range of cultural influences on this work: the Quran, other

---

57   Eli Yasif, "Parables of King Solomon", *Jewish Studies in Hebrew Literature*, (9), 357–373.

58   The same is true for *Midrash Al-Yithallel*, which we find printed in Jellinek, Grünhut, and then Eisenstein. The former makes brief mention, as with *An Episode*, about a connection to *Emeq HaMelech*.

59   Jellinek, *Beit HaMidrasch*, "Salmo's Wanderjahre," vol. 2, xxvi. Our translation. This is the complete text of his introduction to the midrash.

60   Jellinek, *Beit HaMidrasch*, "Salomo und die *Ameise*," 5, p. xi. Our translation:
       This essay, "Solomon and the Ant" occurs at the end of the *Midrash Wajoscha*, a manuscript originally belonging to the Hon. N. Coronel and then passed on to the library of Cambridge University. Later on it was published, together with the earlier mentioned [*Midrash Wajoscha*] without pagination, partly with "quadratic" and partly with "rabbinic" font.

61   Jellinek, *Beit HaMidrasch* "Salomo und die *Ameise*," xii, 5.

"Mohommedan origins" and haggadic teachings to Psalm 6:6 (which we find in *Midrash Mishlei*). All of these clues are remarkably helpful for tracing the influence of Muslim legends on the Jewish expansion of understanding King Solomon; they also lead us to understand that this Hebrew text was created in a land and time when the Crescent reigned. Of course, this affords us no greater specificity as to a potentially precise date for this Midrash other than a span of at least seven centuries.

Sometimes, we do have a clear textual history of a given midrash. For instance, regarding *The Throne and Hippodrome of King Solomon*, Eisenstein summarizes:

> This haggadah regarding the throne of the king and his hippodrome (or a field for games) is copied from a manuscript in Munich, number 222, that was published by Joseph Pereles in a manuscript in the year 1872, and also in a dedicated volume (Breslau, 1872). The haggadah about the throne also appears in the *Targum Sheni to Esther*, in *Midrash Bamidbar Rabbah, Midrash Abba Gurion* (Buber press), and in the *Sefer Kol Bo*. And the *aggadah* of the appearance of the throne was published by Jellinek in *Beith HaMidrasch* 2, and the Throne and Hippodrome there in volume 5.[62]

We might be hopeful that such a clear textual history would allow us to discover a clear date for the creation of a given midrash. But even those hopes are likely to be dashed. The science of carbon dating, despite its prohibitive expense, doesn't offer precision: many tests only provide a hundred-year range for a given manuscript. Even then, we really only uncover the latest date on which a midrash was committed to parchment, not the first time its legends were told. Were we, for instance, to be able to date Munich MSS 222 to the 16th century, we might still wonder what led a scribe, in that late year, to record legends that seem to have blossomed in Byzantium five hundred years beforehand.

The Throne and Hippodrome of King Solomon and *The Form of the Throne of King Solomon*, as we shall see later in greater detail, do have their origins in historical realities attested in other literature. The work of Perles referenced by Eisenstein goes into great detail about the actual Hippodrome at Byzantium that seems to serve as model for the midrashic throne of Solomon. We know from a variety of Byzantine testamentary sources not only of a "Throne of

---

62   Eisenstein, *Ozar Midrash*, 526. Interestingly, Eisenstein omits information Jellinek provides about the Throne material: that the *Yalqut* contains extensive details and that further information may be found in Cassel, *Wissenschaftlicher Berichte*, Akademie, Erfurt, Vol. 1, 37ff.

Solomon" that stood in Constantinople, but also about the remarkable physical automata that produced its apparent magic.[63] However, even hearing first-hand references to a real-life Throne of Solomon that seems so much like the one described in our midrash can only take us so far: some contemporary scholars wonder if the entire model of Solomon's Throne was only a metaphor, while another—in the absence of being able to form a clear mental picture of Byzantium or discover archaeological remains of said throne—concludes that we ultimately will always "be reduced to conjecture".[64]

Our Medieval Midrashim do not tell us who wrote them, nor do they purport to tell us where they were first told. Sometimes the tales told within, or the cultural references we can trace, provide us with temporal pins to place parts of a particular tradition on a general historical timeline. While it is somewhat unsatisfying, the truth about the canon of Medieval Midrashim is that, while individual texts might be able to be connected to a particular region or era, the entire genre comes from a timeframe nearly one millennium in length.

Scholarly Vagaries: Lists of Lists

The only good news about setting this very broad period for the creation of Medieval Midrashim is that it seems to be the one aspect of this study on which all scholars agree. Eisenstein himself addressed this issue when turning the genre into a canon:

> These midrashim (excluding the example) were mostly written in the time of the Geonim, and fewer of them close to the time of Rashi and the Rambam . . . and also from the remainder of the period of dispersal; they are in manuscripts and treasuries of Jewish literature not known to most readers, and even those rabbis who study and expound in the known midrashic collection like Midrash Rabbah, Midrash Tanhuma, the Yalkut and the like, they do not know from these Minor Midrashim except for a

---

63 On the former, Ra'anan Bouston, "Israelite Kingship, Christian Rome, and the Jewish Imperial Imagination: Midrashic Precursors to the Medieval 'Throne of Solomon,'" in *Jews, Christians, and the Roman Empire: The Poetics of Power in Late Antiquity*, ed., Natalie Dohrmann and Reed, Annette Yoshiko, (Philadelphia: University of Pennsylvania Press), 2013, 167–182; on the latter, Gerard Brett, "Throne of Solomon," *Speculum*, 29:3 (1954), 477–487.

64 Priscilla Soucek, "Solomon's Throne/Solomon's Bath: Model or Metaphor?," *Ars Orientalis*, 23, 1993, 109–134. Gerard Brett, Ibid. 487.

few like Midrash Vayosha, Midrash Tadshe and Midrash Aseret HaDibrot and another two or three. Certainly people will be astonished and amazed to hear and to see here collected two hundred midrashim like this.[65]

Eisenstein admits these Medieval Midrashim were from the period of the Geonim, Tosafists, and even later. He openly acknowledges that these texts are likely to have eluded even the most erudite of scholars. Writing ten years later, Moses Gaster expounds:

> It must be remembered, however, that it is not an easy task to do full justice to a literature which covers a period of close upon twenty centuries, and it is not unlikely that other references will be found in works not noticed by me. Again, if a scientific purpose were to be served, it was necessary to follow a new method. It is of the utmost importance to try and establish as far as possible the chronological sequence of the Hebrew books referred to, a task rendered extremely difficult when one considers that by far the largest portion consists of anonymous works. Opinion as to their date and antiquity differs very widely amongst scholars; it must be borne in mind, however, that the largest section consists of compilations which, passing from hand to hand, have undergone those changes which are so characteristic of popular literature.[66]

Gaster is honest about the enormity of the scholarly project to date just a single Medieval Midrash precisely; he only hints at the impossibility of dating the entire genre into any narrow time frame. Subsequent scholars seem to have been wary of this difficulty, as we can surmise by a near-universal tendency to shy away from discussing any matter of dating these works. In fact, the only attention academia seems to have paid these Medieval Midrashim was to continue—without much commentary—to list their names and the dates of the 19th Century publication.

Judah Theodor of Posen, who authored the article "Smaller Midrashim" for the *Jewish Encyclopedia*, lists 18 individual works, provides a bibliography including the collections we noted above, and describes these texts most generally as "a number of midrashim exist which are smaller in size, and generally later in date, than those dealt with in the articles Midrash Haggadah and Midrash Halakah."[67] Hermann L. Strack, in his formative *Introduction to the*

---

65   Eisenstein, *Oẓar Midrashim*, x.

66   Gaster, "Bibliography," *Exempla*, xlv ff.

67   *JE*, vol. VIII, 572ff.

Talmud and the Midrash, provides the standard *Wissenschaft* bibliography with the usual cast of characters, and adds only this terse commentary to the entire genre he titles *Midrash Collections and Translations,* "The texts of almost all these Midrashim are found in Jellinek's *Beth HaMidrasch*."[68] Sixty years later, when Strack's work was updated by Stemberger, the academy had extended the categories that included Medieval Midrashim: a few more of these works are described (usually briefly) on lists with names "Homiletical Midrashim," "Midrashim on the Five Megillot," "Other Exegetical Midrashim," and the likewise generalizing, "Other Haggadic Material". However, in that span of time, very little scholarship had been advanced. In the volume's final paragraph on Midrash, we only read, "A number of additional midrashim are contained in the collections of..." preceding a remarkably unchanged biography from the days of the *Jewish Encyclopedia.*[69]

In the century since Eisenstein, the academy has not altered its assessment about the timeframe from which we inherit the midrashim he compiled. In fact, continued scholarship in this field has almost exclusively consisted of making lists and maintaining bibliographies. The apogee of this approach we find in the grand indexed list of Townsend, who sought once-and-for-all to put in one place the entire list of Medieval Midrashim along with the printed history—notably *not* the manuscript history—of every work. At length, Townsend addresses the difficulties about which previous scholarship kept silent:

> Many of these short pieces are still in manuscript. Some have been published and then forgotten. During the past 120 years, however, a number of these works have been gathered into anthologies.
>
> These so-called Minor Midrashim have presented various problems, especially to Christian scholars. First of all, many fail to realize that this literature generally stems from an era far too late to provide much help in the study of Christian origins. While some may have roots in the first centuries of the Christian era, or even earlier, the vast majority comes from medieval times, i.e., from the sixth through the thirteenth century. A few are even later.
>
> A more difficult problem is that the midrashic collections form a labyrinth in which few can navigate. Even those relatively familiar with the literature sometimes have trouble. Moses Gaster, for example, was

---

68 Hermann L. Strack, *Introduction to the Talmud and the Midrash,* (Philadelphia: Jewish Publications Society), 1931. We note especially that this is an earlier version of the work before G. Stemberger entered the editorial process.

69 Strack/Stemberger, 359.

familiar with Jellinek's *Beth ha-Midrasch*; but apparently he did not real-
ize that what he had extracted from the Torah commentary of Menahem
Tsiyonne ben Meir and translated under the title, *The Revelation of Moses,
B*, could be found in Jellinek as *Aggadat "Shema Yisrael"*.[70]

Townsend sets out to "provide a guide to this labyrinth of midrash" by providing an alphabetical index of all the midrashim contained in the classic
Wissenschaft des Judentums collections, but was unable to speak any more
clearly about a narrow dating of this material than Eisenstein could before
him.

The scholarly literature in this small field has a clear three-fold tendency:
name the midrashim, provide a brief description of the material therein,
and supply the same general bibliography that has remained unchanged for
a hundred years. The best and brightest working in the field of Rabbinics,
Midrash and Jewish Literature do not address issues of dating or authorship
on any large scale. Most of their lists mention only 20% of the tales contained
in Eisenstein's *Treasury*. Some, like Gaster and Townsend, are openly honest
about these shortcomings; others address our lack of knowledge on this issue
through silence. Perhaps David Stern, attempting to assess the impact of these
kinds of tales, best captures why so much remains hidden, or perhaps lost:

> The "narrative" of classical Jewish narrative that we have told in these
> pages (despite ourselves, perhaps) thus culminates somewhat incon-
> clusively, its impact and influences upon contemporary Jewish writing
> partly hidden, partly lost. A conclusion of this kind is perhaps especially
> appropriate for a group of narratives that began with midrash and its sto-
> ries disguised-as-commentaries.[71]

Whether it is literarily appropriate, or simply an academic truth, we are unable
to find anything more than the most general, historic time frame regarding the
partially hidden and partly lost origins of most Medieval Midrash.

Medieval Midrash: A Broad, but Honest, Definition

What we are able to know about Medieval Midrash is limited. Our conclusion
is that the best "date" we can provide for this material has a remarkably wide
range, what we call the Medieval Period: between the close of the Rabbinic Era

---

70   Townsend, 333.
71   David Stern, "Introduction" to Stern and Mirsky, *Rabbinic Fantasies*, 28.

and the beginnings of the Enlightenment in Europe. What our thesis lacks in specificity, it gains in honest evaluation of how little we know about the individual midrashim, many of which we know *only* from their being printed by a scholar/collector of the *Wissenschaft* project. While certain texts might allow us to conjecture certain claims regarding cultural composition, the ability to discover even a slight historical connection or geographical association will be sporadic and idiosyncratic to particular pieces.

Although it is a broad response, we do finally have a response to the first question often asked about these midrashim: *When* were they written? With this knowledge—and its necessary limitations and shortcomings—we can turn to address the next question students of Medieval Midrashim are likely to pose: *What* was happening to the Jewish people during this era? *What* defined Jewish life during this period?

Jewish Life in the Medieval Era

Just as this historical era is defined as resting between two epochs, so is Jewish life in the medieval period defined by being between two dominions: Byzantium in Europe, and the Muslim realm that arose in Arabia and expanded beyond. Life in each of these empires posed different problems for the Jews who lived in them; however, the opposition between these imperia also offered unique opportunities for Jewish communities. These circumstances, we shall see, directly contributed to the creation and flourishing of Jewish literature, including the creation of Medieval Midrash.

The Byzantine Empire

The Byzantine Empire survived the fall of Rome in the 5th Century, and continued until conquered by the Ottoman Turks in 1453. During that near-millennium, the realm—centered in Constantinople—was the most powerful economic, cultural and military force in all of Europe. In greater focus, the Byzantine Empire was of immense importance to the development of Judaism, as Samuel Krauss claimed, "...the fate of the Jewish People was decided in Constantinople."[72] A more receptive climate was created for Jews in the days following Diocletian, who in 285 CE partitioned the Roman Empire into eastern and western administrative districts. In 330, Constantine officially moved the capital from Rome to Byzantium, renaming the city and becoming

---

72   *JE*, vol. III, 451.

its eponym. While Constantine famously granted Christianity imperial preference, it was Theodosius I who in 381 began to implement a series of anti-
pagan policies that promoted Christianity as the state religion. By the time of
the Theodosian Code, enacted by Theodosius II beginning in 404, Jews were
(unlike pagans) tolerated by the state, but proscribed from holding civil and
military posts.[73] The "anti-Jewish" attitude of the Byzantines towards the
Jews, Cecil Roth explains, "is well known," as Justinian in the 6th Century and
Heraclitus in the 7th "hampered every detail even of [the Jews'] religious life
to a fantastic extent".[74] However, Jews were permitted to continue on as merchants and manufacturers, which proved to be of great importance.

Of the daily life and religious organization of Byzantium's Jewry we know
precious little. The 12th Century travelogue of Benjamin of Tudela, which cata-
logues his visits to many communities, provides a rare yet precious insight.[75]
Likewise, a family chronicle attributed to Ahimaas of Oria (in southern Italy)
paints a portrait of how Jewish life was lived in the days of the Empire. However,
a contemporary understanding of Byzantine Jewry remains in some way as a
clouded academic field. Nicholas de Lange, in attempting to assay the current
state of research in this arena, indicates how little we truly know with introductory hedges along the lines of "very little is known," "another area where
little is known," "no scientific study actually exists," and "given the dearth of
other types of Jewish *realia*". Indeed, he opens his essay with the following:

> A century and more of research on Byzantine Jewry has lifted a corner of
> a curtain, but little more. We are still woefully ignorant about the physical
> dimensions of the Jewish presence in Byzantium—how many Jews there
> were, and where they lived—and about many aspects of Jewish life.[76]

Despite the fact that there are great limits to what we can know about Jewish
life in Byzantium, certain pertinent information is available to us. For instance,
Jewish communal leadership passed from the hands of wealthy archons (who

---

73   Andrew Sharf, *Byzantine Jewry from Justinian to the Fourth Crusade*. (New York, Shocken
      Books, Inc.), 1971, 21ff.

74   Cecil Roth, *The Jews of Italy*, (Philadelphia: Jewish Publication Society), 5706–1946, 49.

75   The text in its entirety is translated in Joshua Starr, *The Jews in the Byzantine Empire 641–
      1204*, (Athens: Verlag der Byzantinisch-Neugriechischen Jahrbücher), 1939. That volume,
      together with Steven Bowman, *The Jews of Byzantium 1204–1453*, (Tuscaloosa: University
      of Alabama Press), 1985, remains the apogee of scholarship for this historical period.

76   Nicholas De Lange, "Research on Byzantine Jewry: the State of the Question," in Jewish
      Studies at the Central European University IV, 2003–2005, eds. Andras Kovacs and Miller,
      Michael L., (Budapest), 2006, 41–51. This article provides a current bibliography of aca-
      demic evaluation of Jewish life in this period.

were of primary importance in the late days of the Roman Empire) into the studious meritocracy of the rabbis. Jewish communities in the areas controlled by Constantinople developed their own identities: new rituals were developed in the Romaniote rite,[77] hundreds of hymns were created,[78] and *responsa* responded to "distinctive practices of Byzantine Jews."[79] Some of these practices seem to indicate an admixture of Christian and Roman influences on Jewish life. A good example of this blending is evident in Jewish marriage rituals, where the *Ketubah*'s commitment to the dowry belonging inalienably to the bride is influenced by Byzantine law, while the emerging ceremony of *stefanomata* is connected to Christian use of crowns at weddings.[80]

The Jews of Byzantium, about whom little truly is known, do seem to have played an important role in the creation and transmission of traditions, and their location between cultures here seems to be key. Jews found themselves between religion as represented by Christianity and imperial power in Constantinople: as we saw with wedding traditions, Jews created new rituals based in foreign cultures (and perhaps other religions), yet adapted them to and appropriated them for particularly Jewish settings. Socially, being neither Christian nor pagan, the Empire allowed Jews to live as Jews, but proscribed their options and impelled many of them to engage in international trade (which again brought Jews betwixt and between cultures). Finally, in Byzantium Jews found themselves on an important middle ground between the two primary Jewish communities of late antiquity: Palestine and Babylon, each represented by its own Talmud. Ta-Shma indicates that the Jews of Byzantium were connectors of these two different *Jewish* cultures, and played a key role in transmitting Talmud study to Ashkenaz, the Mediterranean, and even Spain.[81]

Jewish life in the Byzantine Empire was defined by opposites: acceptance and marginalization, success and suppression, rest and upheaval. Likely, except during times of physical persecution and forced conversion, the Jewish community learned to lead their lives in ordinary, prosaic ways. However, it seems, this life was always led on the edge, on the border. Jews were obviously peripheral to the

---

77   G. Drettas, and Arom, S., "A Journey through Romaniot Space," *Bulletin of Judaeo-Greek Studies* 27 (2000–2001), 30–33.

78   Leon J. Weinberger, *Jewish Hymnography: a literary history*, [London: Vallentine Mitchell] 1998.

79   DeLange, "Research," 47.

80   Bowman, *Byzantium*, 121ff.

81   Israel Moses Ta-Shma, "The History and Cultural Relations between Byzantine and Ashkenazi Jewry," *Meah She'arim*, ed. Ezra Fleischer, et al., (Jerusalem: Magnes Press), 2001, 61–70.

state religion, Christianity; likewise they were, at best, second-class citizens of the Empire that often disempowered them. As merchants and manufacturers, Jews were not infrequently on the edges of invention, and through trade often were crossing the very physical boundaries between towns, provinces, nations and even empires. The theme we retroactively apply to the Jews of Byzantium is that they lived their lives defined by, living on, and crossing borders.

The Muslim Empire

Across the border from Byzantium, and most often opposed to it, was the Muslim Empire. A comprehensive combination of religion and polity was the goal from the days of Mohammed, who by 632 united the entire Arabian Peninsula into a single society, free of paganism, and devoted to Islam. Following Mohammed's death, first the Rashidun and then the Umayyad Caliphates continued the commitment to conquest, and spent much of the subsequent centuries engaged in war with the Byzantine Empire. By 750, the Muslim Empire in the West had crossed the Strait of Gibraltar into Spain; influence in the East extended through Mesopotamia to the Caucasus. The extent of the empire—and its unifying power that led to uniformity of culture—is captured by the poetic history of Edward Gibbon in his *The History of Decline and Fall of the Roman Empire*:

> Under the last of the Umayyads, the Arabian empire extended two hundred days journey from east to west, from the confines of Tartary and India to the shores of the Atlantic Ocean. And if we retrench the sleeve of the robe, as it is styled by their writers, the long and narrow province of Africa, the solid and compact dominion from Fargana to Aden, from Tarsus to Surat, will spread on every side to the measure of four or five months of the march of a caravan. We should vainly seek the indissoluble union and easy obedience that pervaded the government of Augustus and the Antonines; but the progress of Islam diffused over this ample space a general resemblance of manners and opinions. The language and laws of the Quran were studied with equal devotion at Samarcand and Seville: the Moor and the Indian embraced as countrymen and brothers in the pilgrimage of Mecca; and the Arabian language was adopted as the popular idiom in all the provinces to the westward of the Tigris.[82]

---

82   Edward Gibbon, *The History of the Decline and Fall of the Roman Empire*, with notes by Milman, Guizot, and Wenck, Smith, William, Ed., (New York: Charles C. Bigelow & Co. Inc.), Vol. v, assumed date of publication 1920s, 404–405.

The role of the Jew in the Muslim empire continues to be a focus of extensive academic study.[83] Given they were adherents to a scriptural faith that *preceded* Islam, Jews were afforded status as "People of the Book". The best of this group, and their merit of reward, were described in the Quran:

> And, behold, among the followers of earlier revelation there are indeed such as [truly] believe in God, and in that which has been bestowed from on high upon you as well as in that which has been bestowed upon them. Standing in awe of God, they do not barter away God's messages for a tri-fling gain. They shall have their reward with their Sustainer—for, behold, God is swift in reckoning![84]

As People of the Book, Jews were protected in accordance with the concept of *dhimma*, which indicates protection by treaty. Religious groups permitted to live in keeping with this concept were termed *ahl al-dhimma*, or "protected people". More commonly, individual Jews were referred to as *dhimmi*, namely non-Muslims with certain legal rights (including the ability to practice their faith in private) and protections (of the state). *Dhimmi* communities, like the Jewish community, were subject to special tributes such as the *jizia* poll tax or the *kharaj* land tax, and further were expected to organize themselves as a community *under* Caliph rule. This granted Jews a certain limited autonomy, but also confirmed their (obvious) outsider status in Muslim lands.

Despite this outsider status, Jews often integrated into society in the are-nas of politics, sciences and—most notably—international trade. The accep-tance of Jews in Muslim lands was dependent on the orientation of the ruling authority and culture, and often held great tension at its heart:

> There were variations in the attitude towards Jews. Instances will be mentioned below of Jews who, through their own talents, rose to politi-cal leadership in Moslem Spain, among them Hasdai Ibn Shaprut in the tenth century, Samuel Hanagid and his son Joseph in the eleventh, and the Ibn Ezra family (which initially served Moslem rulers and later some if its members served Christian rulers). Reference has already been

83   For three recent evaluations of Jewish life in this period, see: Bat Ye'or, *The Dhimmi: Jews and Christians under Islam.* (Teaneck, NJ: Fairleigh Dickinson University Press), 1985; Bernard Lewis, *The Jews of Islam,* (Princeton: Princeton University Press), 1984; Martin Gilbert, *In Ishmael's house: a History of Jews in Muslim Lands,* (New Haven: Yale University Press), 2010.

84   *The Quran,* Surat 'Ali 'Imran, 3:199.

made to the court bankers, who played so important a role in the political economy of the caliphate and who lived like noblemen. These were
favourable exceptions to general circumstances. Moslems frequently
reacted furiously to the elevation of 'degraded ones'. Sometimes the fury
of the masses erupted against both the Jewish minister and his brethren,
as happened in the Grenada riots of 1066, when the whole congregation
was killed together with Joseph Hanagid. This was a violent expression of
the immanent tension and dialectic involved in the rise of a gifted member of a minority who surmounted or breached the rigid limitations fixed
for the *dhimmi*, a situation fraught with both promise and danger to the
man and his community.[85]

Moses Maimonides and Jewish Life in the Muslim Empire

Moses Maimonides is perhaps the best example of the ability of the individual Jew to flourish or decay in the medieval Muslim Empire. Many are familiar with his service as a court physician to Muslim authorities in Egypt: in
1185, al-Fadil, appointed vizier of Egypt by none other than Saladin, brought
Maimonides into the royal retinue at Cairo. All the while he continued to
serve as religious leader in Fostat, journeying between the two. Bridging that
distance (or perhaps reflecting it) are the two great literary works Maimonides
crafted during this period: *Mishneh Torah*, a Hebrew guide for Jewish practice, and *The Guide for the Perplexed*, a book of philosophy—based not just
in Aristotle, but also Averroes—written in Judeo-Arabic. Maimonides, during his tenure in Egypt, served with the Jewish community and the Muslim
community, and drew inspiration and learning from both sources of human
knowledge.

Yet Maimonides did not lead a life free from religious persecution. He was
forced to flee his childhood home in Cordoba, when it fell into the hands of the
religiously intolerant Almohads as Maimonides turned the significant Jewish
age of thirteen. He and his family narrowly escaped forced conversion and
death, making their way from Fez to Acre. Even after finding calm on the east
side of the Mediterranean Sea, Maimonides knew of the suffering of his people
at the hands of Islamic authorities. In 1172 he penned his *Iggeret Teiman* to
the Jewish community in Yemen; he advised them not only how to survive the
religious persecution of the Shi'ite authorities there, but also how to avoid fall-

---

85   H. H. Ben-Sasson, (ed.) "The Middle Ages," in *A History of the Jewish People*, (Cambridge:
      Harvard University Press), 1976, 405–406.

ing prey to false messiahs or the enticing lure of conversion to Christianity or Islam. Men like Maimonides knew from personal experience that Jews could rise to the apex of Muslim society and status, and that many others were often segregated into ghettoes, or lived their lives on the edge of the sword. The Jewish experience in the varied Islamic empires of the Middle Ages was hardly consistent: golden ages alternated with persecution; tolerance and acceptance in one place could be replaced by ostracism and violence in another. In this fashion, Jewish life under the Crescent in the East was not so different from Jewish living under the West's Cross.

The Link between Empires

Here we arrive at a crucial intersection: the life of the Medieval Jew was not materially different regardless of the empire in which that Jew lived. Whether in East or West, under Islam or Christianity, the place of the Jew was on the border of society, often tolerated, sometimes subjugated, but never fully incorporated into the body politic. However, beyond these, one further similarity must be brought to the surface, because of its direct impact on our literary study. For Jews did not just live on the borders of Byzantium or on the edges of the Islamic world: Jews often straddled the border between these two cultures as well. This, primarily, was a result of their function as cosmopolitan merchants: Jews were engaged in trade from India through Spain. In times of conflict, when Christian and Arab aggression prohibited trade between the two, Jews often served as agents bringing goods across imperial boundaries. The Jewish mercantile class [at least] was not only versed in the languages of different lands, but had Hebrew to unite them to their coreligionists across the globe. Thus, as Simon Dubnov explains, the Jews were not only often the bridge between the two great Medieval empires, but also as result reaped the benefit of a resurgence of their language and culture:

> A Jew who spoke Italian in Lombardy and Rome would resort to Arabic when in Sicily. Naturally he would converse in Greek in Apulia, and in Constantinople, Macedonia, Thessalia, or Greece. But in addition to this polyglot of languages in everyday practice, the Jews had one literary language that united them which, of course, was Hebrew.
>
> Now we shall see the resurgence of this language in the living monuments of literators. This was brought about by the influx of fresh forces from the spiritual centers of the eastern countries. The road from Palestine and Babylon to Western Europe proceeded through Italy and Byzantium;

those countries, together with Spain since the Arab conquest, were way stations on the Jewish culture's journey from East to West.[86]

There is no doubt that a substantial portion of the medieval Jewish mercantile class was not only multilingual, but also highly literate. Jews in Byzantium created rituals influenced by Christian culture, and those in Muslim lands developed philosophies under the sway of Islamic thought: likewise, Jews who crossed the borders between these two empires were impacted not just by the culture of *one* empire, but more so by the great confluence of these two often opposing geopolitical tides. Thus some subset of Medieval Jewry was influenced not by Byzantium, and not by Islam, but by the meeting of these different empires and the customs, cultures, practices and religions they represent.

Coda: Being "Between"

For our canon of midrashic material, we have arrived at geopolitical and temporal definitions that nest our literature in the spaces "between": historically between the end of the Talmudic Era and the dawn of the Enlightenment, and culturally between the dominant Christian and Muslim imperial forces of that millennium. These liminal delineations capture the threshold role Jews often played during this era: trading between cultures, whether in the realm of religious practice, philosophical speculation, or material merchandise. While much of the Jewish history of the medieval period can certainly be written about the results of Jews existing on the outside of virtually every society, it is precisely the placement of Jews between cultures that gives rise to our genre and canon of Medieval Midrashim.

---

86   Simon Dubnov, *A History of the Jews: 2, from the Roman Empire to the Early Medieval Period*, tr. Moshe Spiegel (South Brunswick: Thomas Yoseloff), 1968, 596.

Traditions: Making Midrash

Literary Undercurrents: Seismic Shifts

Medieval Midrash is a literature that took root and blossomed in the "in-between" places: these works were created between two great literary epochs [that of the Talmud and the Enlightenment], while the Jewish people lived amid and amongst two expansive empires [the Islamic and Byzantine]. Perhaps part of the reason that this literature was so fruitful is that the soil in which it grew was so dramatically overturned: the puissant expansion of Islam in the century following the death of Muhammad was momentous. Geographic terrain and borders seemed to melt before the advancing armies of the new faith. Tribes and nations of diverse ethnic composition willingly yielded to its conversionary fervor or swiftly learned the deadly consequences of their failure to submit. The geographic dimensions of the Islamic conquests were monumental. The contiguous, conquered landmass in the east extended from Turkey across all the eastern lands to the Hindu Kush mountain range in India. In the west, Egypt, Ifriqia [Tunisia, western Libya, and eastern Algeria], all the way across the Maghreb to Morocco on the Atlantic Ocean, and Andalus came under its sway. The effects of these conquests were more than military, more than political: they were seismic. All the diverse cultures: Animist, Buddhist, Zoroastrian, Byzantine and Coptic Christian fell before the passionate invaders. The effect of these conquests permeated the varied cultures, replaced or augmented their alphabets and languages, and reshaped their arts, literature, and even their diets.

Medieval Jewry—including that segment living in Byzantine lands—was not immune to the monumental cultural change brought about by this upheaval. Within the limited scope of our present study, we will examine those societal shifts that will help us address specific questions about Medieval Midrashim: how were these texts fashioned? Who are the people that might have created them? In order to get nearer to the heart of these matters, we will examine the earliest literary figures and works that emerged as a result of the cultural upheavals of the Middle Ages, and that would prove directional for the formation of the canon of Medieval Midrash.

Literary Pollinators: Geography and Commerce

As we explored above, Jews played a unique cosmopolitan role ranging between the Byzantine and Muslim empires. The Jewish mercantile class not

© KONINKLIJKE BRILL NV, LEIDEN, 2017 | DOI 10.1163/9789004331334_004

only transferred material goods from place to place; the international travels of this multilingual set also built a literary bridge that provided for a relatively free exchange of culture from East to West. The international transmission of literature was abetted serendipitously by the geographical position and the commercial endeavors of Jewish merchants. Nowhere, perhaps, are the cultural benefits of such coincidence better demonstrated than in Southern Italy in the early 11th century.

Southern Italy was under the control of the Byzantine emperors. The extensive Mediterranean coast of Italy was home to Roman Catholic Christians, with Byzantine Christians situated in the south, in towns like Bari and Otranto. A cursory look at a map of Italy in 1025 [before the Norman invasions] demonstrates not only the physical propinquity of different Christian communities living on the Italian mainland, but also depicts the proximity of areas under the hegemony of Islam, namely the island of Sicily and the coastal states of North Africa. Jews resided in and travelled between all of these geographic regions ruled by three different cultures; thus were they compelled to master the languages of the people with whom they traded. In order truly to master a language, one must understand the people—and thus the culture—that speaks it in daily life. Merchant Jews were culturally proficient in Catholic, Byzantine and Islamic lands.

In this way, the Jewish mercantile class served as the connective link between Greek, Roman, and Muslim culture. Jews moved back and forth between the varied—and remarkably proximate—domains with ease. All the while, the Jews from all of these geographic areas shared Hebrew as a unifying language, Hebrew literature as an integrating force, and religious rituals as a stimulus to consolidate an international community. In the Byzantine territory, a network of academies flourished and great literary works were produced that, importantly, were spread to Jewish communities in other empires. The historian Joshua Starr cites an epigram based on a verse in the biblical book of Isaiah, which accentuates the vitality of Jewish learning in Byzantine Italy: Isaiah's words, *For instruction will go forth from Zion and the word of the Eternal from Jerusalem*,[87] were recast and applied locally in the form of this aphorism, "From Bari comes forth the Law, and the word of God from Otranto."[88]

---

87   Isaiah 2:3.

88   The origin of this maxim is found in Rabbi Jacob Tam's (Rabbeinu Tam, 1100–1171), *Sefer haYashar l'Rabbeinu Tam*, and is often cited. See, Ḥeleq haShe'alot v'haTeshuvot, ed. Shraga Rosenthal, (Berlin: Zvi Hirsch Issakovski Press, 1898), New Edition, (Jerusalem) 1972, p. 90. See further, Starr, "The Jews in the Byzantine Empire", 60; Roth, *History of the Jews of Italy*, 61; Robert Bonfils, *Tra due mondi, cultura ebraica e cultura cristiana nel*

In their packs, luggage, saddlebags, and mercantile crates were more than the goods Jewish merchants came to trade. They also transported parchment and vellum manuscripts acquired during their extensive travels. Perhaps the majority of the Hebrew literature carried across continents was not folkloric in nature, but legal: the medieval period is widely known for the rise and spread of Responsa literature that sought to deliver the legal rulings of international experts to far-flung communities. However, it was not exclusively the ruling of Rabbenu Gershom from Germany or Isaac Alfasi of Andalus that travelled with merchants from port to port. These traders also heard stories, legends, and fables on their travels, and they carried back home with them the details of those tales. On their scrolls and in their ears were the stories, legends, and narratives of other cultures that served to stir the imagination and to open the channels of Jewish creative genius. These factors added yet another layer of complexity to the medieval image of the Jew as literary mediator between cultures, nations, and empires: in feeding their own appetite for tales and legends, the Jews disseminated stories from one world to another.

Literary Bridge Builder: Petrus Alfonsi

A crucial figure in the literary transmission from the Islamic East to the Christian West was Petrus Alfonsi, an apostate Jew. Born Moses Sefardi in the 11th Century in Islamic Andalus, Alfonsi formally converted to Christianity on St. Peter's Day 1106, and adopted as his new namesake the patron saint of that day. Alfonsi, who gained renown as a Jew before his conversion, is paradigmatic of the crucial role historians and scholars of medieval folk literature acknowledge Jews played in the preservation, dispersion, and transmission of folk literature from East to West. Coincidental with the time of his conversion, Alfonsi wrote *Disciplina clericalis*, a moralizing collection of folktales that could serve, according to its translation, as *A Training School for Clergy*. The *Disciplina clericalis* is a compilation of stories derived from Sanskrit, Persian, and Arabic sources. It introduced new story motifs like the tale of *Sinbad the Sailor* into the West and influenced the development of the European novella.[89] This collection of thirty-three medieval folktales, written in Latin,

---

medioevo, (Naples: Ligouri), 1996, 100, for a view of Byzantine-Italian Jewish life consonant with the spirit of this adage.

89 Israel Zinberg, *The History of Jewish Literature, The Arabic Spanish Period*, Bernard Martin, trans., (Cleveland and London: The Press of Case Western Reserve University), 1972, Vol. 1, 186.

demonstrates the enduring influence of Jews as mediators of folk literature in the Middle Ages. The polyhistorian manuscript collector, Moritz
Steinschneider, said this of Alfonsi's work:

> Whoever wishes to chart the path over which the Oriental tales migrated
> to Europe must take account of Alfonsi's *Disciplina* as one of the major
> milestones marking this way.[90]

Literary Journeys: The *Panchatantra*

Alfonsi is but one example of how Jews served as transmitters of fables and
stories across the geographic expanse of the medieval world. Another summary
illustration may be found not in a historic personage, but in a literary text itself:
the *Panchatantra*. As we saw, the success of Islam led to the encounter with the
vast and rich literary heritage of the peoples it conquered. Local storytellers or
itinerant bards transmitted some of that literature orally, while some of it was
already in a written form. The *Panchatantra*, perhaps the foremost contribution in belles-lettres from India, was in this fashion mediated to the West in
a literary exchange after the Islamic conquests. The *Panchatantra*, originally a
Buddhist text, was compiled in the Kashmir in 200 BC.[91] Over time, the less fan-
tastically-oriented Brahmin enemies of the Buddhists expurgated the legends,
fables, animal tales, and magic stories. This expurgation diminished the size of
the original work and reduced it to five (*pancha*) parts, or "books" (*tantra*).

During the Sassanid period of the Islamic Empire, the *Panchatantra* in
its entirety was translated into Pahlavi, a literary language of Persia. It was
translated by a learned Persian physician named Barzau, who also wrote an
extensive introduction to it.[92] The fifth book of these Indian animal legends
was translated into Arabic with the title, *Kalila wa-Dimna* (Literally: The
Lioness and the Horseman).[93] Subsequently, Barzau's original Pahlavi translation was lost but another Arabic translation was rendered during the reign

---

90   Ibid.

91   Johannes Hertel, *The Panchatantra-Text of Purnabhadra-Critical Introduction and List of
      Variants*, (Cambridge, Massachusetts: Harvard University), 1912, 5.

92   Jaako Hameen-Antilla, *Maqama: History of a Genre*, (Wiesbaden: Otto Harrassowitz
      Verlag), 2002, 316.

93   Joseph Jacobs, *Jewish Contributions to Civilization, An Estimate*, (Philadelphia: The Jewish
      Publication Society of America), 1919, 154. Jacobs notes that these stories were known
      by several names, among them, *"Fables of Bidpai"* (or Pilpay), *"Kalilah wa-Dimnah,"*
      "Directorium humanae vitae" . . . 154.

of the caliph Al Mansur, between the years 754–775.[94] Purportedly, one Rabbi
Joel completed the first Hebrew translation of the *Kalila wa-Dimna* in the
12th century.[95] In 1283 at the commission of the Jewish physician and patron
Benveniste, Jacob ben Eleazer of Toledo completed a second translation into
Hebrew.[96] In this version, Jacob ben Eleazar rhapsodized about the importance
and beauty of the *Kalila wa-Dimna*. Israel Zinberg captured the spell it cast:

It was created in ancient days by the great sages of India. This work is their
most precious treasure. It is their Torah, their prophet, their guiding star.
In it are told the stories of beasts, fishes in the sea and birds that ascend to
the heaven. The old understand the wisdom hidden in it. Children laugh,

---

94   Zinberg, Vol. I, 195.
95   Jacobs, 155.
     The chronology and authorship of the Hebrew translations of the *Kalila wa-Dimna* are
     disputed by scholars. Joseph Jacobs asserted that a Rabbi Joel made the first translation
     into Hebrew. [*JE*, Vol. VII, 418.] Following this view, a second, longer translation of the
     Kalila wa-Dimna was rendered by Rabbi Eleazer ben Jacob (Ibid.) In a separate study,
     Jewish Contributions to Civilization, An Estimate, Joseph Jacobs made a strong endorse-
     ment of the influence of Rabbi Joel's translation in the transmission of the *Kalila wa-
     Dimna* into European languages.
         Joseph Derenbourg (1811–1895) published both textual versions of the *Kalila wa-
     Dimna* in one volume, *Deux Versions Hebraique du livre de Kalilah et Dimnah* (Paris: F.
     Vieweg, Librarire-Editeur), 1881. On the front page, numbered VII, in the French section
     we read, "La version hebraique, attribuee au rabbin Joel. . . ." In the Hebrew section, on the
     same page, he wrote יואל ר' אחד לחכם המתיחס שמו (an uncertain R. Joel).
         C. Brockelmann endorsed this chronology when he wrote:
     "The version of Rabbi Joel was translated into Latin by the baptized Jew John of
     Capua between 1263–1278 with the title *Directorium vitae humanae*, published
     and annotated by J. Derenbourg in the Bibl. de l'Ecole des Hautes Etudes, fasc. 72,
     Paris 1887." *C. Bockelmann, The Encyclopaedia of Islam, New Edition,* E. van Donzel,
     B. Levis, and Pellat, Ch., eds. (Leiden: E.J. Brill), 1978, Vol. IV., 505.
     Israel Zinberg dissented from this view and asserted that "the poet and philologist Jacob
     ben Eleazar" received the commission to translate the work from the Jewish physician,
     Benveniste in the first half of the 12th century. [Zinberg, Vol. I, 196] He further argued that:
         Around the year 1250 a second translation of the *Kalilah Ve-Dimnah* appeared. The
         name of the translator has remained unknown. Some scholars have called the trans-
         lator Joel, but this is no more than a conjecture. Zinberg, Vol. I, 197 and footnote
         45 ad. loc.
     We concur that Zinberg's conclusions: (1) that Jacob ben Eleazar's translation preceded
     the so-called Rabbi Joel version and (2) the proposed name of the translator, Rabbi Joel, is
     no more than conjecture.
96   Zinberg, 195.

and think these are merely lovely stories. When the child matures, he will know how to appreciate the depth of wisdom of this book, how beautiful are its pearls and wise its words.[97]

In the 13th century an apostate Jew, John of Capua, translated a Hebrew version of the *Kalila wa-Dimna* into Latin and gave it the title *Directorium Vitae Humanae*. This Latin translation then generated translations into Spanish, French, Italian, English, German and Dutch. Another apostate Jew, Simeon Seth, a court physician to the emperor Michael VII Doukas of Byzantium, translated the *Kalila wa-Dimna* from Arabic in 1081. His Greek version generated the various Slavic translations.[98] While Jews were not solely responsible for the *Panchatantra* traveling from India to Europe, this fabulous collection only crossed from Islamic lands to Christian realms because of the translation efforts of those raised in the world-mediating culture of the Jewish community.

We have traced the journey of the great legends of India through Persia and across the Islamic world to the doorstep of Christian Europe. It is important to take note, that—aside from delivering literature from one Empire to another—in the process these tales came to inform the moral lives of the Jews. These stories were not mere fables: they touched an important historic chord at the core of Jewish consciousness. The narratives they preserved, translated, and transmitted served a deeper purpose. They became an *aide memoire*, recalling their own historic Jewish roots, their ancient homeland, and the glory of their own heroes and heroines. In a way, these Indian tales, en route from being Muslim to informing Christians, served as Jewish stories as well:

> ...these tales were woven into homilies for delivery in the synagogue, and were included in collections that passed from one community to another throughout the Jewish world. In the process the Jews not only absorbed themes, motifs, and entire tales from their surroundings but also served as transmitters of such materials to the cultures among which they moved. As in the field of philosophical speculation, so in the area of the tale: Jews served as the bridge between East and West, between Islam—with its borrowings from the East via India and Iran—and Christendom with its Graeco-Roman and Germanic heritage.[99]

---

97   Ibid., 196.

98   Ibid., 197.

99   William M. Brinner, Introduction and translation, Ibn Shahin, Nissim ben Jacob, *An Elegant Composition Concerning Relief and Adversity*, (New Haven and London: Yale University Press), 1977, xv.

The Emergence of the Medieval Jewish Folk Literature

Literary bridge builders like Alfonsi, and cross-cultural connectors like the legends of the *Panchatantra* helped foster the emergence of a specifically medieval Jewish literature based in folk tales. In his comprehensive study of folklore, Eli Yasif noted that the "Middle Ages" of Jewish folk expression commenced with the rise of Islam. That historic datum is a significant parallel for our examination of Medieval Midrash:

> According to modern historiography, the Jewish Middle Ages begin with the Muslim conquests and expansion in the second half of the seventh century. The demarcation has great significance in the history of Jewish culture. For the first time, there is a clear division between those sectors of the Jewish people located in Christian Europe, and the larger and more important communities (at least in the early part of the period) in the lands under Islamic rule, from Yemen in the east to Spain in the west. This division is essential to understanding medieval Jewish culture, and yet more important as regards the folk literature of the period. As a result of this division, Jews absorbed the surrounding Muslim or Christian culture, and links were forged between elite Jewish and folk cultures. The people's position astride two cultures gave rise to new narrative genres and social tension.[100]

At the height of the Geonic Period (8th–9th century CE) Hebrew literature moved away from the literary model employed in the Talmudic Age with its comprehensive, integrated style. The dawning age tended in the direction of the separation of literary genres. In this era, specific works of a legal, grammatical, philosophical, or exegetical nature proliferated. Yosef Dan suggests that one of the distinguishing factors in the history of medieval Hebrew literature was:

> ...its liberation from the framework of the [Classical] aggada and midrash and its transformation into a subject in its own right. Between the 7th and 11th centuries the first collection of Hebrew stories was edited. Its essential purpose was to bring to the reader stories arranged within a literary structure.[101]

---

100 Yasif, *The Hebrew Folktale*, 245–246.

101 Dan, *The Hebrew Story*, p. 69; Ibid., Yasif, 246; Stern and Mirsky, *Rabbinic Fantasies*, 92; The author of this section of *Rabbinic Fantasies* is Joel Rosenberg; Berdichevsky, Micah Joseph,

Among the earliest examples of this emerging medieval Jewish narrative art
are *The Midrash of the Ten Commandments* and the *Alphabet of Ben Sira*. Eli
Yasif argues that these works:

> ...were produced in the cultural expanse of Babylonia and Persia dur-
> ing these centuries. These are the first texts in the history of Hebrew
> Literature with an unreservedly literary orientation, and which can be
> defined as groupings of artistic-fictional tales, almost entirely devoid of
> overt ideational-didactic objectives.[102]

The earlier Talmudic literature was replete with didactic narratives. The anonymous writers of these two early Medieval Midrashim were well aware of this
tradition, even as they consciously moved away from it. Nonetheless, they carried certain rabbinic literary forms with them as they shaped and reshaped
their new compositions with decidedly different aims, and under the influences of the legends of definitively distinct cultures. Yasif's research helps
us understand this latter, vital factor in the emergence of this new literary
creation:

> ...the phenomenon would not have unfolded, it seems, if not for the sec-
> ond factor: the existence of story groupings in Arabic in the same cul-
> tural region. Kalila wa-Dimna, The Tales of Sendebar, and early versions
> of The Arabian Nights were widespread in Babylonia and Persia at the
> time; Jews were also familiar with them. The combination of the two fac-
> tors, namely, the internal legitimization by means of borrowing literary
> models from the Talmudic literature, and the inclination to adopt modes
> from the Arab culture, apparently led to the barrier-breaking new phe-
> nomenon in Jewish culture.[103]

To understand better how these literary barriers were broken in the early
medieval period, we will turn to a brief examination of these emergent styles.
We will see how *The Midrash of the Ten Commandments* and *The Alphabet of
Ben Sira* stick to classic aggadic forms even as they merge with multi-cultural
folklore as they begin to expand the very definition of "midrash". Then we will
turn our attention to two anthological works with known authors: *An Elegant*

Emanuel Bin Gorion, ed., Dan Ben-Amos, ed., *Mimekor Yisrael: Classical Jewish Folktales*,
(Philadelphia: Jewish Publication Society of America), 1976, Vol. 1, xliii.

102   Yasif, 246.

103   Ibid.

Composition Concerning Relief after Adversity of Rabbi Nissim ben Jacob, and Joseph ben Meir ibn Zabara's *The Book of Delights*. These later works consciously combined Greco-Roman and Arabic legends and styles into intentionally Jewish contexts. Together as two pairs, these four works paint a clear picture of how the medieval Jewish mediation between cultures fostered the formation of new narrative forms.

The Midrash of the Ten Commandments

The Midrash to the Ten Commandments (and *The Alphabet of Ben Sira*) reflect the medieval movement away from earlier literary forms. *The Midrash of the Ten Commandments*, traditionally dated to the early 10th century, preserves some of the features of the classical midrashim: citation of individual biblical verses to serve as lemma; seemingly homiletic interpretation; illustrative tales; and an *inclusio* structure that connects the concluding moral passage with the opening words of the midrash. The Midrash unfolds seriatim through the Ten Commandments. It uses materials drawn from the Talmud and gives us an account of how those stories were retold in a medieval setting. It also uses material from the Apocrypha and Pseudepigrapha; the story of Judith, which is related without mentioning her name; and the legends of the anonymous mother and the martyrdom of her seven sons, told in II Maccabees 7.[104]

Despite appearing to cling to traditional aggadic forms, however, the *Midrash of the Ten Commandments* takes certain liberties. It is evident, for example, that the connective material between each commandment and the unfolding tale is at best "tenuous and forced".[105] While each individual commandment frames many particular tales, many of those stories have little, or no, thematic or substantive linkage to the commandment. A striking example of this is found in a story related in the section on the Third Commandment, *You shall not take the Divine Name in vain*:

A tale is told of a certain man who placed a gold dinar in trust with a certain widow. She placed it in a jar of flour and kneaded it into a single loaf, and gave it to a pauper. After some days, the owner of the dinar came and said to her, "Give me my dinar." She replied, "May I enjoy death if I have

---

104 See, Shelomo Buber, *Midrash 'Aicha Rabba*, (Vilna: The Widow Rom and Sons), 1898, 1:48, 86–87. This early midrashic account of the same martyrdom tale was also available to the author/editor of *The Midrash to the Ten Commandments*.

105 Eli Yasif, "The Hebrew Narrative Anthology in the Middle Ages," Prooftexts, 17, (1997), 154.

profited in any way from your dinar!" Not many days passed when one of her sons died. When the sages heard of this matter they said, "And if this one, who swore truthfully, could lose her sons—for one who swears falsely, how much the moreso!"[106]

While the widow's oath is unintentionally false, it is easy to discover a logical flaw in the Sages' connection to the third commandment: the widow in no way swore in the name of God. Joel Rosenberg, who translated this *Midrash*, appended a footnote to this section that makes our claim emphatically:

> The widow's act is technically a theft and a violation of a trustee relation, but these are committed for the sake of charity. None of the details of the brief episode has a rational explanation, nor is there any clear-cut way to sort out the rights and wrongs of the woman's action or its apparent divine recompense. The sages' "explanation," by relating the event to the Third Commandment, is appropriately off the point. The total montage thus supplies, perhaps inadvertently, an accurate portrait in the difficulty of the relation between legality, morality and divine justice.[107]

Here we see that the writers/editors of *Midrash to the Ten Commandments* seem ambivalent: one foot appears planted in the world of the older, more classic literary style, while the other foot finds itself extended towards a new literary form in which the homiletic context is no longer central but, rather, it is the story itself that attracts the focus of the writer(s). There is a wonderful story to be told: a moral fable with a watchword about being careful about speech. Clearly the authorial desire to include this story in *The Midrash of the Ten Commandments* trumped the clear fact that the story has a tenuous—at best—connection to any of the Ten Commandments.

This work also clearly demonstrates the emergence of a new style of literature in its implementation of tales from other cultures. As we have seen, this Midrash, in part, draws from Jewish folklore, and, in part, from international sources. Furthermore, however, the overall narrative sets aside the more reverential tone of classical aggadah in favor of a grittier, or at least more realistically *human*, portrait of daily life. Joel Rosenberg captures the transition from the more pious tone of the Talmud to the unidealized images in this collection:

---

106   Stern and Mirsky, *Rabbinic Fantasies*, 98.
107   Ibid., 114–115.

... the collection elicits fascination for its exclusively irreverent and satirical tone. Behind the veil of orthodox exhortation, it portrays unapologetically sordid or extreme behavior: familial treachery, uxoriousness, false accusation, random violence, sexual chauvinism, idolatry, adultery, materialistic rapacity, divine refusal, horrific divine castigation.... As is frequent in satire, the moralist and the immoralist merge in the one editor, and we cannot say to which vision he is most drawn.[108]

The Midrash of the Ten Commandments, as it relates to its Rabbinic predecessor, both perpetuates inherited forms even as it invents—or perhaps simply makes room for—new styles and wider understandings. The work is new because it gives voice to literary styles that range far from the standard Rabbinic prototypes; the book is continuous with the past because it presents itself in and preserves the forms of classical midrash. With *The Midrash of the Ten Commandments*, perhaps the earliest work of the medieval period, something new is emerging in an old form.

The Alphabet of Ben Sira

The Alphabet of Ben Sira was also created in the Geonic period, and has been dated between the 9th and 10th Centuries CE.[109] Like *The Midrash of the Ten Commandments*, the author(s) of this work remains unknown. The *Alphabet*, as we will see, reflects a Muslim aura, and is built on a tripartite structure. The birth of Ben Sira is related in part one, followed by twenty-two aphorisms unfolding in the order of the twenty-two letters of the Hebrew alphabet, to each of which Ben Sira responds in turn. In part two, King Nebuchadnezzar summons the prodigy Ben Sira to his court and addresses him with twenty-two questions; Ben Sira responds to the king with twenty-two narrative tales. In part three, twenty-two proverbs are given; here, only a few of these have a correlating response or illustration. The narrative of *The Alphabet of Ben Sira* is aggadic in style and employs, perhaps for the first time in Hebrew literature, parody. The work "treats various biblical characters and Rabbinic motifs irreverently, at times almost to the point of insanity."[110] This nearly nonsensical material is represented in the following of the prodigy's responses to the king:

---

108   Ibid., 92.
109   Strack/Stemberger, where Stemberger claims that the work originated in Babylonia and dates from the 9th–10th century CE, 334.
110   Stern and Mirsky, *Rabbinic Fantasies*, 167.

Nebuchadnezzar asked Ben Sira: "Why does the ox have no hair under the nose?" "Joshua was a stout man when the Israelites and Joshua were encircling Jericho in order to bring it down, and they brought him first a horse to ride, then an ass, and then a mule, but all of them died under him. Finally, they brought Joshua an ox, and it managed to carry him. When Joshua saw this, he kissed the ox on its nose, and that is why it has no hair."[111]

Such stories do not beggar belief. Instead, they seem intentionally ironic and unconventional. Norman Broznick noted this in his introduction to his translation of *The Alphabet of Ben Sira*.[112] He asserts that the intent of the work was:

> a kind of academic burlesque—perhaps even entertainment for Rabbinic scholars themselves—that included vulgarities, absurdities, and the irreverent treatment of acknowledged sanctities ... read as popular entertainment in most Rabbinic communities throughout the Middle Ages. In some quarters, however, it enjoyed an unusual respectability.[113]

This burlesque is quite literally apparent in one particular response Ben Sira provides to the King. This story bears relevance on our study, as it is an early medieval depiction of King Solomon, who in this instance not only demonstrates consummate wisdom, but one that serves a concomitant lust:

> First, he asked him how he shaved the hare's head.
> "With a lime solution," Ben Sira answered.
> "Of what kind?"
> Ben Sira replied, "A depilatory solution of lime, composed of lime and arsenic. Solomon used his wisdom to invent this solution in the days of your mother, the queen of Sheba. When she came bearing gifts to Solomon in order to observe his wisdom, he found her very attractive and wanted to sleep with her. But Solomon discovered that she was very hairy. He took lime and arsenic, minced the lime by hand with a knife, crushed the arsenic, and mixed them together in water, and so made a depilatory solution of lime. Then he smeared her with the solution and bathed her,

---

111   Ibid., 187.
112   We see parts of our own study reflected in the version Broznick chose to translate: he based his English on the version first published by Mortiz Steinschneider and later reproduced by Judah David Eisenstein in his *Oẓar HaMidrashim*.
113   Stern and Mirsky, *Rabbinic Fantasies*, 168.

and her hair fell off. He had intercourse with her right away. And she said to Solomon, 'I did not believe all these things until I saw them with my own eyes.'"

Nebuchadnezzar asked Ben Sira, "How do you know all this?"

"I am a prophet," he answered. "The Holy One, blessed be He, reveals to me all that is unknown"[114]

Here, we do seem to have something that breaks sharply with the past of Jewish, or at least Rabbinic literature. *The Midrash of the Ten Commandments* exemplifies the transitional stage of Hebrew storytelling in the early Middle Ages, as its creators, stylistic invention aside, preserve many modes found in the classical aggadic literary tradition. The author/editor(s) of *The Alphabet of Ben Sira*, however, breaks more sharply with the past and abandons the stylistic norms of earlier Hebrew literature. Eli Yasif speculates that this abandonment might, in part, be connected to an attempt to reach a new audience:

[*The Alphabet of Ben* Sira] presents the narrative material as part of a new literary pattern, apparently intended for an audience of readers other than Torah scholars and study-hall devotees.[115]

The audience for which any of these emerging medieval works was written is a matter of speculation. But what is clear with both *The Alphabet of Ben Sira* and *The Midrash of the Ten Commandments* is that old midrashic forms are being filled with a novel kind of material: the result is works that looks like, or can be presented as, midrash, but begin to appear like something new. How completely distinct or how strikingly similar may be an arena for academics and aesthetes to debate. However, by the dawn of the medieval period, Jews began using the midrashic forms of antiquity to express emotions and ideas infrequently found in previous Jewish literature. Soon after, as we will explore below, Jewish literature felt free to distance itself even further from the classical Rabbinic terminology, frameworks, and standards.

---

114   Ibid., 180.
115   Eli Yasif, "The Hebrew Narrative Anthology in the Middle Ages," 155.

Nissim Ben Jacob ben Nissim Ibn Shahin

An Elegant Composition Concerning Relief after Adversity
Two additional medieval works illustrate—each in its own way—how Jewish
medieval literature maintained its connection to the past even as it broke new
literary ground in its own day. Both of these works, it is important to note, are
attributed to authors: *An Elegant Composition Concerning Relief after Adversity*
to Nissim ben Jacob ben Nissim Ibn Shahin of Qairouwan in North Africa
(modern Tunisia), and *The Book of Delights* to Joseph ben Meir ibn Zabara
of Barcelona. Each of these works follows a very different form in laying out
its narrative material and moral message. In a very narrow way, both of them
share textual similarities in their description of the life of King Solomon with
the Medieval Midrashim that are at the core of this study. Despite their notice-
able differences, however, it has even been speculated that the two renditions
(at least of the Solomon Material) flow from a common Arabic version of the
story.[116]

The *Elegant Composition* is an anthology of Hebrew stories and folk tales
written in the early 11th Century. Reading the work, it seems Rabbi Nissim's
purpose was motivational: to lift the human spirit, to strengthen belief, to rein-
force faith, and to inspire a higher morality in his readers. To achieve this end,
Rabbi Nissim employed legends and tales to such an extent that Ta-Shema
claims the work was "possibly the first prose Hebrew storybook in medieval
Hebrew literature."[117] These stories were drawn, in large part although not
exclusively, from early Hebrew sources; thus the *Elegant Composition* has
proven important for the study of Rabbinic literature. Furthermore, this singular opus provides literary insight into the life of the Jews in Qairouwan, which
was a vital religious and cultural way station between the ancient Jewish center in Babylonia and the emerging center of Judaism in Andalus. In cataloguing
the assets of the work, it should be noted that its value as a resource for the
biography of its author is incalculable. Lastly, and perhaps of greatest importance to our study, the *Elegant Composition* inspired many later literary works.
Brinner claims:

[it not only gave] rise to numerous similar ma'assiyyot, as such stories
came to be called, but it opened a new era in the publication of Hebrew

---

116   Eli Yasif, "Meshalim shel Melech Shelomo," ("Parables of King Solomon"), Jewish Studies
        in Hebrew Literature (9), 365.
117   Israel Moses TaShema, in *Encyclopaedia Judaica*, (Jerusalem: Keter Publishing House
        Ltd.), 1971, vol. 12, column, 1184.

tales and legends directly inspired by, or even translated from, Arabic literature.[118]

The connection to Muslim culture here comes to the forefront: *An Elegant Composition* was written in Judeo-Arabic, that is, the form of the Arabic language spoken by Jews in the Muslim world, but written in Hebrew script. It seems certain that Rabbi Nissim wanted to speak directly to the hearts of his fellow Jews and used the quotidian language of his people in the same fashion that Jewish immigrants to New York's Lower East Side translated the hits of Tin Pan Alley into Yiddish. This blending of Jewish with Arabic went beyond language itself: Rabbi Nissim crafted oft-told stories drawn primarily from classical Jewish sources but sometimes infused them with details and *realia* drawn from the Muslim world in which he and his audience lived. In his recasting of the traditional sources, Rabbi Nissim sought to inspire his listeners and readers with courage and faith in the face of the adversities of life. While a thorough examination of the *Elegant Composition* is not our current task, the following brief episode highlights many of the aspects salient to our study: the reflection on moral values, the presence of Scriptural texts in non-traditional aggadic fashion, and the dangerous—although perhaps salvific—lot left to Jews who lived at the mercy of foreign kings.

The Child Taken Captive While Holding a Scroll of the Book of Genesis

The Sages tell a story of a man in Israel who had an only son. When he reached the age of three, the father had [a scroll of] the Book of Genesis made for him and sat him down in the synagogue before the teacher. One day an army entered the city and took its inhabitants captive, including the boy who was taken holding the Book of Genesis in his hand. They took him to the city in which the king resided and imprisoned him together with the other prisoners, while the Book was deposited in the king's treasury.

One night [thereafter] the king, finding himself unable to sleep, ordered that any books that were in his treasury be brought up, so that they might be read to him and provide entertainment for him. The Book that belonged to the boy was found [among them], but none of the chiefs and scholars knew what was in it.

---

118   Brinner, p. xxx.

One of the king's servant then said, "There is a Jewish boy imprisoned here. Perhaps this is in their script, and he may know it and be able to read it." So the king ordered him to be summoned, and when he was brought in the king's presence he was given the Book to read. But when the boy saw it he wept bitterly, whereupon the king asked him, "Do you know what is in it?" to which the boy replied, "Yes, master."

The king said, "Read to us," and the boy recited to him from *In the beginning* to *And the heaven and the earth were finished.*[119] Thereupon the king said to the boy, "Interpret it," and the boy did so. When the king heard this interpretation, he rose to his feet [from his couch] and knelt down upon the ground for a whole hour. Then he said, "Blessed be God Most High, creator of heaven and earth." He then ordered the boy to be clothed in a handsome robe, seated him beside him, and asked him for his story.

The boy replied, "Master, I am the only child to my parents and was taken captive while I was reciting from this Book before my teacher. Now I know the distress my parents are suffering on account of me, and their weeping and worry."

The king said, "I have no doubt that God had caused this sleeplessness [of mine] tonight solely for your sake. So be of good cheer, for I am going to order that you rejoin your parents, and let your heart rest easy." The next morning the king ordered the boy to be given money and clothing and to be conveyed in a litter until he reached his family. All this was done for him, and he [finally] reached his parents with his heart at ease.

When they asked him, "Son, how did you attain this favor, and how did you return to us? We had already given up hope for you," he recounted to them all that had happened, and they gave thanks to God Most High for His favor in reuniting them with their son after they had despaired of him, he being their only child. And even though the custom is for our children to begin their recitation of the Torah with the Book of Leviticus, yet the man was inspired by God Most High to begin teaching his son with the Book of Genesis, so that it might cause his salvation.[120]

It is with a rather calm detachment that Rabbi Nissim begins this tale of the kidnapping of a three year-old Jewish boy; little seems to be out of place for his audience with foreign rulers having their way with the Jewish community on their campaigns and crusades. The protagonist himself is passive,

---

119   Genesis 1:1 and 2:1, respectively.

120   Brinner, 86–87.

arriving at salvation only after patiently abiding an unknown sentence in jail. Furthermore, our hero—to the extent we can call him that—is no great Torah scholar. Unlike the Talmudic tales of Rabbis outwitting Emperors with Scriptural dexterity, here the boy's interpretation doesn't even merit inclusion in the story. In fact, his tears seem to compel the King to mercy even more so than his ability to read and illustrate Genesis. Ultimately, the entire legend serves to undermine a core Rabbinic practice: commencing the study of Bible with the Book of Leviticus.

This story barely resembles midrash, and certainly doesn't act like it. In fact, excepting the presence of a religious message, it appears to be an inversion of many of the standards of earlier Rabbinic literature. Were it not written in Hebrew letters, or couched as a cautionary tale of the "Sages of Israel", we might have a hard time discerning any connection it might have to previous Jewish literature. However, *An Elegant Composition* enjoyed popularity in its own time, and comes down to our age as a sterling example of the formative Jewish literature of the medieval period.

Joseph ben Meir ibn Zabara: *The Book of Delight*

The creation of *An Elegant Composition* in the 12th century marked, therefore, the beginning of a fertile century in the spiritual and creative life of the Jews.[121] Joseph ben Meir ibn Zabara, the author of *The Book of Delight* was fortuitously born during this period in Barcelona, Spain in 1140. He was a contemporary of many Jewish luminaries of Spain and Provence whose influence in poetry, philosophy, and translation made that era golden: among them were, Moses ben Maimon, Judah al-Harizi, and the Ibn Tibbon family. Joseph ibn Zabara, following in the footsteps of his father, studied medicine, and wrote on medical topics; he drafted works on philosophy, astronomy, and physics as well. His thirst for knowledge brought him to the south of Spain, and later to Narbonne, in Provence, where he learned at the feet of Joseph Qimḥi. After those years of wandering and growth, ibn Zabara ended his wanderings and returned to Barcelona.

In his literary achievement *The Book of Delight*, ibn Zabara demonstrates his broad knowledge of Jewish sources, specifically the Hebrew Bible, and the two Talmuds. However, in the stories it amasses and tales it tells, *The Book of Delight* not only reveals knowledge of Greek philosophy but also employs fables, folktales, aphorism, satiric epigrams, humor, and apologues. No resource

---

121   Judith Dishon, *The Book of Delight*, (Jerusalem, Reuben Maas, LTD.), 1985, 13.

of any foreign culture—Indian, Greek or Arabic—is cast aside in helping ibn
Zabara attain his aim, which is the moral education of his readers even more
than their mere entertainment. Davidson, in introducing his translation of *The
Book of Delight*, notes how profoundly fashioned it is by the influences of both
the Byzantine and Muslim Empires:

> In the Book of Delights, more than in any other book of its type, the impact
> of all three cultures that dominated Hebrew thought in the Middle Ages
> is discernable, the Greek, the Arabic, and the Indian.[122]

It is not just its wide-ranging sources that make *The Book of Delight* so excep-
tional an example of the cross-cultural bridges being built in medieval times.
In constructing the book, ibn Zabara relies upon two modes of writing to guide
his stylistic artistry: an ancient literary, international genre, the framework narrative; and also an inherently Islamic style, the *maqama*.

The framework narrative is one of the earliest techniques for unifying groups
of disparate stories; it has been likened to an umbrella spread open to shelter
individual tales under a single cover.[123] *The Alphabet of Ben Sira* employs the 22
Hebrew letters as its narrative frame; Scheherazade's attempt to tell stories to
escape execution is the framework narrative of *Arabian Nights*.

The other stylistic mode ibn Zabara employs, the *maqama*, is a unique product of the Middle Ages. It is a "rhymed-prose narrative" intentionally modeled
after a parallel genre in Arabic literature said to have been invented by the
10th century author Badi al-aman al Hamadhhani.[124] While differing in literary style, the *maqama* in many ways parallels the ribald, real-life storytelling
personified by *An Elegant Composition*. David Stern provides important insight
into the history of the *maqama* tradition:

> The tradition, the only one in medieval Jewish narrative that might be
> considered authentically secular, initially grew out of the same soil as
> the lyric poetry of the Spanish Hebrew Golden Age in the twelfth cen-
> tury. Modeled upon an Arabic genre, Hebrew maqama was both ornately
> rhetorical and highly conventionalized. Thus the various maqamat that
> together form a collection usually share a common narrator, who, in each
> episode, describes a character whom he has met on his journeys. The

---

122   Israel Davidson, tr., *Sefer Sha'ashu'im of Rabbi Joseph ben Me'ir Zabara*, (Berlin: Eshkol
      Publishers), 1925, 15.
123   Eli Yasif, *The Hebrew Folktale*, 67.
124   Stern and Mirsky, *Rabbinic Fantasies*, 25.

latter character is typically also the common hero of all the maqamat in the collection, and his exploits generally include some kind of hoax or deception that he perpetrates upon the innocent victim. While their narratives center upon the illicit but comic machinations of the protagonist, maqamat also portray a host of richly imagined characters, including forsaken lovers, village yokels, pretentious philosophers, disreputable poets, corrupt rabbis, unfaithful wives, essentially the array of social types who populate Spanish Jewish culture in all its worldly and unworldly varieties. In the hands of some of the later authors, maqama even became a satirical tool for social criticism, directed in particular against the ambitious, aristocratic courtier classes that dominated Spanish Jewry.[125]

The author of *The Book of Delight* had a plan, a larger design as he contemplated his literary opus. Joseph ibn Zabara invented the rather exotically named giant, *Enan Hanatash* the son of *Arnan Ha-Desh*, to escort him on his narrative journey, to be his companion, and to share his knowledge and wit.[126] Ibn Zabara arranged the opus around his beliefs, which are reflected in the many tales and moral aphorisms found in *The Book of Delight*. He distilled from his scientific knowledge, the essence of his medical expertise and shared it with his readers. Merriam Sherwood attempted to encapsulate ibn Zabara's wide-ranging expertise and focused purpose in his insightful introduction to the English translation by Moses Hadas. In doing so, he also located ibn Zabara's place in a long line of medieval Jewish middlemen exchanging stories between cultures:

> In its conception *The Book of Delight* proves, upon analysis, to be a more ambitious undertaking than the usual framework narrative; it is not, *The Thousand and One Nights*, the *Decameron, The Canterbury Tales*, a collection of stories merely. In it the author attempts to set forth, frequently by the common medieval device of questions and answers, the sum of his knowledge and of his beliefs, literary, moral and scientific. The largest amount of space devoted to the last is to be explained by his profession, that of physician. But the moral tales which he tells form an important part of the work; they are the most interesting part for us because of the relation they bear to the narrative writings of his contemporaries in other lands. Zabara's scientific, especially his medical knowledge is essentially that which was traditional in his time among the Arabs and which was

---

125 Ibid., 125–127.
126 Israel Abrahams, *The Book of Delight and Other Papers*, (Philadelphia: The Jewish Publication Society of America), 1912, 28.

spreading throughout Europe as Christians, whether through commerce or crusades or through the Jews as middleman, became more and more intimately acquainted with Mohammedan culture. But the stories in *The Book of Delight* arrest our attention particularly because, with some of them are tales that were the common property of East and West in the Middle Ages, others seem not to have been generally known, perhaps at all, to the Christian literature of Western Europe. These were not known, at least in the form in which Zabara recounts them. The themes are, for the most part, common enough—for example, several of them deal with faithlessness of women—but the tales themselves apparently have no parallels in the Christian West.[127]

Ibn Zabara's work is punctuated by satire and medieval science, folktales about the powerful and wealthy, and animal fables filled with commonsensical wisdom. The author is also remarkably well versed in a wide-range of folklore and philosophy; demonstrating this mastery is among the most cherished and enduring sections of *The Book of Delight*, ibn Zabara's discourse on love:

> For they asked Plato, "What is a lover?" When one saith, "Thou art he; thou and none beside thee," he replied. When Galen was asked, "What is love?" he replied, "Similarity of soul"; and it is the wont of similars to be conjoined, for that they are of a single nature. Another sage was asked, "What is love?" "Brotherly nighness of soul," he replied, "and not brotherly nighness of body." They asked of Aristotle, "What is love?" "One heart," said he, "Divided into two bodies."[128]

Ibn Zabara was a Hebrew author who intentionally and overtly incorporated non-Jewish traditions into his writings. While he did rely heavily on the Jewish tradition as well, he was unafraid to disagree directly with the Rabbinic tradition he clearly knew well. This can best be seen through a few of his parables, whose morals directly contravene dicta of the Sages. Parable #34 reads, "When is silence better than speech? At the time of lustfulness."[129] This seems contrary to the spirit of *Pirqei Avot* 1:17, which indicates the value of keeping quiet when in the presence of Sages in the house of study, "There is nothing better for the body than silence." Similarly, ibn Zabara seems to be building on and departing from the Rabbinic traditions about acceptable prevarication when

127   Joseph ben Meir Zabara, Moses Hadas, tr., Merriam Sherwood, *Introduction, The Book of Delight by Joseph ben Meir Zabara*, (New York: Columbia University Press) 1932, 12.

128   Ibid., 155–156.

129   Ibid., 104.

he teaches in Parable #87, "Lying is justifiable in only three instances: in war, for then it is cunning strategy; in making peace between man and his neighbor; and when a man giveth pleasure to his wife."[130] Here we seem to have a blending, if not an intentional distortion of inherited tradition. The Rabbis of the Talmud at BT *Yebamot* 65b argue that a white lie is permitted to keep peace in a marriage; ibn Zabara relocates the permission for such a fib in the relationship between neighbors, and places a different allowance for prevarication between husband and wife. For all that *The Book of Delights* is built upon a solid Jewish foundation, so too does it both incorporate foreign texts and invert traditional Jewish norms. Because of this, and in many other ways as well, it is the appropriate place for us to depart from our cursory overview of early medieval Jewish literature, and return to examine how these works inform the origins and development of Medieval Midrash.

Literary Creation: Medieval Midrash

Of the four medieval Jewish works we have examined, only one of them bears the title of *Midrash*. Regardless, the fashion in which all of them expand the boundaries of Jewish literature beyond the bounds of pure scriptural interpretation sets the stage for the types of narratives found throughout the canon of Medieval Midrashim. Some Medieval Midrashim, like the *Aggadat Tefillah Shemoneh Esreh*, or "The Legend of the Eighteen Benedictions", follow the lead of *Midrash on the Ten Commandments* and use traditional Jewish texts—in this case the statutory eighteen prayers that constitute the *Amidah*—as a quasi-midrashic narrative frame.[131] Others, like *Ma'aseh Torah*, or "Torah Deeds", tell moral tales with ostensible—but remote—connections to Jewish themes; such works seem to be under the influence of *An Elegant Composition*.[132] Still more midrashim, such as *Sefer Oreḥot Ḥayyim*, or "The Book of the Paths of Life", are in keeping with the *Alphabet* insofar as they are aimed at an audience that extends well past the House of Study and the Rabbis who dominate it.[133]

---

130   Ibid., 109.

131   This text exists in two versions: recension A, (Jellinek, V:54–55, and Eisenstein, 2:584–5) and recension B, (Jellinek, V:55–6, and Eisenstein, 2:585).

132   Jellinek printed this midrash with this name in II:92–101. According to Townsend, it is also known by the names *Midrash Shelosha v'Arba*, *Pirqei Rabbenu haQodesh*, and *Ḥuppat Eliyahu*.

133   Eisenstein, 1: 28–31. The Hebrew text and English translation appear side-by-side as "The Paths of Life by R. Eleazar the Great," in Abrahams, I., *Hebrew Ethical Wills*, (Philadelphia: Jewish Publication Society), 1926, 1:31–49.

Finally, like the brilliant *Book of Delight*, nearly all of the Medieval Midrashim demonstrate a profound connection to Indian, Greco-Roman or Muslim literature, if not all three combined. *Ma'aseh Avraham Avinu 'Alav HaShalom*, or "The Deeds of our Father Abraham, Peace be upon Him!", was perhaps originally written in Arabic and draws heavily from Muslim traditions;[134] *Ma'aseh Yehudit*, or "The Deeds of Judith", draw heavily from Hellenistic sources.[135] The upheavals that marked the end of Antiquity overturned the literary soil of the Jewish people and allowed for new directions in the growth and development of Jewish literature. Our small subsection, the canon of Medieval Midrash, is certainly part of the produce of that fruitful garden.

Coda: Returning to Questions

Just as we have discovered that Eisenstein's *Oẓar Midrashim* loosely addresses the question "What are Medieval Midrashim?", so too have we been able to answer—although rather loosely—the issue of *when* these works were written. Likewise, we see that these works have their origins throughout the realms of Islam and Christendom; *where* they were composed was anywhere Jews lived during the Middle Ages. Because so little is known about authorship, we will not likely know *who*, individually, wrote each of these individual pieces. Finally, through tracing the general development of Jewish literature in these same Middle Ages, we see *how* they were written: different styles and content from wide-ranging cultures were amassed, repackaged, and exchanged by perhaps the same Jews who amassed, repackaged, and exchanged so much merchandise through medieval times.

Admittedly, these are general answers to questions that might hope to achieve more focus. However, the limits of the literature and the scholarship that attends them leads us to be honest in attesting what we can say to be true, and candid in admitting the vast amount of information that presently seems unknowable, and—without massive and unforeseeable scientific and literary intervention—will likely remain so for generations. Of course, for particular midrashim from our medieval canon, more answers are available than for others. However, for most texts in this canon, these general statements will need to suffice, especially on the fronts of *who, what, when, where, and how*. However, *why* each piece is written is a doorway open to interpretation,

---

134   Jellinek, I:25–34.

135   Jellinek, II:12–22. For parallels, see also *Midrash l'Ḥanukkah*, (Jellinek, I:132–136), and *Midrash Aḥer l'Ḥanukkah*, (Jellinek I:137–141).

to study, and to evaluation. The remainder of this work will try to evaluate the range of meanings that lead various anonymous authors to craft works of Medieval Midrash. By using the lens of those works written around the figure of King Solomon, we will attempt to evaluate the wide range of reasons that seemed to compel medieval Jews to take advantage of the literary environment of their time and create new works, wonderful pieces of Medieval Midrash.

PART 2

Six Midrashim of Solomon

∵

Overview

Midrashim about King Solomon: An Illustration

Medieval times witnessed a major expansion of the boundaries of Jewish literature. By the dawn of the modern era, the pioneers of a scientific study of Judaism not only anthologized this widened array of texts and tales, but also categorized them under the name Midrash. Here, as illustration and overview of this genre, we will explore the diverse views of Solomon as found in the Medieval Midrashim arranged around his personality: *Midrash Al Yithallel, An Episode concerning King Solomon, The Episode of the Ant, Parables of King Solomon, The Form of the Throne of King Solomon,* and *The Throne and Hippodrome of King Solomon.*[136] These narratives serve as an appropriate introduction to this field of literature, because these six texts encompass the wide range of style and content found in Medieval Midrashim. Some, like *Midrash Al Yithallel,* look like classical Midrash, and follow the lead of Scriptural text to offer their insights; others offer moral tales loosely linked to a verse from the Bible, as may be seen in *The Parables of King Solomon.* A few of these tales, such as *The Episode of the Ant,* are clearly connected to Islamic culture, while the two narratives about King Solomon's throne are profoundly influenced by the Byzantine Empire. While the best way to understand the field of Medieval Midrashim would be to read the hundreds of texts anthologized in the collections, these six stories revolving around King Solomon provide a most thorough introduction to the field.

Our translation and commentary of these texts will continue to trace the larger tropes of the form and function of Medieval Midrashim. However, insofar as these works are connected to the figure of King Solomon, we will also explore the themes that emerge connected to his character, and to the symbolic role King Solomon played in medieval Jewish communities. Thus, in addition to our overall aim of illustrating the development of Medieval Midrash, an added goal is not only to provide thorough translations of and critical commentary to these texts, but also to analyze the figure of this complex king in post-biblical Jewish literature. Of particular importance to our

---

136 Our work here builds upon the work commenced by Bernard H. Mehlman in his translation and commentary of *Midrash Al Yithallel*, one third of which focuses upon the character of Solomon. Originally published by Bernard H. Mehlman, "Midrash Al Yithallel—Do not Boast: Introduction, Translation, and Exposition," *CCAR Journal: A Reform Jewish Quarterly*, Spring 2014, 88–101.

larger study, the connecting figure of King Solomon will allow us to compare and contrast the various apparent motives behind the creation of these pieces. This second level of interpretation, ultimately, will bolster us in evaluating the still lingering question about Medieval Midrashim: *why* different authors (or communities) were moved to create these works of literature.

King Solomon of the Bible: The Dichotomy

To understand the depiction of King Solomon in Medieval Midrash, we must first understand King Solomon in the Bible. Solomon was in many ways the embodiment of an earthly man: he sought and discovered women, wealth, and power. Yet Solomon also received the divine imprimatur: he was endowed with heavenly wisdom and was ordained to build God's Holy Temple. The dichotomy that is King Solomon is captured in the tension between the biblical books of Kings and Chronicles. In Kings, we read of Solomon's human range: he is born of adultery, attains kingship through civil war, receives the gift of divine wisdom, marries foreign wives, amasses great wealth, makes treaties with surrounding nations, builds the Holy Temple, and leaves a disaster of succession in his wake. I Chronicles cleans up his act: for the first time, Solomon's name is specifically linked to the peace he will bring. In this telling, he attains the throne through unchallenged inheritance; only here is he depicted as attaining a regal majesty unparalleled in the history of Israel.

Solomon was born of the illicit union of David and Bathsheba; while his mother names him in the second book of Samuel,[137] we learn nothing more of him until the opening of I Kings. Amazingly, the first seventeen times Solomon's name is mentioned in the Bible, he is passive:[138] either spoken about by others, or the subject of verbs in the passive form. The first action Solomon himself takes—and this is of critical import to our study—is when he sits on the Throne to rule.[139] By the end of the second chapter of I Kings, Solomon has literally executed his father's dying wishes, and through a series of vengeance killings "secures the kingdom".[140] The biblical narrative quickly turns from Solomon's bloodthirsty nature to other passions: we begin to see his lust for both women and political power as he marries the daughter of the

---

137   II Samuel 12:20.
138   Including the Samuel citation and the first sixteen mentions in I Kings Chapter 1.
139   I Kings 1:46.
140   II Kings 2:46.

Pharaoh.[141] With these remarkably human traits firmly in tow, Scripture tells perhaps the paradigmatic story about Solomon; it explains why he is associated with wisdom:

> [4]The king went to Gibeon to sacrifice there, for that was the largest shrine; on that altar Solomon presented a thousand burnt offerings. [5]At Gibeon Adonai appeared to Solomon in a dream by night; and God said, "Ask, what shall I grant you?" [6]Solomon said, "You dealt most graciously with Your servant my father David, because he walked before You in faithfulness and righteousness and in integrity of heart. You have continued this great kindness to him by giving him a son to occupy his throne, as is now the case. [7]And now, Adonai my God, You have made Your servant king in place of my father David; but I am a young lad, with no experience in leadership. [8]Your servant finds himself in the midst of the people You have chosen, a people too numerous to be numbered or counted. [9]Grant, then, Your servant an understanding mind to judge Your people, to distinguish between good and bad; for who can judge this vast people of Yours?"
>
> [10]Adonai was pleased that Solomon had asked for this. [11]And God said to him, "Because you asked for this—you did not ask for long life, you did not ask for riches, you did not ask for the life of your enemies, but you asked for discernment in dispensing justice—[12]I now do as you have spoken. I grant you a wise and discerning mind; there has never been anyone like you before, nor will anyone like you arise again. [13]And I also grant you what you did not ask for—both riches and glory all your life—the like of which no king has ever had. [14]And I will further grant you long life, if you will walk in My ways and observe My laws and commandments, as did your father David."[142]

It is the Solomon of this second paragraph, the wise and discerning Solomon who never sought the life of his enemies, who becomes the figure of I Chronicles. The Chronicles account of the tales told in Kings whitewashes the human, lustful, imperfect Solomon; Chronicles presents Solomon [*shelomo*] as a near-perfect [*shalem*] bringer of peace [*shalom*]:

> [7]David said to Solomon, "My son, I wanted to build a House for the name of Adonai my God. [8]But the word of Adonai came to me, saying, 'You have shed much blood and fought great battles; you shall not build a House for

141   I Kings 3:1.
142   I Kings 3:4ff.

My name, for you have shed much blood on the earth in My sight. [9]But you will have a son who will be a man at rest, for I will give him rest from all his enemies on all sides; Solomon will be his name and I shall confer peace and quiet on Israel in his time. [10]He will build a House for My name; he shall be a son to Me and I to him a father, and I will establish his throne of kingship over Israel forever.'"[143]

Chronicles mentions no struggle in Solomon's succession of David;[144] it re-tells the divine gift of wisdom at Gibeon, yet fails to preface it with any mention of Pharaoh or his daughter.[145] Solomon's riches and preference for foreign horses are depicted in Chronicles, but only insofar as they are the necessary prerequisites for building God's Temple in Jerusalem. Even when Solomon wages war, he does so in the service of the Kingdom of Israel whose borders he increases and security he enhances. In fact, when at the end of such a campaign he brings the daughter of Pharaoh to Jerusalem as captive, he does not bring her into the royal palace lest he taint the sanctity of God's Holy Temple.[146] The books of Chronicles, in retelling many of the same tales, present a near-perfect Solomon who is such a marked contrast to the passionate, earthly, and rather human ruler of the books of Kings.

Beyond these differing descriptions, the ascription of the existentialist *Qohelet* to Solomon's pen further complicates the biblical picture of this King. Granted, the Bible itself only ascribes the Book of Proverbs to King Solomon; his authorship would be in perfect keeping with the Divine Wisdom endowed on him at Gibeon. However, subsequent tradition identifies Solomon as the Son of David, King in Jerusalem, who in Ecclesiastes is only named Qohelet.[147] As we will see, *Qohelet*'s themes of futility and uselessness—of life being so much 'striving after vanity and the wind'—will surface in the Medieval Midrashim about King Solomon.

These varied biblical accounts of Solomon set the stage for the dichotomies and differing perspectives that remain connected to this King through *all* later

---

143   I Chronicles 22:7ff.

144   I Chronicles 23:1, 29:3ff.

145   II Chronicles chapter 1.

146   II Chronicles 8:11.

147   In a sense, this identification of Solomon as the son of David who served as King in Jerusalem seems obvious. However, seeing as the biblical phrase "son of David" could mean anyone of the Davidic monarchic line, in fact Qohelet could be any descendant of David who ruled over the Southern Kingdom.

literature, be it Jewish, Gnostic, Christian, Muslim, or Esoteric. Throughout our analysis, we will continue to trace how the different aspects of Solomon's characterization continue to frame the varied approaches of the Medieval Midrashim associated with him.

The Texts and Their Histories: An Overview

We have seen how the work of Jellinek and Eisenstein frame, in many ways, the establishment of the genre of Medieval Midrash. Fittingly, editions of all six midrashim are found in both *Beit HaMidrasch* and *Ozar Midrashim*. Our translations of these texts are eclectic in the sense that we relied upon the texts of both books; on the infrequent occasions when they differed, we often opted for Eisenstein's rendition.[148] As discussed previously, the dating of these texts is not a precise science. As Ra'anan Boustan noted in his chapter on the Throne of Solomon, "it is impossible to fix with precision the dating of the compilations" in which this literature is found.[149] However, we do have some information about these manuscripts. According to Jellinek, *An Episode concerning King Solomon* is taken from the book *Emeq ha-Melech* [14d–15a], authored by Naftali Hertz ben Yaakov Elchanan and published in Amsterdam, 1684. *The Episode of the Ant* appears at the end of *Midrash VaYosha* in a manuscript presently at Cambridge University, while *Parables of King Solomon* and *The Form of the Throne of King Solomon* seem to appear first in Jellinek's publications.[150] More is known about *The Throne and Hippodrome of King Solomon*: Jellinek informs us it is housed in codicil 222 of the Royal Library in Munich, and was first published by Perles in *Graetz's Monthly Bulletin*, 1872. In 1962, Evelyne Ville-Patlagean argued that the text was produced in tenth century Byzantium; Boustan argues this is more likely the date of redaction than the date of

---

148 Partial translations of some of these works appear in the *JE*, "Solomon", and in the retelling of the midrashic tradition by Ginzberg, *Legends of the Jews*.

149 Ra'anan Boustan, "Israelite Kingship, Christian Rome, and the Jewish Imperial Imagination: Midrashic Precursors to the Medieval 'Throne of Solomon," in Natalie B. Dohrmann and Reed, Annette Y., eds., *Jews, Christians and the Roman Empire: The Poetics of Power in Late Antiquity*, [Philadelphia: University of Pennsylvania Press], 2013.

150 It should be noted that Jellinek does make reference to *Proverbs* appearing in *The Collection of Const.*, a work we have not been able to locate.

composition.[151] In our introductory material to each midrash, we will detail the manuscript and textual history of each piece to the extent possible.[152]

The stories related in these legends have a far more traceable history. While we will, in the critical commentaries, go into deep detail for the parallels we were able to discover, these texts generally borrow widely from Rabbinic, Byzantine, and Islamic literature. These tales often repeat stories of the Midrashim and Talmudim, and also make multiple direct references to the Quran. Specifically, the two texts on Solomon's Throne are built upon earlier traditions found in *Targum Sheni* to Esther and *Midrash Abba Gurion*. The difficulty in precisely dating this material is in part connected to their technique of artfully combining legends whose origins span vast swaths of time and geography.

Cultural origins of these midrashim, as we set forth in the previous chapter, connect their seemingly Jewish writers to Islamic and Byzantine settings. Furthermore, the preponderance of rabbinic material present argues for the cultural influence of Greece, Rome, Babylon, and Persia on our stories as well. The authors draw on well-known motifs, themes and tropes from the wider world in which they found themselves, and thereby testify to a cosmopolitan setting in which Jews sat at the center of cultural crossroads. We share a few illustrative examples here.

"The Ring inside the Fish" is a common folkloric motif traced back to Herodotus.[153] There, Polycrates, ruler of Samos, discards a prized ring to put himself through a trial; later, regretting his decision, he discovers the ring in the belly of a fish he is given as tribute.[154] Our Sages were familiar with this motif, and tell a version of the tale in BT *Shabbat* 119a. These strands are woven together in *An Episode Concerning King Solomon*, in which his wife Na'amah discovers his prized signet ring inside the belly of a fish Solomon purchases in the market.[155]

---

151   Boustan, 170–171.

152   While some history exists for each narrative, the details are scant for *An Episode concerning King Solomon*, *The Episode of the Ant* and *The Form of the Throne of King Solomon*. We are able to provide much more analysis of sources for *Midrash Al Yithallel*, *Parables of King Solomon*, and *The Throne and Hippodrome of King Solomon*.

153   Beert Verstraete, "The Ring and the Fish: A Comparison of the Use of a Similar Folklore Motif in Herodotus and a Dutch-Frisian Folktale," *The Afriadian Journal of Netherlandic Studies*, 14–18.

154   Herodotus, *The Histories*, (Oxford: Oxford University Press), 2008, 3:3.

155   Further complicating the cultural milieu, W. A. Clouston argues that this legend also involved the Muslim motif he labels "the demon enclosed in a bottle". W. A Clouston, *Popular Tales and Fictions*, 2 vols. (London: Blackwood and Sons), 1887, 381.

Proverbs 6:6, purportedly written by Solomon, reads, "Go to the ant, lazy one; see her ways and become wise." Islamic tradition expands the association of Solomon and the ant into a complete Sura of the Quran, 27:18–19:

> When they came to the Valley of the Ants, an ant said: 'Go into your dwellings ants, lest Solomon and his warriors should unwittingly crush you.' He smiled at her words, and said: 'Inspire me, Lord, to render thanks for the favours You have bestowed upon me and my parents, and to do good works that will please You.'[156]

The Episode of the Ant ascribes to Solomon unique powers over the wind, demons, and all birds, specifically the vulture. The Quran (and subsequent Hadith traditions) also describe Solomon as possessing these powers, and are likely sources for our stories.

Boustan teaches that our Throne of Solomon traditions likely come from a political *sitz im leben*:

> The existence of an actual throne of Solomon at the Byzantine court is first attested in the tenth-century *Book of Ceremonies* as well as in the contemporaneous eyewitness accounts of the Ottonian diplomat Liudprand of Cremona. These sources locate the throne of Solomon in the Great Triklinos of the Magnaura Palace, the hall where important reception of foreign embassies took place. Like the thrones from which late antique emperors—Roman or Persian—had greeted foreign visitors, the throne of Solomon in the Magnaura stood as a material projection of the universal claims of Byzantine imperial power over all the peoples of the *oikoumene*.[157]

However—and importantly—the existence of an actual Throne of Solomon postdates certain Jewish speculation about his regal chair. The earliest Jewish traditions regarding the Throne are found in *Targum Sheni*, which some date as contemporaneous with the *Tosefta*.[158] Hence our Midrashim about this

---

156   N. J. Dawood, (Tr.), *The Koran*, (London: Clays LTD.), 2004, 265–266. The entire chapter [Sura] is called in Arabic, *al Naml*, "On the Ant".

157   Boustan, 173.

158   Bernard Grossfeld, *The Aramaic Bible: The Two Targums of Esther*, (Collegeville, MN: The Liturgical Press), 1991, 2.

astonishing seat connect centuries of Jewish imagination with the realities of medieval geopolitics.

In these ways, and many more to be noted, the texts of these midrashim were written in a cultural context that was open to a wide variety of influences. Our stories evolved with the passage of time as our history became interconnected with different peoples and cultures. This is, in part, why these Medieval Midrashim regarding King Solomon provide such a helpful illustration of the breadth and scope of this genre. Ecclesiastes says, "Of making of books there is no end,"[159] and there is no limit to the connections between the legends in these midrashim and stories Jews and their neighbors have told for centuries.

The Portrayal of Solomon

While our primary goal remains an evaluation of Medieval Midrash, through analyzing these six works, we are also able to assay the medieval understanding of the figure of Solomon. The differing portrayals of Solomon in I Kings and I Chronicles continue through the midrashic tradition. In some of our legends, Solomon is aggrandized for his power, wealth, and wisdom. In contrasting stories, the king appears humbled, and sometimes humiliated by being powerless or ignorant in the face of certain challenges. Likely, these varying portrayals of Solomon reflect the different reactions of the Rabbis to royal rule reflected in this powerful episode from BT Shabbat 33b:

> R. Judah, R. Jose, and R. Simeon were sitting, and Judah, a son of proselytes, was sitting near them. R. Judah commenced [the discussion] by observing, "How fine are the works of this people! They have made streets, they have built bridges, they have erected baths." R. Jose was silent. R. Simeon b. Yohai answered and said, "All that they made they made for themselves; they built market-places, to set harlots in them; baths, to rejuvenate themselves; bridges, to levy tolls for them."

The Parables of King Solomon aggrandizes his intellect; our two *Throne* texts likewise magnify his natural, magical, and political power. The throne itself is a paradigm of artistry: it contained work in precious metals and stones, along with seemingly magical mechanisms. Twice, Solomon is given credit for the

---

159   Ecclesiastes 12:12.

actual building of this throne;[160] the glory of this cathedra is meant to reflect God's Throne of Glory and thus distinguish Solomon as God's chosen servant on earth. In ascending the throne, Solomon demonstrates his mastery over birds, beasts, and demons; his wisdom is also manifest in quoting endlessly from the Torah's juridical passages. From the throne itself, Solomon issues law for all Israel with powerful appurtenances of pyrotechnics and outlandish zoological cacophonies. These depictions clearly capture the perspective of Rabbi Judah, who so greatly appreciated the magnificent works of Rome.

Solomon's name is synonymous with wisdom. In the biblical text, Solomon prays for and receives the gift of God's insight, adjudicates brilliantly the case of the baby claimed by two prostitutes, and answers the questions of the Queen of Sheba. This motif is expanded upon in the *Throne* midrashim, but receives even more attention in *The Parables of King Solomon*. There, Solomon not only settles complicated cases of law, but does so specifically when others fail to reach a decision. His wisdom exceeds the capacity of all other men, all other kings, and sometimes even otherworldly creatures as well. His gifts range from the sciences to a deep understanding of human nature. The singular scope of his intellect is captured in these tales.

Solomon's wisdom is also associated with the book of Ecclesiastes. Outside of that scroll's two final verses, the subject matter revolves around the futility of wisdom and earthly possessions, which hardly seem to fit the perspective of such a successful sovereign. BT *Megillah* 11b speculates that Solomon lost the kingship during his lifetime (and questions whether or not he later resumed the throne). This notion, that Ecclesiastes was written by Solomon because of a humbling trial in his life, informs the attitude of the parallel narratives of *Midrash Al Yithallel* and *An Episode Concerning King Solomon*, specifically, and *The Episode of the Ant* more widely. The former depicts Solomon's hubris in the face of Asmodeus, King of the Demons. The tragedy that ensues forces Solomon to wander the earth unknown to all. It is only at the end of that episode that Solomon, through either a miracle or a simply well hooked fish, resumes the throne (perhaps from which he penned his reflective *Qohelet*). Similarly, *The Episode of the Ant* captures many aspects of Solomon's bravado; in turn, the wind, an ant, and an architectural marvel outsmart him. These two *Episodes* seem to reflect the perspective of R. Simeon ben Yohai regarding the egotism and selfishness of those in power. The Rabbis, like the Bible they

---

160 *The Throne and Hippodrome* first describes Solomon as the builder of the throne, and later says that God built it.

cherished, were of two minds about Kings, and about Solomon in particular. Our midrashim reflect precisely this dichotomy.

The Traits of Solomon

The Bible depicts Solomon as blessed with wisdom, wealth, and women. His relationship to all three of these becomes thematic for our midrashim. Thus these works not only allow us a prism through which to understand how the authors perceived Solomon's character, but also afford the reader insight (and perhaps even guidance) regarding those personality traits that relate to mind, money, and marriage. As we might imagine, Wisdom remains lauded in this literature. Wealth is appreciated, but not without reservation. And save a few precious counterexamples, women unfortunately are derided in these mostly misogynic tales.

Because Solomon is a synonym for wisdom, and because wisdom is so consistently valued throughout Jewish history, it is not surprising that our texts continue to valorize the gifts of the mind. In 1 Kings 3:9, Solomon asks of God "Grant, then, Your servant an understanding mind to judge Your people, to distinguish between good and bad; for who can judge this vast people of Yours?" *The Parables of King Solomon* shows the breadth of the gift of wisdom Solomon was granted. In "The Man with Two Heads", Solomon creates a practical test to adjudicate a difficult matter; in "The Servant and the Son", he relies upon the secret of a special forensic examination. Distinguishing between good and bad was the blueprint for Solomon's throne: in *The Form of the Throne* we see how its mechanisms were designed to ensure that witnesses would deliver truthful testimony.

While Solomon's intellect is a crowning feature in all these midrashim, in a few of them this trait touches on hubris.[161] In *The Episode of the Ant*, Solomon is rebuked by the Queen of those creatures, who quotes *Mishnah* at him to tame his swelling ego. Later on in that text, even as the King navigates the tricky passages of a magical castle, his search for wisdom meets the grim reminder that even such a great mind is destined to die. Likewise, *An Episode concerning King Solomon* depicts how his quest for knowledge may be both his success and his undoing. Even *The Throne and Hippodrome*, which describes so much of Solomon's success, places the prophets Nathan and Gad at his side to rein in any autocratic action. While Solomon's excessive wisdom is never in doubt, it is not always seen as an exclusively positive trait.

---

161   This is certainly the case in *Midrash Al Yithallel*.

The same may be said of Solomon's wealth. Vast riches and visual glory are the object of the ekphrasis of the two *Throne* midrashim; these leave little doubt that the tellers of our tales wanted to dazzle their audiences with the splendor and opulence of his majesty. In *The Parables*, "The Three Brothers" tells how the youngest sibling chooses wisdom over wealth and is thus rewarded with both; the subtlety here is that Solomon made the same choice, and received the same rewards. In contrast to these celebrations of wealth, *An Episode* depicts the King as a penniless beggar, driven into servitude for a period of three years. It is not the wealth he left behind in Jerusalem that ultimately saves him, but a combination of his wisdom with good fortune. In the midrashic material, as in the Bible, Solomon's riches are obvious and vast, but they do not always bring out the best in his character.

These midrashim do not bring out the best in their author's character when it comes to their depiction and denigration of women. This is unfortunately not entirely surprising given our genre of literature:

> ...folk literature's perspective of the attitude towards women— expressed primarily in the genre of the novella—indicates polyphony: even if, qualitatively, the tales expressing hatred or anxiety of women and femininity outnumber the others, the voice of the others counterbalances them with their power and authenticity.[162]

Our texts mirror precisely this pattern: on the main, they take a low view of women, but the presence of two strong and salvific female characters "counterbalances" these negative tales. Those two women—whom we prefer to put first—are Na'amah, daughter of the King of Ammon and an unnamed (but ultimately recompensed) widow from the *Parables*. The latter, whose wealth is stolen in the wake of her husband's death, ultimately has her cause

---

162 Eli Yasif, *The Hebrew Folktale*, 345. In this chapter, Yasif specifically speaks to our texts, which fit into a cultural pattern of misogyny:

Since most texts on this theme were created in the region of Arab influence, and but few misogynic tales are known to us from the rabbinic period, and also as a significant portion of narrative material of this sort has known variance in the non-Jewish cultures, it appears that the bulk of such material reached Jewish narrative of the Middle Ages from without. A story cycle that represents this misogynistic attitude is *Meshalim shel Shlomo ha-Melekh* (Parables of King Solomon), created at the end of the Middle Ages, 346.

One countervailing example to Yasif's well-made point about rabbinic literature is the incident of Beruriah's suicide, hinted at in BT Avodah Zarah 18b, and expounded upon by Rashi's comments there. For more background on this episode, see Calderon, Ruth, *A Bride for One Night*, (Philadelphia: Jewish Publication Society of America), 2014, 133ff.

upheld by wise Solomon.[163] In *An Episode*, Na'amah's devotion to Solomon—whom she does not know as a king, but as a lowly servant—leads her at first to abdicate her royal position, and in the end to be the key to Solomon's second ascension to the throne.

These two women are outweighed in our texts by consistent tropes of misogyny. The best example of this may be seen in the *Parables*, specifically the sections explicating Ecclesiastes, "I found only one man in a thousand, and the one I found among so many was never a woman." Both "The Wayward Wife and the Brigand" and "The Test of a Man and a Woman" demonstrate Yasif's claim that this kind of tale:

> . . . takes a model of romantic love and knocks it down to expose its insincerity. It claims that a woman's integrity is a sham that crumbles after the concluding stage of the novella, i.e., marriage, which she uses as a mere stepping-stone in her head-long rush to satisfy her appetite; the continuation in the misogynic tale reveals her true colors.[164]

Yasif also argues that the paradox here that our midrashim seek to negotiate is the need for women (as represented by the commandment to be fruitful and multiply) and the fear of women (given "knowledge" of their true and devious nature). We see Na'amah and the widow as two stalwart examples of trustworthy marriage; the other female characters challenge the fundamental underpinnings of the nuptial ritual. The best that may be said of our collection of stories is that they stand astride this unfortunate (masculine) divide in attempting to understand the role of women and marriage.

The biblical Solomon is connected with wisdom, wealth, and women. The post-biblical Solomon maintains these three relationships, but one new one is added to the dimension of his character. Specifically, Solomon becomes transformed into an "Esoteric King" whose supernal knowledge leads him to intimate relationships with all sorts of demons, and grants him magical spellbinding powers. According to Pablo Torijano, this expansion of Solomon took root in the Second Temple period; he argues that the caves at Qumran contain the earliest evidence of King as Magus.[165] Rabbinic literature is replete with examples of Solomon interacting with Asmodeus, King of the Demons.

---

163 As we will explain later, the text reads that it is King David who upholds her case, but that is likely a textual corruption and should be read as Solomon.

164 Ibid. 348–349.

165 Pablo A. Torijano, *Solomon the Esoteric King: From King to Magus, Development of a Tradition*, (Leiden: J. Brill), 2002, "Conclusion".

BT *Giṭin* 68b, in fact, contains the seed of the confrontation between these two rulers that ultimately blossoms into our *Episode concerning King Solomon*. Throughout our midrashim, Semitic *shedim* like Uza and Azael, as well as foreign demons such as Shed-Ad, make their appearance as if their presence was as normative as a Queen of Sheba or one of Solomon's trusted advisors. There is no doubt that the post-biblical King Solomon extended his rule beyond Israel, and came to reign over a whole host of supernatural beings.

These six midrashim build upon the characterization of King Solomon in the biblical and post-biblical traditions. They deepen our understanding of his personality more than they provide us with innovations of his character. In the end, the Solomon who was enigmatic for our Rabbis remains the same in these texts. He is haughty and in need of humbling; he is wise, grand, regal, and deserving of respect. He commands the demons, the animals and the wind; he is left without even command of his kingdom. He loves women and comes to their rescue; he tells bawdy tales of wives' infidelities that sicken the heart. Just as the Bible is torn between the picture of Solomon in Kings and in Chronicles, so too do our midrashim depict the bifurcated life of our second-most-famous King.

The Midrashim: A Note on the Presentation

Our translation and commentary of these six pieces of Medieval Midrash will follow the same format. For each work, we will provide both a literary introduction as well as a textual history (to the extent such is possible). Subsequently, we will offer our translation of the text. As mentioned above, we based our translations on *both* the Jellinek and Eisenstein texts; those places where we had to choose between the two will be duly noted. We present our commentary through two methods. The first is the more critical apparatus of footnotes to the translation themselves: there we will note Scriptural citations, cultural allusions, and narrow academic insight to certain terms. The second form of commentary will be a more general exposition that follows our translation. In those final overviews, we will trace the two major themes of our work: the development of the figure of King Solomon in Medieval Midrash, as well as the literary expansions and continued development of this emerging area of literature.

Finally, the order of presentation of our midrashim regarding King Solomon is also of import. We begin with *Midrash Al Yithallel* because it seems, in many ways, the mostly closely in keeping with classical modes of midrash. We will then move to *An Episode of King Solomon*, which continues a connection to much of Rabbinic tradition, but clearly moves in new directions. The theme of Solomon's arrogance and humbling takes us next to *The Episode of the Ant*; that work's obvious influence by Islamic culture will lead us to examine *The Parables of King Solomon* in its wake. Finally, we will move to the two works that focus on Solomon's role as ruler, and study first *The Form of the Throne of King Solomon*, and then *The Throne and Hippodrome of King Solomon*. By that time, we will have crossed from the Muslim world to the Byzantine Empire, and seen the complete cosmopolitan portrait of King Solomon painted by the works of Medieval Midrash.

Midrash Al Yithallel[166]

Textual History

There have been three Hebrew publications of *Midrash Al Yithallel*, "Do Not Boast". Jellinek published his edition, based on a Munich manuscript in his *Beit ha-Midrasch*, Grünhut published another version of the midrash based upon a Yemeni manuscript in his *Sefer ha-Likkutim*, and Eisenstein published both Jellinek and Grünhut's editions with notes in his *Oẓar Midrashim*.[167] Unlike some Medieval Midrashim that appear in only one of these collections, *Midrash Al Yithallel* seems important enough to have been in three of them.[168] We posit that the potential explanation for this, in part, is that this work seems to bridge the classical form of Rabbinic Midrash with new types of literature subsumed under the title "Midrash" in the Medieval period. Retaining inherited styles and blending them with emerging literary trends marks *Midrash Al Yithallel* as a key work for understanding how this new literary creation came into being.

Literary Introduction

In keeping with its Rabbinic roots, *Midrash Al Yithallel* opens with a prophetic text, which serves as its interpretive springboard:

---

166   Originally published by Bernard H. Mehlman, "Midrash Al Yithallel—Do not Boast: Introduction, Translation, and Exposition," *CCAR Journal: A Reform Jewish Quarterly*, Spring 2004, 88–101.

It should be noted that of all six pieces translated and studied in this section, this is the only one to contain the word "Midrash" in its title. In keeping with academic convention, we will therefore refer to it as such [*Midrash Al Yithallel*] and not, as we will with the other texts, by its translation.

167   The text of the following translation is based primarily upon Eleazer Grünhut's version of the Yemeni manuscript found in his *Sefer ha-Likkutim*. We have also drawn upon insights from Adolph Jellinek's text in his *Beit ha-Midrasch*, along with footnotes and suggestions from J. D. Eisenstein's, *Oẓar Midrashim*.

168   Perhaps attesting to the popularity [and maybe importance] of *Midrash Al Yithallel*, Rabbi Yom-Tov Lipmann ben Natan ha-Levi Heller, in his 16th Century commentary to the Mishnah, makes the same connection between Jeremiah 9:22 and the text in *Pirqe Avot* 4:1 that is at the foundation of *Midrash Al Yithallel*.

> *Thus said Adonai: Let the wise not boast of their wisdom,*
> *Let the strong not boast of their strength,*
> *Let the rich not boast of their riches.*[169]

The midrash is an elaboration of this verse and draws upon earlier Rabbinic texts, sometimes combining and embellishing them. When citing Jeremiah's admonition against boasting about human wisdom, strength, and riches, the writer of the midrash, no doubt, associates—and will later explicate—an earlier rabbinic teaching found in *Mishnah, Pirqe Avot* 4:1:

> *Ben Zoma said:*
> *Who is wise? One who learns from every person . . .*
> *Who is mighty? One who conquers the impulse to do evil . . .*
> *Who is rich? One who is happy with one's portion . . .*
> *Who is honored? One who honors the creations . . . .*

Three of the four questions posed by Ben Zoma in *Mishnah, Pirqe Avot* 4:1 become the crux of the midrashic expansion. The midrashist assigns a well-known biblical personality to each of Ben Zoma's questions. The wise person, we learn, is none other than the sage-king Solomon; the mighty person is the warrior-king David; and the wealthy person is Korah, though this is a midrashic amplification, as the biblical text itself suggests nothing of Korah's "wealth." Ben Zoma's fourth question is not developed in *Midrash Al Yithallel*.

In addition, *Midrash Al Yithallel* connects with other literary sources. The Solomon episode, as we will see, is completely parallel with *An Episode Concerning King Solomon*,[170] which also relates Solomon's "exile" from Jerusalem as a wandering penitent, his life as an expert court chef, the fabulous story of his signet ring, and how he regained his throne from the impostor, Ashmedai.[171] David's fate at the hands of Ishi-benob, the brother of the slain giant, Goliath is also detailed in *Midrash Goli'at ha-P'lishti*, "The Midrash of Goliath the Philistine".[172] *Midrash Al Yithallel* is further enhanced by the narrative elements about Abishai son of Zeruiah and Ishi-benob that are derived from BT *Sanhedrin* 95a, and certainly were available to the author/editor. Lastly, the section explaining Korah as both spokesman for the destitute widow and her daughters and as the one who confronted Aaron and Moses, is more

---

169   Jeremiah 9:22.

170   Jellinek, Vol. II, 86–87. See next section for translation and analysis.

171   Ibid., XXVI, citing *'Emeq ha-Melech*.

172   Ibid., Vol. IV, 140.

extensively developed in *Midrash Tehillim*, "The Midrash to Psalms".[173] That *Midrash Al Yithallel* is steeped in Rabbinic text and is deeply connected to the emerging project of Medieval Midrashim is evident.

The Text with Annotation

Thus said Adonai: Let the wise not boast of their wisdom,
Let the strong not boast of their strength,
Let the rich not boast of their riches.

[The words] *Let the wise not boast of their wisdom* apply to Solomon at the time that he reigned over his realm. He boasted and bragged and said, "There is no one like me in the world."[174] Furthermore, he transgressed what was written in the Torah [Deuteronomy 17:17]: *And he shall not multiply wives to himself.*

What did the letter Yod in the Hebrew word "multiply" do?[175] It stood before the Holy One[176] and said, "Sovereign of the universe, is there a single, irrelevant letter that You wrote in Your Torah?"

God responded, "No."

The Yod asked, "Has not Solomon rendered me irrelevant and married a thousand wives as it is written [1 Kings 11:3]: *He had seven hundred royal wives and three hundred concubines?* In this way Solomon transgressed what was written in the Torah!"

The Holy One retorted to the Yod, "It is My responsibility to argue your case and render a judgment on your behalf."

Immediately the Holy One of Blessing said to Ashmedai, king of the demons,[177] "Go to Solomon and remove his signet ring from his hand, impersonate him,

---

173 Solomon Buber, ed., *Midrash Tehilim*, (New York, Om Publishing Co.), 1947, Psalm 1:15,ß 7b–8a.

174 This verse appears in a pericope in Deuteronomy 17, opening in verse 14 and closing in verse 20 that details the proper behavior of an appointed Israelite monarch. Solomon transgressed the law elaborated in verse 17 by taking numerous wives.

175 The initial letter in this Hebrew verb structure is the letter *Yod*, which is personified for the purpose of the midrashic teaching.

176 This is our rendering of, הקדוש ברוך הוא, literally, "The Holy One, Blessed be God".

177 In BT *Giṭin* 68a Ashmedai is called מלכא דשידי, *the king of the demons*. Bernard J. Bamberger amplifies our image of him as a king: "Ashmedai is mentioned as king of the demons, but nowhere do we find him actually ruling. His one important appearance is in the legend of his dealings with Solomon. There he is pictured as a rather genial sort, of great might and crude good nature, inclined to drink and to lust, but by no means vicious."

and sit on his throne." At that time, Ashmedai went and removed [Solomon's] signet ring from his hand and disguised himself [as Solomon] and sat upon his throne [deceiving] the Israelites [who] thought that he was [really] Solomon.

But [the real] Solomon was wandering in the cities and villages and said [Ecclesiastes 1:1]: "I am Solomon, *I am Qohelet... king* over Israel." This went on for three years.

Now people [began] saying to one another, "Look at what a fool this person is! Indeed the king is sitting on his throne and this person says [Ecclesiastes 1:12]: *I Qohelet was king.*" And he [continued] wandering [Genesis 4:12]: [as] *a ceaseless wanderer.*

The Holy One of Blessing said, "I have already rendered judgment for Yod."

What did Ashmedai do during those three years? He passed among the wives of Solomon until he came to one of them who was menstruating.[178]

When she saw him, she said to Solomon, "Why have you changed your usual habit by which you conducted yourself with us?"[179]

He immediately became silent.

She said to him, "You aren't Solomon."

Furthermore, he went also to Bathsheba, the mother of Solomon and said to her, "My mother, I want such and such from you."

She answered him, "My son didn't you [already] gain [financial] benefit from the place you [just] left? If you do this, you aren't my son."

She immediately went to Benaiah and said to him, "Benaiah, my son, Solomon has demanded such and such from me."[180]

Benaiah immediately was so outraged he rent his garments and tore out his hair and said, "Certainly this person is not Solomon, rather he is Ashmedai! And that young man who has been wandering about and saying, 'I am Qohelet,' he is really Solomon."

[Benaiah] immediately sent and called out to that young man and asked him, "My son, tell me who you are?"

He responded, "I am Solomon, the son of David."

[Benaiah] asked him, "How did this happen?"

Bamberger, Bernard, J., *Fallen Angels*, (Philadelphia: The Jewish Publication Society of America), 5712–1952, 104.

178   BT *Ketubot* 2b.

179   Jellinek, Vol. VI, 106, Since the word, טעמך/ta'amcha does not appear in this version, I have deleted it in the translation. This manuscript reading is smoother and consonant with the main idea of the sentence.

180   Benaiah son of Jehoiada, II Samuel 23:20ff; whom King David appointed over his bodyguard, *Targum Jonathan* to II Samuel 23:23.

He responded, "One day I was sitting in my place when something like a windstorm came and swept me out of my place. From that very day until now my sense was taken from me. It is for this reason that I was wandering about."

[Benaiah] asked him, "Do you have evidence to prove who you are?"

He answered, "Yes. At the moment that I was made king, David, my father, took one of my hands and placed it in your hand, and my other hand he placed in the hand of Nathan, the prophet, while my mother stood and kissed my father's head.[181] That is the evidence I have."

What did Benaiah do when he heard his words? He called to the Sanhedrin and said to them, "Go write for yourselves the Tetragrammaton and affix it over your hearts."[182]

They went and came to him. They said to him, "We are terrified of the name engraved on his heart."[183]

He responded, "Can one name prevail against seventy names?"[184]

What did Benaiah do? Benaiah took [his sword] in his hand and gave Ashmedai a single blow, took the signet ring [from him], and was about to slay him. A *Bat Qol* went forth and proclaimed, "Do not touch him because the command originated with me [because Solomon] transgressed what was written in the Torah."[185] The signet ring was immediately returned to Solomon's hand, his appearance was restored, and he regained his realm.

Solomon immediately exclaimed, "What my realm? What my power? They did not help me at all! But all who humble themselves in this world, The Holy One raises. There is nothing [as precious] in this world as humility and meekness, as it is written [Psalm 51:19]: *Sacrifices to God are a broken spirit. A broken and crushed heart God will not despise.*"

∴

[The words:] *Let the strong not boast of their strength,* apply to David, son of Jesse, king of Israel. When he would wage war, he could shoot the arrow and slay 800 at one time. As it is written [11 Samuel 23:8][186]: *These are the names of David's warriors: Josheb-basshebeth, a Tachemonite, the chief officer—he is*

---

181   The text follows Jellinek's Munich MS. here.

182   Benaiah is identified as the head of the Sanhedrin in BT *Berachot* 4a and this detail gives nuance to the midrashic account here.

183   Ashmedai's heart.

184   The words, "You do not have God's favor," are deleted from this translation.

185   *Bat Qol,* literally, *daughter of a voice.* It has its origins in the book of Daniel 4:3. In Rabbinic texts it is a voice, which emanates from an invisible, heavenly source expressing the divine will.

186   See also BT *Mo'eid Qatan* 47b.

Adino the Eznite—[he wielded his spear] against eight hundred and slew them on one occasion. When he saw this, he bragged and said, "There is no one like me in the world and after me there will be no one like me."

The Holy One asked David, "Why are you bragging so much about your strength? What [good] is your strength to you now?" What did The Holy One do to him? God appointed for him a deer. The deer lured him, and the land shrank[187] before him until it brought him to Ishbi-benob.[188]

Ishbi-benob said, "This is David, who slew Goliath the Philistine, my brother." He took [David's] hand and took him and placed him in an olive press[189] and pressed on him in order to break him. [David] immediately uttered [these words of Psalm 18:37], *"You have lengthened my steps under me, And [yet] my feet have not slipped,"* and the earth beneath him became like a spring of water.

When Ishbi-benob finished his food, he took David and flung him into the air above for he thought that he would land on the tip of the spear, thereby becoming a protective shield on it. Then David said [Psalm 18:3], *"My shield, my horn of rescue, my high tower."* [Once David was on] the tip of the spear, [Ishbi-benob would flip it and thereby] would cast him under, then David would say [again, the words of Psalm 18:37], *"You have lengthened my steps under me."*

In spite of all this, Israel did not know where David had gone until Abishai, son of Zeruiah,[190] entered the bath-house in order to bathe and saw that the water in his hands had turned into blood. Rav and Samuel disagreed. One said he saw blood and one said he saw a wildly fluttering dove before him. He said to himself, certainly the king is in trouble. Abishai immediately went to the royal palace but did not find him. He inquired about him but they told him

---

187   According to BT *Sanhedrin* 95a-b, the land shrank for three people: Eliezer, Abraham's majordomo, Gen. 24:42–43; Jacob, Gen. 28:10; and in the incident with Abishai, II Sam. 21:17.

188   Ishbi-benob, was a Philistine giant who wanted to slay David but who was slain by Abishai. II Sam. 21:16.

189   The two printed versions of the story, J. D. Eisenstein, (the Yemenite version) and Jellinek (the Munich manuscript) have the word מרטף/(storeroom, cellar). Jastrow, Marcus, *A Dictionary of the Targumim, The Talmud Bavli and Yerushalmi, and the Midrashic Literature*, (New York: Pardes Publishing House, Inc., 1950), 848. BT *Sanhedrin* 95a–b has a different rendition of parts of this story. In the Talmudic version in place of store-room or cellar we read, בדייא בי (olive press) with an alternative reading cited in the margin of the text, סדייא. The tightening of the olive press in order to squeeze out the olive oil fits the image here quite well.

190   Abishai ben Zeruriah was the son of King David's sister. I Chron. 2:16. David restrained him from slaying King Saul with these words, "Don't do him violence! No one can lay hands on YHWH's anointed with impunity." I Sam. 26:9. *Midrash Al Yithallel* reflects the Rabbinic account of Abishai ben Zeruriah's aid to David found in BT *Sanhedrin* 95a.

they did not know where he had gone. What did Abishai do? He took the king's donkey, mounted and rode it until he reached Ishbi-benob who had David in his power, and was sporting with David with the spear. What did Abishai do? He dismounted from the donkey and engaged Ishbi-benob in battle and gave him a single [fatal] blow. He found David walking weakly, his strength sapped from great fear and sadness as it said [II Samuel 21:17], "*But Abishai son of Zeruiah came to his aid.*" What did Abishai do? He took David's hand, bound it behind him, lashed him, and made him swear not to enter Jerusalem unless he was standing on his feet. Thus he led him up to Jerusalem on his feet. Then David said [Psalm 102:24]: *God weakened my strength in the way; God shortened my days.*

Israel said to David, "You sought to annihilate only the enemies of Israel. For if the Philistine had slain you [Numbers 27:17, I Kings 21:17]" *Israel would have been scattered like a flock without a shepherd.*"

David responded, "My transgressions have caused this for me." Immediately, David's people declared that he should not leave his house, as it is written [II Samuel 21:17]: *It was then that David's men declared to him on oath, "You shall not go with us into battle any more, lest you extinguish the lamp of Israel!"*

Immediately, King David of blessed memory said, "What my strength, what my power."

∵

[The words] *Let the rich not boast of their riches,* apply to Korah, the Levite, the keys of whose treasure-house were a load for three hundred white mules.[191] [If this is true about his] keys, how much the more so his money. Where did all his money come from? From the money that Joseph the righteous collected in Egypt.[192] It filled three towers. The depth of each tower was one hundred *amas*, its breadth one hundred, and its height one hundred *amas*.[193] And all the money was given [directly] into the house of Pharaoh and not even five silver coins were given to his children. Why? Because it was done as an act of faith, as it is written [Genesis 47:17]: *Now Joseph brought the money into the house of Pharaoh.*

---

191   BT *Pesaḥim* 119a, b; *Sanhedrin* 110a.

192   See *Esther Rabba*, 7:5; *Targum Pseudo-Jonathan*, Num. 16:19.

193   *Ama* was an ancient Hebrew measure based on the span of the fingers on the human hand. There is debate about the precise size of an *ama*. Some Sages say it is the equivalent of five handbreadths and others six handbreadths.

When Korah discovered one tower he bragged about his wealth. The second was revealed to Antoninus [Severus],[194] and the third is hidden way until future time.[195]

Was the beginning of the disagreement with Korah [or] with Moses, or with Aaron? [It began] over [the case of] a widow who had one ewe. When the time came to shear its wool, Aaron heard about it and took the wool.[196]

She went to Korah protesting and weeping and said to him, "Aaron did such and such to me."

Korah went to Aaron and asked, "What is the problem between you and this poor widow? Return her wool to her."

Aaron answered him, "According to the Torah, the wool is mine, as it is written [Deuteronomy 18:4]: *and the first shearing of your sheep.*"

What did Korah do? He took four silver coins and gave them to her. She went on her way but Korah enraged, walked on. A short while later the ewe bore a male sheep. Aaron heard about it and took the first-born sheep. The widow went to Korah protesting and weeping. Korah asked Aaron, "What is your problem with that poor widow?"

Aaron retorted, "It is mine. For it is so written in the Torah [Deuteronomy 15:19]: *You shall consecrate to Adonai your God all male firstlings that are born in your herd and in your flock.*"

But Korah enraged, went on his way. When the widow saw this she went and slaughtered the ewe. Aaron heard [about this] and came and took the shoulder, the cheeks, and the stomach. Korah said to him, "What is the problem between you and this poor widow?"

Aaron retorted, "It is mine. For it is written in the Torah [Deuteronomy 18:3]: *Everyone who offers a sacrifice, whether an ox or a sheep, must give the shoulder, the cheeks, and the stomach to the priest.*"

Korah said to him, "Son of Amram, why do you lord it over us?[197] [Numbers 16:14]: *Should you gouge out those men's eyes? We will not come!*" They did not

---

194   There are several Roman noblemen named Antoninus in the Rabbinic literature. Louis
       Ginzberg identifies him as Antoninus Severus in Ginzberg, *Legends of the Jews*, 2, 125.
       There is a wide range of scholarly opinion about him and it remains an unsettled matter.
       See also Jacob Schachter and H. Freedman, trs., *The Babylonian Talmud, Seder Neziqin*
       (London: Soncino Press), *Sanhedrin*, vol. 3, 756 and a more equivocal opinion in the same
       volume, 610, n. 7.

195   Schachter and H. Freedman, *Sanhedrin*, vol. 3, 610, n. 11.

196   This episode is more fully developed in Buber, *Midrash Tehillim*, Psalm 1:15, pp. 7b–8a.
       The details of the parable of Korah and the widow vary in other sources. See *Bamidbar
       Rabba* 18:7; *Tanhuma*, Qoraḥ 12; *Yalqut Shimoni*, Qoraḥ, 750.

197   An allusion to Numbers 16:13.

utter this verse except for Moses and Aaron. In the morning 250 people gathered near Korah, some with their fire-pans, some sacrificing, and some offering incense.

Immediately, Moses, our teacher stood in prayer before God and said, "Sovereign of the universe, [as for] this prophecy that you sent to us, is it true?"

God answered, "Yes. Now you will see what I shall do to Korah." Why was his name called Korah? Because in his lifetime he was plucked out of Israel. [198]

Moses further exclaimed before the Holy One of Blessing [Numbers 16:29], [199] *"If these men die as all humans do, if their lot be the common fate of all humankind, it was not Adonai who sent me."*

The Holy One responded to Moses, "Have you become a heretic?"

Moses retorted to The Holy One [Numbers 16:30], [200] *"If God creates a creature."*

The Holy One responded, "I will do your will." Immediately, The Holy One pointed toward the earth and it swallowed the people [as far as] their bellybutton.

Korah and all his household cried out, "Moses, Moses have mercy on us."

Moses retorted [Numbers 16:7], *"You have gone too far, sons of Levi!"*

They were swallowed up immediately, and the remainder were burned up, as it is written [Numbers 16:33]: *They went down alive into Sheol, with all that belonged to them; the earth closed over them*; and it is further written [Numbers 16:35]: *And a fire went forth from YHVH and consumed the two hundred and fifty men offering the incense.*

And those who went down under the earth remained [down] there. They assumed that they would never rise up until Hannah[201] came and prophesied [1 Samuel 2:6]: *God deals death and gives life, Casts down into Sheol and raises up.* Nevertheless, they did not believe that they would rise up until the Temple was destroyed and the Temple gates were swallowed up, as it is written [Lamentations 2:9]: *Her gates have sunk into the ground.* Then they came to Korah and they grasped hold of them. They immediately believed and said, "When these gates are raised up we will also rise with them." Guards were

---

198   BT *Sanhedrin* 109b. There is a play on the name of Korah. In Hebrew, the meaning of, קרח/ qrḥ is related to baldness, the plucking out of the hair of the head.

199   See *Bamidbar Rabbah*, 18:12.

200   The terse response in the Hebrew biblical verse is more forceful because of its assonance, יברא ,בריאה/ yivra, beri'a (the verb "create" and the noun "creature"). The midrashic understanding depends upon a literal translation of Num. 16:30 and is dependent upon the earlier midrash, Bamidbar Rabbah 18:13.

201   *B'reishit Rabbah*, 98:2.

appointed over those gates until [the time that] they would rise up. Thus Korah and his riches perished from the midst of the community. Therefore it is written: *Let the rich not boast of their riches*, for all riches belong to The Holy One, as it is written [Haggai 2:8]: *Silver is Mine and gold is Mine—says Adonai of Hosts.*

Conclusions: King Solomon

Midrash Al Yithallel, in keeping with its rabbinic precursors, explores the tensions between different texts of Torah. We previously explored the dichotomy between the rather human Solomon depicted in Kings and the more immaculate version of the King presented in Chronicles. Here, our Midrash picks up on what appear to be a series of subtle disapprovals of Solomon's actions we discover in the laws of Deuteronomy 17. In fact, the protagonist for the King's downfall in this Midrash—aside from his hubris in abrogating deuteronomical law—is the very letter Yod of the Torah verse Solomon transgresses. Hence our story here aggrandizes the arrogance of Solomon by adding to the portrait of him from Kings the additional information of his wantonly breaking God's commandments.

In *Midrash Al Yithallel*, Solomon begins at the apogee of arrogance, yet ends humbled and meek. It is not surprising that this nimble narrative pivots this change in the King's character around a verse from Ecclesiastes: *I am Qohelet, King of Israel.*[202] Solomon's humility is immediately connected to the existential anguish captured in his purported book of wisdom, Ecclesiastes. Solomon is made so low not only that none in his own kingdom recognize him, but also by the narrative making another the protagonist of his story. Benaiah, whom King David had appointed as bodyguard, becomes the active hero of our tale: when Benaiah hears Bathsheba's report about the king not being whom he seems, Benaiah takes all the necessary actions—including striking the Demon-king with his sword—that banish Ashmedai and restore Solomon to his rightful throne. The humbling of Solomon, so important for a Midrash named "Do Not Boast!", is complete in his final query, "What my realm? What my power?" The mighty commandment-breaking King has realized that no earthly ruler has any power or might compared with that of the Holy One.

202　　The full verse of Ecclesiastes 1:12 reads: *I, Qohelet, was King of Jerusalem over Israel.*

Conclusions: Literary Expansions

Midrash Al Yithallel has much in common with classical Rabbinic Midrash. To begin with, it relies upon the textual frame of a passage from Jeremiah that links its subsequent literary units. This kind of frame narrative begins to appear in *Leviticus Rabbah,* and gets further developed in such later collections as *Pesiqta deRav Kahana* and *Pesiqta Rabbati.*[203] In further keeping with classical Midrash, the text here continues beyond the narrative frame to employ biblical passages as both proof-texts and opportunities for further exegesis. The implementation of scriptural passages here is quite remarkable: words of Solomon [from *Qohelet*] come to teach about Solomon's humbling; words of David [from *Psalms*] likewise appear to describe David's humiliation; even Torah's words about Aaron's due are here spoken by Aaron in claiming the tributes due to him. *Midrash Al Yithallel* is the product of close readings of many different parts of the Bible that are woven together with masterful skill.

The artistry of *Midrash Al Yithallel* allows it to make a rather focused point. The midrashic use of the Jeremiah text is meant to be a prescriptive warning. The narrative then moves in order to apply each verse-stitch of the Jeremiah frame to an individual biblical human being: one wise, one powerful, and one affluent. Contrary to the thinking of each protagonist, the midrashic teaching reaffirms that boastfulness leads to the diminution of self, and not to greater personal glory. As a whole, our Midrash illustrates how boastful behavior leads to the attenuation of the leadership of each character and in the end, results in disservice to the people of Israel. The midrashic pedagogy is pellucid: it allows each of us, as readers, to see the effects of boastfulness on Solomon, David, and Korah, as it simultaneously urges us to beware of the pitfalls of arrogance in our own lives. If Solomon, David and Korah succumbed to the appeal of boastfulness, we, all the more, need to guard ourselves against its destructive allure. This kind of clear moral message, along with the method in which it is delivered, are in keeping with the Rabbinic tradition.

We should note, however, that while *Midrash Al Yithallel* shares much with the midrashic literature that preceded it, it does seem to blaze new trails past the boundaries of the Rabbinic period. While fantastic tales certainly fill the pages of Talmud and Midrash, neither of the two remarkable stories here told about the humiliations of David and Solomon have a precursor in the Rabbinic canon. Likewise, all three sections of *Midrash Al Yithallel* have remarkable inversions of our expectations: David and Solomon appear as

---

203 See especially, *Pesiqta deRav Kahana, Pisqa* 13 which uses the opening verse of the Book of Jeremiah to frame an extended commentary on the nature and character of Jeremiah.

anti-heroes, unable to serve as protagonists even of their own tales; the biblical villain Korah is here represented in the almost flattering light of trying to protect a poor person from the venal priestly hands of Aaron. These depictions seem to exceed, or at least push up against, the limits of how the Rabbis were able to understand—or at least depict—characters such as Korah, David and Solomon.

Lastly, we noted that one of the potential markers of Medieval Midrash was its appeal beyond the walls of the traditional house of study and an audience of scholarly disciples. The fantastic tales told here, and the focus on little-known characters who assume great roles, indicate that these tales were perhaps more for a popular audience. Serious scholars might have scoffed at David being upended by Goliath's brother; a crowd in the marketplace would have listened to every last word. A top disciple might never be able to understand any decency behind Korah's rebellion; a poor person often subjected to the whims of the ruling class might have more sympathy with the widow than esteem for a corrupt minister. In some fashion, *Midrash Al Yithallel* would fit neatly within the walls of a Rabbinic house of study, and, in other ways, it seems tailor-made for a wider world. As such, it serves as a perfect bridge that will connect the classical world of Rabbinic exegesis with the literature of Medieval Midrash that developed in its wake.

An Episode Concerning King Solomon

Textual History

While it is easy to recognize the many sources that come together in *An Episode concerning King Solomon*, it is more difficult to discover the textual history of this telling of the tale. According to Jellinek, our text is taken from the book *Emeq ha-Melech* [14d–15a], authored by Naftali Hertz ben Yaaqov Elḥanan and published in Amsterdam, 1684.[204] That seems to be the solitary situation of the story of which we know today.

Literary Introduction

There is no doubt *An Episode of King Solomon* is connected to *Midrash Al Yithallel.* In many ways, it is a better told version of the first third of that *Midrash*; however, textual history being as cloudy as it is, it is impossible to determine whether *An Episode* is a refined version of *Midrash Al Yithallel,* or if the latter based itself on the former. One could easily argue that the author of *Midrash Al Yithallel* based the Solomon section on the tale as told in *An Episode*; conversely, it is not hard to conceive of *An Episode* as a fully developed narrative of the themes addressed in *Midrash Al Yithallel.* Either way, these two tales are closely connected.

This terse tale of *An Episode of King Solomon* is exactly as advertised: it narrates in one brief tale how hubris humbles Solomon, while wisdom and fortune restore him to his throne. Our legend here is not built directly on a biblical foundation: nowhere in the Solomon stories of Kings and Chronicles do we read of him losing his regency for even a short spell.[205] However, our *Episode* seems centered around a Rabbinic tradition found at BT *Megillah* 11b, which discusses—likely in speculation as to how this successful and majestic monarch came to write the existential *Ecclesiastes*—Solomon's loss of the kingship.

Next to *Midrash Al Yithallel* that it so resembles, *An Episode* is the most deeply steeped in rabbinic tradition of our Medieval Midrashim regarding King Solomon: legends of the *Shamir* come from *Tosefta*; the *Bavli* tells how

---

204   *Bet Eked Sefarim, Bibliographical Lexicon,* Ch. B. Freidberg, and Freidberg, Baruch, (1951–1956: Israel), Volume 3, 804, Entry 918.

205   In fact, our *Episode* in one instance directly contravenes the Bible: 1 Kings 14:26 has Solomon marry Na'amah while his father David is still alive (and thus King); here they wed during Solomon's exile.

Asmodeus casts Solomon into exile; *Ruth Rabbah* describes the King begging at doors; and the *Zohar* describes Uza, Azael, secrets and magic rings.[206] Furthermore, this tale is also informed by Islamic aspects of Solomon, specifically the Quran's teaching of his punishment and exile, which the *Hadith* literature subsequently connects to a story of a magic ring.[207] That legendary ring, as noted in our introduction, is a remarkably well-travelled motif in folk literature. With its combination of sources, its fantastic flights, and its trials and tribulations, *An Episode concerning King Solomon* is a tale very well told.

The Text with Annotation

An episode[208] concerning King Solomon, peace be upon him, who would roam[209] every day up to the firmament to hear the secrets/counsel from Uza and Azael.[210] [Solomon] had no fear or terror, and all the hosts on high were

---

206   Respectively: T *Sotah* 15:1, BT *Gittin* 68b, *Ruth Rabbah* ii 14, and *The Zohar* 112b.

207   *The Quran* 38:33–34, Clouston, *Popular Tales*, 381–383.

208   "Episode" is late 17th cent. (denoting a section between two choric songs in Greek tragedy): from Greek *epeisodion*, neuter of *epeisodios:* 'coming in besides,' from *epi* 'in addition' + *eisodos* 'entry' (from *eis* 'into' + *hodos* 'way').

209   cf. Satan's activity in Job 2:2ff. Clearly, the reference to Job [and the arrival of the satanic Uza and Azael in a moment] hover ominously over this passage.

210   In the *Zohar* [112b ff.] this pair of demons appear alongside Solomon in the context of counsel, secrets, and a magic ring. However, their history well precedes this medieval mystical work. This pair makes their first appearance in *Targum Yerushalmi* to Genesis 6:4. Likewise in *Targum Psuedo-Jonathan*, Azael is one of the two נפלים/*nephilim*/*fallen angels* described in Genesis 6:1–4, Numbers 13:30–33. His partner is there named Shamhazai. [Karel van der Toorn, Becking, Bob and van der Horst, Pieter W., *Dictionary of Deities and Demons in the Bible*, (Grand Rapids: Eerdemans), 1999, 619; see continuance of this note for potential equivalence of Aza and Shamhazai]. Furthermore:

   "There are indications that the story as found in *1 Enoch* combines older sources, one of which names the leader [of the Watchers] Semihazah and focuses on the sin of illicit mingling with human women, while the other names him Azael > Azazel and emphasizes the sin of illicit revelation (Hanson 1977)." [*Deities and Demons*, 894.]

   Yoma 67b, in a discussion of Azazel, Soncino explains, "Uzziel who atones concerning the episode of Uzza and Azzael" is a reference to the legend of fallen angels, based partly on Genesis 6:4 and also on foreign lore. See Leo Jung, *Fallen Angels in Jewish, Christian and Mohammedan Literature* (New York: K'tav), 1926.

   Devarim Rabbah, V'zot HaBerachah 10, contains the following information introduced as evidence by Moses' soul as she argues with God to remain connected to the body of Moses:

bowing low and prostrating[211] themselves before the Holy One, and were prais-
ing God for having established a king like this in Israel, and they would fulfill
all of his will, as it is said [1 Chronicles 29:23]: *Then Solomon sat on the Throne
of Adonai to rule*, he would rule over [beings] heavenly and earthly.[212] He
issued a decree and they brought stones and building materials to the Temple,
and when he requested the *Shamir*,[213] they brought him Ashmedai, King of
the Demons, in chains of iron, as well as the ring with the Tetragrammaton
engraved upon it, which he took to his place and which remained with him for
many days after the building of the Temple.

And when [Ashmedai] finished the engraving,[214] he requested that [his
chains] be loosened for him, and that then he would reveal a certain secret
whose essence was mighty and awesome. So [Solomon] loosened [Ashmedai's

---

"Thereupon the soul replied, "Master of the Universe, two angels, Uzah and Azael,
came down from near Your Divine Presence and coveted the daughters of the earth
and they corrupted their way upon the earth until You suspended them between
earth and the heavens.""

Ginzberg explains the following in an extended note [n. 56] to the tale of "The Fall of
the Angels," in *Legends of the Jews*, V:152, n. 6:

"The two fallen angels bear the names of Uzza and Azzael, Shemhazai and Azazel.
The identity of Azzael with Azazel does not require any proof; but it has not hith-
erto been noticed that Uzza or Azza were originally the same as Shemhazai. Since
nearly all the names of angels are theophorous (this was already noticed by the
old Midrashim; comp. PK 12, 108b, and the parallel passage cited by Buber, which
reads: The name of God is combined with every angel), Uzza and Azza are therefore to be taken as abbreviated forms of Jehouzza and Jehoazza .... This abbrevia-
tion is due to the fact that it was not considered proper to combine the names יהו
and יה with the fallen angels. Another way of avoiding this combination was the
substitution of שם "the Name" for יה."

211   While we are familiar with this language from our *Aleinu* liturgy, the biblical reference has
      naught to do with God, but instead with political prostrations [Esther 3:2]: *All the king's
      courtiers in the palace gate bowed low and prostrated to Haman.*

212   This precise interpretation of 1 Chronicles appears at BT *Megillah* 11b, and in Rashi's com-
      mentary to BT *Sukkot* 53a.

213   The *Shamir* is the legendary tool (others, perhaps later, a magical worm) employed by
      Solomon in the miraculous construction of The Temple. See BT *Giṭin* 68a, BT *Soṭah* 48b,
      which echo earlier descriptions from T. *Soṭah* 15.1 and M. *Avot* 5:6:
          Our Rabbis taught: The *Shamir* is a creation about the size of a barley-corn, and was
      created during the six days of Creation. No hard substance can withstand it.

214   We are entertaining two possibilities: either, "when he finished the engraving", read-
      ing verb as *ligmor*, and ignoring the suffix of "*h*"; or "when he had caused the ring [the
      unnamed object of the verb represent by the suffix of "*h*" with a *mapiq* in it] to do its
      engraving".

chains] for him. Then [Ashmedai] asked of [Solomon] to give him his ring that had the Tetragrammaton engraved upon it. (Solomon trusted him [only] because God brought it round to repay him double for his transgressing three negative commandments, [for which Solomon subsequently paid the penalty] specifically that he walked three years in exile.)[215] And when [Ashmedai] took the ring, he cast it into the sea and a certain fish came and swallowed it; then did he cast him [Solomon] four hundred parsangs into the lands of the nations and expel him from his rule [so that] he lost his majesty.[216]

[Ashmedai] cast [Solomon] far, so that he was [reduced to] begging at doorways and saying, "I am Solomon. I was King in Jerusalem." They mocked his speech, and said, "A king such as this? Begging at the doorways?" And he endured trouble such as this for three years for having transgressed three commandments of the Torah: regarding not increasing wives; not increasing horses; and silver and gold not to increase greatly for himself.[217] [Solomon] failed in all of them. And at the end of this set period of three years, The Holy One wanted to take mercy on him for the sake of David, His servant, and for the sake of Na'amah[218] the righteous, daughter of the King of Ammon, with whom he conjoined and brought to the Land of Israel, and from whom the Davidic Messiah will descend. The Holy One brought [Solomon] to the Land of Ammon, and he entered the royal city, named Mashkemam.[219] And he would stand in the streets of the city of Mashkemam, and the chef of the King, master of the kitchens, who prepares and cooks the food of the King, came to take what was needed for his work. He found Solomon standing there, and he took him in indentured servitude—[namely] to carry what he took—and he led

---

215   This is an artless insertion foreshadowing the remainder of our tale.

216   Solomon's exile fits the model established in BT *Gittin* 68b, *Ruth Rabbah* 2:14 and *Qohelet Rabbah* 1:12 that Solomon lost his throne during his lifetime. In the passage from *Ruth Rabbah*, as here, he ultimately regains rule of the realm.

217   The citations for these prohibitions are found in Deuteronomy, as follows: 17:17, against increasing wives; 17:16, against increasing horses; 17:17, against increasing silver and gold. The sequence in our text is odd.

218   This sentence is poorly constructed (and timed), yet suits the purpose of introducing the heroine of our tale (as well as the reason God makes her the heroine). Here our midrash is contrary to what we discover in I Kings 14:21, where Solomon marries Na'amah *during* King David's rule (and lifetime). However, the notion of God favoring Na'amah—despite her Ammonite heritage—is a rabbinic tradition found in BT *Baba Qama* 38b and BT *Yevamot* 63a.

219   As per Ginzberg [*Legends*, VI, 300, note 90], the city called מׁשכמם/*Mashkemam* is probably an intentional corruption of עַם כמׁש/*'am kemosh*, which for Moab in Numbers 21:29, might be taken for Ammon in accordance with Judges 11:24.

him to the kitchens. And he saw what he was doing, and Solomon said that he would remain with him and serve him, and that he only wanted the food alone, and he would be satisfied with it. And he dwelled, and served and assisted him.

After some time, [Solomon] said to [the chef] that he would cook food for the King as was him custom, as if he were a great artist in these foodstuffs, and the chef was satisfied with him. So he prepared and cooked the delights of the King, and when the King ate the delicacies that the chef brought him, and tasted the particular spices, the King inquired of the chef, "Who cooked these foods? Until now you never brought the likes of them!" He related to him the complete story of the event with this man, and [the King] commanded his servants to summon [Solomon]. He came before the King, and the King inquired of him if he wanted to be his chef. He responded, "Yes." [The King] dismissed the [former] chef, and put Solomon in his place to cook all his foods.

Sometime later, the daughter of the King of Ammon, named Na'amah, saw him, and said to her mother that she wanted to take this man, the chef, as her husband. Her mother rebuked her, and said to her, "Aren't there in your father's kingdom many minister and grandees, that you might take one of them who pleases you?" She said, "I don't want any of them besides this chef." She implored her greatly, but to no benefit, because she said on every occasion, "My will is not for any other man except for this one," until she compelled her mother to reveal the matter to her husband, the King, [namely,] that it was the will of his daughter to take the chef for a husband. And when he heard this, he became greatly incensed, and he wanted to kill the two of them, but it was not the will of The Holy One. So God performed a miracle for them, that the King's compassion was kindled for them, and he didn't want to spill innocent blood. He summoned one of his servants, and commanded him to lead them to a desolate desert, so that they would die at the Hand of God. The officer did as the King had commanded, and left them in the desert and went on his way to the King to serve him as he had previously.

As for them, they walked from there to find food to sustain themselves, and they came to a certain city that was on the shores of the sea. [Solomon] went to find food to sustain themselves, and found fisherman selling fish. So he bought one of them and brought the fish to his wife so she might cook it. And when she opened the fish, she found within it the ring with the Tetragrammaton engraved upon it.[220] She gave it to her husband, and he immediately recognized

---

220 The motif of "The Fish and The Ring" is prevalent in folklore throughout the world. An early version, the tale of Polycrates, is found in Herodotus, *History*, 3:3. A version of this tale, starring Joseph *Shomer Shabbat* is at BT *Shabbat* 119a. Lastly, in an important cultural context for our work, a version of this tale is also found in the Quran, 38:33–34.

this ring, and put it on his finger, and immediately his spirit returned to him, and his wisdom [again] resided in him, and he went up to Jerusalem and drove out Ashmedai, sat on his Throne, and placed the royal crown on his head. Afterwards, he sent to summon her father, who was King of the people of Ammon, and he asked him, "Why have you killed two people without permission or fear?" He responded, "Heaven forefend! I didn't kill them, I only drove them into the desolate desert, and I do not know what was done to them." King Solomon, peace be upon him, responded, "If you were to see them, would you be able to recognize them? Know that I am the chef, and your daughter is my wife!" And he sent to summon her. She entered and kissed his hand, and he rejoiced greatly and returned to his land.

Conclusions: King Solomon

In its narrative, our *Episode* is an inversion of Job: Solomon's trials result from his haughtiness, and his reward seems to come more from the grace of God and Na'amah rather than through any moral growth on the part of our protagonist. The Solomon of our *Episode* is at times cunning, but is remarkably reliant on others—demons, mentors, women—for any ultimate success. In this sense, our sad story reflects that biblical understanding of Solomon as remarkably human and frail; he is here hardly the perfect and gallant knight errant of Chronicles. Ultimately, like that book pseudepigraphically attributed to Solomon, our *Episode* too ends with a cheery chorus that seems counter to stark sadness that characterizes the rest of the work. Thus, while the *Episode* underscores Solomon's shortcomings, it stops short of a full condemnation of the King: at the tale's close, Solomon again sits as King in Israel.

Conclusions: Literary Expansions

We noted above that *An Episode Concerning King Solomon* is a tale very well told. Here we should note that, by comparison, it is far better told than the version in *Midrash Al Yithallel*, and, furthermore, clearly liberated from the strictures of classical Midrash. Outside of the initial Chronicles citation, *An Episode* is all narrative, and no exegesis. While biblical and rabbinic allusions suffuse the text, gone are the direct and continued references to Scripture that mark not only *Midrash Al Yithallel*, but all Rabbinic exegesis. We see this most clearly in *An Episode*'s narratives around Solomon's hubris, the Shamir, and Na'amah. Taken in reverse order, we see that Na'amah's heroism is not an invention of the author, but rather grows out of a Talmudic teaching [BT *Baba Qama* 38b and BT *Yevamot* 63a] regarding God's favoring this Ammonite Queen. Similarly, this legendary tool, the *Shamir*, is not some fantastical creation of the medieval literary imagination: it is also introduced in the Talmud.[221] Finally, we see a great distinction between the hubris of Solomon as seen here and as presented in the parallel *Midrash Al Yithallel*. Here, Solomon's transgressions are briefly noted; only a scholar of Torah would understand that the "three transgressions" of Solomon were the three commandments in Deuteronomy 17 he violated. In clear contrast, *Midrash Al Yithallel* does not allow the reader to remain ignorant about Solomon's sin: it is the letter Yod of the very verse of Torah he abrogates that comes to accuse the King. Hence we see that *An Episode* is clearly a step beyond *Midrash Al Yithallel* in crossing over the bounds of classical Midrash.

Two other features of *An Episode Concerning King Solomon* are important to note. The first is the depth of character the story presents: we see the exiled Solomon as constantly working for his own self-improvement; we see in Na'amah a woman who knows what she wants and is unafraid to take the lead and acquire it. *An Episode* spends a great deal of time on mundane details that round out our understanding of the characters, and intrigue us to learn what happens to them. This leads us to the last major distinction between *An Episode* and *Midrash Al Yithallel*. *Midrash Al Yithallel*, from its opening citation of Jeremiah throughout its entire tripartite structure, is organized around the moral principle of its title: do not boast! Each of its three sections ends with the main character admitting their own humble shortcomings and thereby exalting mighty God. Importantly, *An Episode* offers no such moral message. All we are told at the end is that Solomon and his beloved Na'amah return to rule together: in place of any moral message, we are told that the King and Queen live happily ever after. Clearly, with *An Episode Concerning King Solomon*, we have crossed the bridge out of the Rabbinic world, and into the realm of Medieval Midrash.

---

221   BT *Soṭah* 48b.

The Episode of the Ant

Textual History

As with *An Episode concerning King Solomon*, Jellinek can only cite one source of *The Episode of the Ant*. All we know to date, from Jellinek's introduction in *Beit HaMidrasch*, is that this tale appears at the end of *Midrash VaYosha* in a manuscript presently at Cambridge University.

Literary Introduction

Of all the midrashim associated with Solomon, *The Episode of the Ant* is most directly influenced by the Islamic traditions that surround our Jewish King. The Quran itself dedicates an entire *Sura* to the interactions (and subsequent fall-out) of Solomon and a lowly ant. While the King's connection to this small insect might derive from a Jewish text,[222] the stories told in this narrative seem predominantly, if not exclusively, to come from a Muslim context: Solomon's dominion over demons, control of the wind, reliance upon Assaf ben Berachiyyah, and confederacy with the vulture are all well attested themes in the Quran and subsequent traditions, yet barely discoverable in a Jewish context.[223] However, these borrowings from Islamic culture ultimately are framed in a very Jewish fashion.

Thematically, *The Episode of the Ant* resonates with two Jewish strands of Solomon's character: his hubristic boasting, and his experience with suffering and futility that led to his drafting Ecclesiastes. We have seen how *Midrash Al-YitHallel* and *An Episode Regarding King Solomon* center around the arrogance of Solomon, and the comeuppance his pomposity receives. In our *Episode*, Solomon is rebuked by the vapor of the wind, the lowliest of the insects, and a Greek-speaking boy. Furthermore, even though Solomon proves

---

222 Solomon's connection to the ant may be rather thinly traced to the book of Proverbs he purportedly authored: *Lazy one: go to the ant; study its ways and learn* [6:6].

223 Respectively, *The Quran* 21:82, 34:12, Jacob Lassner, *Demonizing the Queen of Sheba*, (University of Chicago Press: Chicago), 1993, and Haim Schwarzbaum, *Biblical and Extra-Biblical Legends in Islamic Folk-Literature*, (Vio: Waldorf-Hessen), 1982.
The only potentially Jewish aspect to this *Episode* is Solomon's uncanny connection to the eagle, which is located throughout Jewish literature: II Chronicles 8:4, *Ecclesiastes Rabbah* ii 25, *Ruth Rabbah* i 17, *The Zohar* 112b.

successful in meandering through the maze of the fantastical castle in the final part of our story, he ultimately is left to confront the futility of earthly existence. Amazingly, this midrash speculates that it was in this Golden Palace that Solomon found inspiration for Ecclesiastes; some of that scroll's most famous passages appear on the palace walls before they ever emerge from Solomon's pen. As much as King Solomon of the Bible (and subsequent tradition) is a dichotomous character, this text clearly chooses to focus not on the grandiose brilliance of his fortune and fame, but rather on his human frailty and failure.

The Text with Annotation

Part 1: The Royal Robe and Retinue

This is what occurred in the days of Solomon the King, peace be upon him. At the time that the Holy One granted the kingship to Solomon son of David and gave him dominion over all species of beasts and creatures in the world, and also over human beings, and also over beasts and birds and also over everything the Holy One created,[224] [God] gave him a magnificent robe upon which he sat.[225] And it was made of green silk woven with fine gold and [embroidered] with all forms of designs in the world. It was sixty miles long and sixty miles wide.[226] Solomon had four ministers: one human minister, a second minister from the demons, a third minister from the beasts, and a fourth from the birds. The human minister was named Asaph son of Berechiah.[227] The demon minister was named Ramirat,[228] the minster of beasts was a lion, and

---

224   Here, the text echoes the Islamic tradition [Quran 21:82] that Solomon had dominion over all worldly creatures as well as demons. As will become important in the subsequent section, the Quran also describes Solomon as commanding the wind [21:81, 34:12].

225   In *Legends*, appropriately, Ginzberg renders this vast garment as a "flying carpet". The Arabic overtones of this tale (see esp. n. 4 below) indicate the precision of that reading. However, we render this flying carpet as a royal robe, as that language is used consistently in the text.

226   2000 cubits, according to Jastrow, 773.

227   See 1 Chronicles 15:17 and 6:24, which list Asaph as one of the Levites who serviced the Holy Ark in the time of David all the way through to the days of Solomon, when it was placed in the Temple. According to Ginzberg [VI:298], this is the same Asaph ben Berechiah (also known as Asaf Judaeus) who was the famed father of Hebrew medicine and author of *Sefer haRefu'ot*/The Book of Medicines, 9th or 10th Century CE. In Muslim tradition, Asaph son of Berechiah is one of Solomon's key counselors. See "Asaph Son of Berechiah" in Lassner, *Demonizing the Queen of Sheba*.

228   In keeping with Ginzberg, *ad loc.*

the minister of the birds was an eagle. [Solomon] only travelled by means of [the robe carried by] the wind. He would eat breakfast in Damascus and dinner in Media, that is to say in the East and the West.

Part II: The Rebuke of the Wind

One day, [Solomon] was boasting, saying, "There is no one like me in the world, whom the Holy One has given wisdom and knowledge, understanding, and enlightenment, and who has been granted dominion over all [God's] creatures." At that very moment, the wind was stirred, and 40,000 human beings fell from off the robe. When Solomon saw this, he yelled at the wind and said to the wind, "Return, O wind, return!" And the wind responded,[229] "You return to your God, and do not boast,[230] and I will return with you." In that moment, Solomon was shamed by the words of the wind.

Part III: The Episode of the Ant

One day, at another time, [Solomon] was walking and passed by a certain river that had ants in it. He heard the voice of one black ant who was speaking to the [other] ants, "Enter your houses so you are not destroyed by King Solomon's soldiers."[231]

When Solomon heard the words of the ant, he became angry, and said to the wind, "Go down to the earth." And he went down. He sent after the ants and said, "Who among you said, 'Enter your houses so you are not destroyed by Solomon's encampments'?"

That same ant said, "I said it to them."

He said to her, "Why did you speak thus?"

She said to him, "I was afraid lest they come to see your encampment and thereby neglect the praises they [usually] praise to the Holy One, and that God would get angry at us and would slay us."

He said to her, "Why did no other ant speak to me except for you?"

She said to him, "I am queen of the ants."

He said to her, "What is your name?"

She said to him, "*Machshema*".[232]

---

229   Literally, "returned" to him, i.e., retorted.

230   Here we discover echoes of *Midrash Al Yithallel/Do not boast!*, in which Solomon is one of three protagonists undone by his boastful behavior.

231   This first paragraph is almost a literal repetition of the Quran, *Sura Al Naml* [About the Ant]. However, Solomon's connection to the ant could be connected to Proverbs 6:6.

232   In both texts, this name is in quotation marks. Furthermore, it is a homophonic corruption of Solomon's question "What's your name?", in Hebrew, מה שמך/*Mah Shemech*?

He said to her, "I want to ask you one question."

She said to him, "It is not customary for me that the questioner be above and the respondent below."

He lifted her up before him. She said to him, "It is not customary for me that the questioner be seated on the throne, and the respondent on the earth. Rather, lift me up on your hand and I will answer you." He took her upon his hand so that she was positioned across from his face, and she said, "Ask!"

He asked her, "Is there a person more grand than me in all the world?"

She responded, "Yes."

He asked, "Who is it?"

She responded, "It is I."

He asked her, "How is it that you are more grand than I?"

She responded, "Were I not more grand than you, the Holy One would not have sent you to me to lift me up in the palm of your hand!"

When Solomon heard the ant's words, he became angry at her, cast her to the earth, and said to her, "Ant! Do you not know who I am? I am Solomon, son of King David, peace be upon him!"

The ant responded, "Do you not know that you are from a fetid drop?[233] Do not boast about yourself." At that moment Solomon fell on his face and was embarrassed and ashamed by the words of the ant.

After this, Solomon said to the wind, "Carry off the robe that we might go."

The wind lifted the robe, and the ant said to Solomon, "Go, but do not forget the blessed Name of God, and do not be too boastful." Then the wind went and ascended on high, between the sun and the earth, and remained there ten days and ten nights.

Part IV: The Golden Palace

One of those days, he saw a magnificent palace[234] made of fine gold. Solomon said to his ministers, "I have never seen a palace such as this in all the world." At that moment, Solomon said to the wind, "Go down below!" The wind went down below. Solomon and his minister, Asaph son of Berechiah, walked and strolled around the palace, and the aroma of the grass was like the aroma of the Garden of Eden, but they were not able to find any doorway through which to enter [the palace]. They were astonished by this matter: how shall we make it so we may enter inside?

---

233 M *Avot* 3:1.

234 Here we follow Ginzberg in reading טריקלין/*triclinium* /the Roman dining sofa as synecdoche for a palace. See, Jastrow, 554.

They were caught up in this matter when the minister of the demons came before the King and said to him, "My Lord, why are you so worried?"

Solomon responded, "I am worried about this palace that has no door. I don't know what to do!"

The minister of the demons responded, "My Lord, the King: I will decree for all the demons that they will go up over the roof of the palace. Perhaps they will find some matter or person or bird or creature." At that moment, he shouted to the demons and said, "Hurry, and go up to the top of the roof, and see if you find anything."

They went and ascended. They came down and said, "Our Lord, we didn't see there any person at all, except for one bird named 'Eagle', and he is sitting on his fledglings."

At that moment [Solomon] summoned the minister of the birds, the Vulture,[235] and said to him, "Go and bring me the Eagle."[236]

The Vulture went and brought the Eagle before King Solomon, peace be upon him, and [the Eagle] opened his mouth in song and sang praises to the King of King of Kings. And then he greeted King Solomon.

King Solomon asked him, "What's your name?"

He responded, "*Al-en-ad.*"

He asked, "How old are you."

He responded, "I am seven hundred years old."

He asked, "Have you seen or known or heard if there is a door to this home?"

---

235   This פרס/*peres* makes its debut in the Torah: Leviticus 11:13 and Deuteronomy 14:12, both times with double *segol* and translated as "vulture" in NJPS.

In Muslim literature, the Vulture is the only creature that knows the location of hidden items. See Schwarzbaum, *Biblical and Extra-Biblical Legends in Islamic Folk-Literature.*

הפרס/*HaParas* seems to be from the root פרס/p-r-s as a segolate noun. In *Ben Yehuda's Dictionary* it is vocalized with a double סגול/*segol*. Ben Yehuda says simply, "A big bird of prey" and at the end of a footnote adds: "The German translation for the bird is *Beinbrecher*" [literally: *Bein*=bone and *brecher*=breaker] "as language of שבירה/*shevira/breaking*, [maybe this is the connection to פרס/*paras/to break into pieces* like a פרוסת לחם/*p'rusat lehem/a morsel of bread*]. Then he ends with this great question: *But who can tell us what the real origin of this word is?* Eliezer Ben Yehuda, *A Complete Dictionary of Ancient and Modern Hebrew*, (New York and London, Thomas, Yoseloff), 1960, Volume VI, 5202, column 1. See also, *Sefer HaShorashim Shel Radaq*, column 598, "A large bird, desert dweller, according to the words of our rabbis *z"l* in BT *Hullin* 62a."

236   In rabbinic literature, Solomon commands the eagles. See *Ruth Rabbah* 1:17, *Qohelet Rabbah* 2:25, as well as II Chronicles 8:4.

He responded, "My Lord, by your life and the life of your head, I do not know. But I have a brother who is two hundred years older than I, and he knows and understands. He lives in the second heaven."

Solomon said to the Vulture, "Lead this Eagle back to his place, and bring me his older brother." He went, and no eye could see him. After a while he came before Solomon with an Eagle even more grand than the first. He recited songs and praises to his Creator, and then greeted King Solomon.

Solomon stood between his wings and asked, "What is your name?"

He replied, "*Al-Of*".

He asked him [Genesis 47:8], "How many are the years of your life?"

He responded, "Nine hundred years."

He asked, "Do you know or have you heard if there is a doorway to this palace?"

He responded, "My Lord, by your life and the life of your head, I do not know. But I have a brother 400 years older than I, and he knows and understands. He lives in the third heaven."

Solomon said to the Minister of the Birds, "Lead this one [back to his place], and bring me his older brother."

He lead him [back], and no eye could see them. After a while the large Eagle came, and he was old and unable to fly, and [other eagles] bore him on their wings and brought him to King Solomon. He expressed exaltation and praise before his Creator, and then greeted the King.

Solomon asked him, "What is your name?"

He responded, "*Alt'mar*".[237]

He asked him, "How old are you?"

He responded, "Thirteen hundred years old."

He asked him, "Do you know or have you heard if there is a doorway to this palace?"

He responded, "My Lord, I do not know. But my father told me that there is an entrance from the West side, but it has become covered by the dust of many years that has passed over it. And if you desire, command the wind to remove the dust from around the house and the door will be revealed."

Solomon commanded the wind, and it blew and swept away the dust from around the house, and the door was revealed. The door was very large, made of bronze, sitting in place as if it had been burned, and worn out from the years. They saw on the door a lock, and this was written upon it:

---

237   Here a homophone of the Hebrew תאמר אל/*al-tomar*/"let it not be spoken".

Know Ye, children of Adam, that we dwelt in this palace in joy and delight for
many years. And when the famine came upon us, we ground pearls in place
of wheat, but it was of no benefit to us. We left the house to the eagles, we laid
down upon the earth, and we said to them, "If anyone asks you about this
palace, say, 'We found it already built.'"

And it was also written:

No person may enter this house, save prophet or king. And if he wishes to
enter, let him dig on the right side of the doorway, and he will see a chest.[238]
Let him break it, and he will discover keys. Let him open the doorway, and
he will find one gate of gold. Let him open it and enter inside, and he will
find a second gate. Let him open it and enter it, and he will find a third gate.
Let him open it and enter it, and he will see an extremely beautiful building,
and inside it there is one chamber[239]*[made] of carnelian, chrysolite and*
emerald,[240] *and pearls, and inside that a single arched chamber made of*
all kinds of pearls. And he will [also] find many fine rooms and pleasant
courtyards paved with bricks alternating silver and gold. Let him look on the
ground, he will see the form of a scorpion. And let him remove the scorpion
that is made of silver, and he will find a second house under the earth. Let
him open [the house] for it has in it innumerable pearls of different variet-
ies, and different varieties of gold and silver. And he will find another door-
way, with a lock on it, and this written on the door:

The former owner of this palace was [great] in strength and honor;
the lions and bears feared his royalty and glory. He dwelt in this palace in
joy and delight, and ruled sitting on his throne. When the moment of his
untimely death arrived, the crown fell off his head. Enter into this palace,
and look, and be astonished!

After this, [Solomon] entered and saw a third doorway. Written upon it was:

They dwelt in honor and great wealth, and the wealth remains. They died,
and the troubles of time passed over them until they journeyed to their
graves. And not one of them remains to walk the earth.

---

238   Jellinek suggests that this chest was made completely of glass.
239   Ginzberg has "apartment".
240   These three jewels, without the subsequently listed pearls, for the first row of stone in the
        Breastplate of Decision. See specifically Exodus 28:17. These three (without the pearls)
        appear later in the story.

[Solomon] opened the doorway and he found one chamber [made] of [Exodus 28:17] *carnelian, chrysolite and emerald*, and [this] written upon it:

> *How much have I learned,*[241] *how much I read, how much I ate, how much I drank, and how much I wore fine garments. How much I frightened, and how I was frightened.*

He walked further and found a pleasant apartment of chrysolite and emerald, and it had three doorways. Written on the first doorway [was]:

> *Child of Adam, let not time lie to you: you will wither as you walk, travel on your way from your place, and then you will lie under the earth.*

Written on the second doorway [was]:

> *Do not proceed quickly; go very slowly, you: for this world will be given from one to the next.*

Written on the third doorway [was]:

> *Take for yourself preparations for the road, and fix food for yourself while it is still day;*[242] *for you will not [forever] remain upon the earth, and you know not the day of your death.*[243]

He opened the door and entered and saw a seated statue, and the one who looked upon it would think it was alive. He went before the statue and drew close to it, and it made a great noise and cried out in a mighty voice, "Come, you children of the demons! See: Solomon has come to annihilate you!" And smoke and fire came out of his nostrils. Simultaneously, there was among [the demons] a great and bitter cry, and roaring and shaking was upon them.[244]

Solomon cried out in a [loud] voice over them and said, "Are you not afraid of me? Do you not know I am King Solomon who rules over all creatures

---

241   Here with Eisenstein, where Jellinek has "How much I stood".

242   Cf. The Parables of King Solomon (IV: The Three Brothers), wherein Solomon's dispensed advice includes, "make camp while it is yet day."

243   Cf. Ecclesiastes 8:8: *there is no authority over the day of death*. See also BT *Pesaḥim* 54b, where, on the Sages' list of seven things hidden from a man, the first is "the day of his death".

244   cf. Isaiah 29:6, which inverts the shaking and roaring.

created by the Holy One? And I want to chastise you with all forms of chastisements, but you rebel against me." And he proclaimed against them the Tetragrammaton.

At that moment they were all silent, and not one of them could speak. All the statues fell upon their faces.[245] Those same children of the demons fled and cast themselves into the Mediterranean Sea, so that they wouldn't fall into the hand of Solomon. Solomon drew near to the statue, and took a golden tablet on a chain from its neck. Written upon the tablet were all the details of the palace. But he was not able to read it, and was extremely troubled, and said to his ministers, "Do you not know how much I wearied myself, and came close to this statue, and now have taken the tablet; but I do not know what is written upon it!"

He reflected and said, "What should I do?"

He looked, and behold: one young man was coming from the desert, and he came before Solomon, prostrated himself, and said to him, "What is with you, King Solomon, that you are troubled?"

He responded, "I am troubled by this tablet, that I don't know what is written on it."

The same boy answered, "Give it to me and I will read it to you. For I was dwelling in my place, and the Holy One saw how you were troubled, and sent me to read the writing for you."

[Solomon] put it into his hand. He looked at it and saw and was amazed for a time. Then he wept and said, "O, Solomon! This writing is in the Greek language, and says:

> I am Shed-ad son of 'Ad. I ruled over thousands and thousands of cities, I rode upon thousands and thousands of horses, thousands and thousands were under my power, and I slew thousands and thousands of warriors. But at the time the angel of death came against me, I could not prevail against him.

And it was further written:

> Any person who reads this inscription will not weary himself greatly in this world, for the end of every human being is to die, and nothing will remain in the hand of any human being except a good name.[246]

---

245 An allusion drawn from the biblical account of the image of the Philistine god Dagon at the temple at Ashdod, which fell to the ground when the Ark of the Covenant was brought into the shrine. [I Samuel 5:1–5].

246 Cf. Ecclesiastes 7:1, "A good name is better than fine oil".

This is what came to Solomon's mind regarding this world.

May all the righteous be remembered for a blessing.
May it be God's will. Amen.
Finished.

Conclusions: King Solomon

The final powerful passages of this midrash leave no doubt as to its intent: despite all of Solomon's majesty—his control of natural forces, his military might, and his uncanny cunning—his life, like all human life, will come to an end. Thus it is his literal chasing after the wind that leads him to that immortal metaphor that frames his Ecclesiastes. In the end, the text Solomon discovers in the dungeon reminds him of his own mortality. The King's experience in the final section of *The Episode of the Ant* resonates with the timeless lines of Shelley about the futility of imperial power:

> I met a traveller from an antique land
> Who said: Two vast and trunkless legs of stone
> Stand in the desert. Near them, on the sand,
> Half sunk, a shattered visage lies, whose frown,
> And wrinkled lip, and sneer of cold command,
> Tell that its sculptor well those passions read
> Which yet survive, stamped on these lifeless things,
> The hand that mocked them and the heart that fed.
> And on the pedestal these words appear—
> "My name is Ozymandias, king of kings:
> Look on my works, ye Mighty, and despair!"
> Nothing beside remains. Round the decay
> Of that colossal wreck, boundless and bare
> The lone and level sands stretch far away.[247]

---

247   Shelley, Percy Bysshe. *Complete Poetical Works.* Boston; New York: Houghton Mifflin, c1901, (Cambridge: Riverside Press); Bartleby.com, 1999.

Conclusions: Literary Expansions

Like *An Episode Concerning King Solomon, The Episode of the Ant* takes us on a series of fantastic voyages well beyond the bounds of Scriptures' tales. Likewise, *The Episode of the Ant* further expands the literary boundaries of Medieval Midrash. To begin with, the classification of this work as "Midrash" is itself perplexing. Scripture is referenced only in passing; citations of Genesis and Exodus are not intrinsic to the text but rather seem like larger cultural allusions, akin to peppering one's speech with famous political paraphrases. Unlike *An Episode Concerning King Solomon*, no biblical verse serves even as the jumping-off point for this series of stories about Solomon; the whole narrative begins with the trite frame, "This is what occurred in the days when King Solomon ruled." If in *An Episode Concerning King Solomon*, a passage from Chronicles is pretext for telling a tale, here no biblical pretense is needed for sharing a series of stories about Solomon. Were *The Episode of the Ant* not included in anthologies of Midrash, it would be hard to make a case it fits any classical definition of that genre.

The Episode of the Ant also presents the clear impact of cosmopolitan culture. As discussed above, *The Episode of the Ant* is teeming with Islamic influences, from the cultural paradigm of the magical flying carpet to the many borrowings from the Quran noted above. However, a world wider than the Islamic empire is present here: from the nonsense names of many of the birds to the "illegible script" found within the secret palace, the audience of *The Episode of the Ant* knew of the existence of foreign languages they couldn't speak, names that held secret meanings that were beyond their comprehension. Furthermore, the remarkable apparition of the young man who speaks Greek testifies that those hearing this *Episode* knew of both great empires that defined Jewish life. Given the obvious presence of Greek and Islamic influences, *The Episode of the Ant* seems to be the product of literary middle men following in the footsteps of Alfonsi and the many cultural predecessors who transmitted stories from one empire to another. Yet here, the author of *The Episode of the Ant* is doing something different from bringing Indian stories to Iraq, or Islamic legends to the Christian world: the author of *The Episode* is bringing the cultural influences of the Muslim world to bear on the creation of a uniquely Jewish story. This is a key marker of the flowering of creativity in the Islamic period: tales from the outside world are translated, as it were, and re-set for a Jewish audience. The inclusion of foreign cultures as potential, imaginative sources for Jewish literature is a major expansion of the literary activity we call Medieval Midrash.

Parables of King Solomon

Textual History

Eli Yasif has written an excellent article that, in part, traces the manuscript history of the *Parables of King Solomon*. Yasif explains that six different manuscripts are connected to this collection, which first was printed in Qushta, (Constantinople) in 1516, as part of *The Chronicles of Moses our Teacher*. The first manuscript is from Oxford, and contains only the story of Solomon, Ashmedai, and the man with two heads;[248] importantly, that story appears only in this Oxford manuscript and is not found in either the first printed Qushta collection of these tales nor in any of the manuscripts that parallel the Qushta edition.[249] A second manuscript contains a section of the parable of the servant and his son that is identical to what is found in the Qushta edition.[250] A third, partial source, is a Hamburg text that contains the stories of the women and the brigand and the three pieces of wisdom, precisely as related in the printed text.[251] Two further manuscripts, from Paris and London, contain the full text exactly as printed in the Qushta edition.[252] The last of these is a text from Parma that not only contains our *Parables* precisely as in the printed edition, but also lacks any "stand alone title" for this series of tales.[253] Yasif speculates that this Parma manuscript is the basis for the first printed edition at Qushta.

Yasif posits something of great importance for our study of Medieval Midrash: that King Solomon serves as the unifying force for these previously existing sets of stories brought together under the aegis of Solomon through the Medieval genre of novella. Yasif explains that the motif of gold stuck in honey jars is found in the Ali Hodja story of *1001 Arabian Nights*;[254] he further shows parallels to the tale of the "fidelity test" in the works of R. Nissim and Ibn Zabara.[255] Yasif is aware that these stories, brought together in the Qushta edition and other manuscripts, were likely created independently of each other.

---

248   Oxford, Bodleian Heb.e.10 [Neubauer 2679].
249   Yasif notes that the first time the tale of the two heads is ever linked to these other parables of King Solomon is in Jellinek's *Bet HaMidrasch*.
250   Oxford, Bodleian, Opp.Add8vo.59 [Neubauer 2589].
251   Hamburg, Levi 153.4.
252   Paris, Heb. 675, a 17th Century manuscript, with pps. 13–29 identical to printed edition; London, Jews College, 35, a 17th–18th Century Persian manuscript.
253   Parma 2294 (Parma Catalogue 194) 44b–48a, a 15th–16 Century Ashkenazic manuscript.
254   Yasif, "Parables," 367.
255   Yasif, "Parables," 365. See also his helpful footnotes numbered 25 and 26.

© KONINKLIJKE BRILL NV, LEIDEN, 2017 | DOI 10.1163/9789004331334_009

According to his dating, only for the tale of the fidelity test does there exist a Hebrew source *earlier* than the first printing. These are stories that, in the main, appear for the first time in Hebrew letters *together*: this is the basis for Yasif's claim that King Solomon was the synchronizing force that unified these disparate tales; he claims, "as a full volume, *The Parables of King Solomon* is a special compilation that was created, it seems, with the first Hebrew printing presses."[256] If this is true, then Adolph Jellinek seems to have continued this synchronic trend by including with our parables the story of Solomon found in a stray Oxford manuscript, of his encounter with Ashmedai and the man with two heads.

Literary Introduction

King Solomon and wisdom walk hand in hand throughout the Bible and all subsequent Jewish literature. These six parables attest to Solomon's outstanding intellect: in half of these stories he adjudicates cases baffling to other judges; in the remainder he demonstrates how much better he knows the ways of the world than most mortals. In the course of our stories, Solomon proves himself wiser than his father, King David, and the entire Sanhedrin of Israel as well. The collective power of these tales demonstrates Solomon's otherworldly wisdom.

The parables here also tell us a great deal about their authors and original audience. To begin with, most of the sources stem from rabbinic tradition: Kings settling confusing cases; wise men choosing wisdom over gold; and even a man with two heads; all of these make their appearance in earlier Jewish literature.[257] With the exception of the trope of the prince being wiser than his father, the king, there appears to be little borrowed from Islamic material.[258] The great novelty here is the unfortunate misogyny associated with Solomon; while his relationship with many women is widely described in the Bible, nowhere do we see quite as vituperative and troubling a depiction of women

---

256   Yasif, "Parables," 360.

257   *Leviticus Rabbah* 27:1, *Midrash Mishlei* 1:1, and *Tosefot* to BT *Menaḥot* 37a, respectively.

258   The notion that Solomon is wiser than his father David is found in Islamic literature. Originally it is in the *Hadith* collections, attributed to Abu Huraira. See Schwarzbaum, *Biblical and Extra-Biblical Legends*, 84.

       However, we should note that while Abraham is not technically a King, there are numerous rabbinic traditions about him being wiser than his father. See, *Bereshit Rabbah* 38:13 and 44:13.

as we do in two of these parables. Women, like King David, the rabbinic court, sneaky servants and avaricious brothers here serve merely as foils for the unparalleled wisdom of one King Solomon.

The Text with Annotation

Parable 1: The Servant and the Son

An episode concerning one man who lived in the days of David, King of Israel: he was exceedingly wealthy, had manservants and maidservants and much property, and also an only son. What did this man do? He purchased much merchandise, and gave it to his son. That same son boarded a boat and emigrated to Africa.[259] He stayed there for many years. During those years his father died, and left his possessions to one of his servants, the Keeper of his Treasury.[260] And this same servant oppressed all the members of the household with strange chastisements, until they left him and went on their way. And he was left alone with all the wealth his master had left, and he feasted and rejoiced out of his lust for wealth. After some time, the same young man returned from the coastal cities,[261] went to his father's house, and found that his father died and was buried. When he started to enter his house, the servant came out to greet him, pushed him, and said to him, "What are you doing in my house, base fellow?" What did the young man do? He took a stick, began to beat him on the head, and said to him, "Servant! You have taken all [the profit of] my labor, and the labor of my father, my teacher! And you've rejoiced on that same wealth."

And there was a great quarrel between them, and there was no one to stop them,[262] until the son of the old man fled and went to complain about the servant to the King. He said, "Long live the King! A certain man took all the money

---

259 Namely, Carthage. Cf. Jastrow, 108.

260 The implication is that he was trusted to share this treasure with the entire household. See Jastrow to *Oẓar*, 32.

261 See BT *Rosh HaShanah* 26a, where "Africa" and these "coastal cities" are referred to in a passage on different ports of call the Sages visited.

262 The translation of אין מציל/*ein maẓil/none to stop them,* here follows NJPS to II Sam 14:4–6, a passage that related a quarrel being brought to King David:

> [4]The woman of Tekoa came to the King David, flung herself face down to the ground, and prostrated herself. She cried out, "Help, O king!" [5]The king asked her, "What troubles you?" And she answered, "Alas, I am a widow, my husband is dead. [6]Your maidservant had two sons. The two of them came to blows out in the fields where there was no one to stop them, and one of them struck the other and killed him.

that my father, my teacher, left me, and said to me, 'You are not the son of the old man, but I am.'"

The king asked, "Do you have witnesses?"

He said, "No."

[The King] summoned that same servant, and asked him, "Do you have witnesses?"

He said, "No."

The King said to the servant, "Go in peace. You do not need to return anything."

When the son of the old man heard this, he began to weep and to wail before the King, once, twice and three times. He cried before the King until the King rebuked him, and said to him, "If you continue any further, I will send my hand against you. If you have witnesses, good! If not, what can I do on your behalf?"

King Solomon heard this matter. He summoned him to the side, and said to him, "Cry out again to the King, and if he gets angry at you, say to him, 'My Lord, the King! If you will render me with justice, put him under the authority of your son Solomon." Then [the King] set him under the authority of his son Solomon, that he would render justice.[263]

Solomon asked the young man, "Do you know where your father is buried?"

He said, "No."

Again he summoned the same servant. He asked him, "Do you know where your father is buried?"

He said, "Yes."

In the Bible, אֵין מַצִּיל/*ein maẓil* is mostly employed to refer to the lack of a physical savior. Outside of the above passage from II Samuel, there is one additional biblical usage of the phrase [Psalm 71:10–13] that seems to take place in a more judiciary setting:

> [10]For my enemies talk against me;
> those who wait for me are of one mind,
> [11]saying, "God has forsaken him;
> chase him and catch him,
> for no one will save him!"
> [12]O God, be not far from me;
> my God, hasten to my aid!
> [13]Let my accusers perish in frustration;
> let those who seek my ruin be clothed in reproach and disgrace!

263 See Schwarzbaum, *Biblical and Extra-Biblical Legends*, p. 152, on the Muslim version of the famous maternity case involving the two prostitutes:

> "The Biblical version has undergone a definite *islamization* by Abu Huraira, and of course, by Umara's other authorities. This is evident from the fact that the lawsuit of the two women is first brought before King David *who fails in his verdict*. Only the young, clever Solomon overrides his father's wrong verdict by offering to cut the child in two."

Solomon said to him, "Go and bring me your father's shin bone."[264] He went and he cut off the shinbone of the old man, and he brought it to him.

[Solomon] said, "Draw blood from them both.[265] Each of them will deposit his blood in his own vessel."

[Solomon] said to the servant, "Dip the bone in your blood". He dipped it but it did not change color.

[Solomon] said to the son of the old man, "You also dip in your blood." The bone changed color and he showed it to all the people.

[Solomon] said to them, "See this blood! From this very bone he came forth!" Immediately, all Israel was astonished, and he returned all the wealth to the young man, and he subdued the servant against his will. Thus it is said [I Kings 5:11]: *Solomon was wiser than all humanity.*

Parable 11: The Wayward Wife and the Brigand

An episode from the days of King Solomon.

A certain man went from Tiberius to Betar to study Torah, and this young man was exceedingly handsome. Immediately, a certain young woman saw him, and said to her father, "I ask of you that you make a match for me with this young man." He [the father] immediately pursued after him. He said to this young man, "Do you wish to marry a woman? I will give you my daughter [in marriage]."

He said, "Yes."

Immediately, he married his daughter and returned to his house and rejoiced with his wife for a full year. At the end of the year, his wife said to him, "I ask of you that you bring me to my parents that I might see them." Immediately he took horses, precious goods, food and drink, and went with his wife to visit her parents. As they went on their way, a certain armed brigand descended on them. When the wife saw the brigand, love for him [the brigand] entered her heart. The wife and the brigand together seized the young man, and bound him in ropes.[266] The brigand bedded[267] the wife with frivolous words, and

---

264   In Hebrew, זְרוֹעַ/*z'roah*, which in the context of Passover is translated as "shankbone".

265   According to *Sefer Ḥasidim*, R. Saadiah ben Yosef adjudicated a similar case with this precise test of dipping the father's bone in two separate blood samples. Yehudah HeḤasid, *Sefer Ḥasidim*, tr. Avraham Yaakov Finkel (New Jersey: Aaronson), *sigla* 525.

266   This is a clear allusion to Judges 16:10ff, namely the episode where Delilah binds Samson with a variety of items, the second of which are our "ropes". It seems significant that our wife here is linked to the betraying Delilah.

267   The Hebrew verb שִׁמֵּשׁ/*shimesh* certainly implies sexual intercourse [Jastrow, 1601]. Note also that this verb maintains the parallels with the story of Delilah and Samson [in Hebrew, שִׁמְשׁוֹן/*Shimshon*].

afterwards sat down to eat and drink together with the wife. The whole time the young man was bound to one tree, and witnessed everything. Afterwards, [the brigand] went to sleep with the young woman, and the brigand took the wine ladle, placed it under his head,[268] and went to sleep. Look:[269] the snake came, drank the wine, and vomited venomous poison into [the ladle]. When the brigand woke from his sleep, he took the wine ladle, drank from it and died. The young man saw the miracle that was done for him.

The young man said to his wife, "I ask of you to release me and loosen the ropes from me."

She said to him, "I am afraid that you will kill me."

He said to her, "I swear I will not slay you." Immediately she examined the brigand, and he had turned to petrified wood. Immediately she took her husband, and the two of them went to the house of the wife's parents. When her parents saw her, they greatly rejoiced, and they fixed food and drink.

The young man said to them, "I will neither eat nor drink until I tell you what happened to me." Immediately, he told them of the entire episode.

What did the father do? He killed his wicked daughter.[270] Thus Solomon said in his wisdom [Ecclesiastes 7: 28]:

[*[23]All this I tested with wisdom. I thought I could fathom it, but it eludes me. [24]What happens is elusive and deep, deep down; who can discover it? [25]I put my mind to studying, exploring, and seeking wisdom and the reason of things, and to studying wickedness, stupidity, madness, and folly. [26]Now, I find woman more bitter than death; she is all traps, her hands are fetters and her heart is snares. He who is pleasing to God escapes her, and he who is displeasing is caught by her. [27]See, this is what I found, said Koheleth, item by item in my search for the reason of things. [28]As for what I sought further but did not find, I found only one human being in a thousand,] and the one I found among so many was never a woman.[271]*

---

268   Cf. Genesis 28:11, 12, 13 and 15. When Jacob slept at Beth El, a very different outcome occurred.

269   The הנה/*hinei* [look!] here is another parallel to the Jacob passage from Genesis 28. That pericope also echoes the Samson and Delilah passage, with its reference to the arrival of the sun, שמש/*shemesh*.

270   This stark act is disturbing to us as modern readers. It, however, reflects the nature of misogynic medieval folktales. It also reminds us of the danger of literalist reading of our traditional texts.

271   NJPS. In our text, only the final verse is present. But the entire passage seems particularly pertinent, as it sets the context for the misogynistic take of these two scenes. For the function of this verse in misogynic folklore, see Eli Yasif, *The Hebrew Folktale*, 345–351.

Parable III: The Test of a Man and a Woman

An episode concerning King Solomon, peace be upon him, who said through the Holy Spirit [Ecclesiastes 7:28]: *I found only one man in a thousand, and the one I found among so many was never a woman.* When the people and the Sanhedrin heard this word, they were astonished.

Solomon said, "If you wish, I will prove it to you."

They all said, "Yes."

He said to them, "Search out one woman from the best of the city, and also a man who is better than all." They examined and found one man who had a good and lovely wife. The King sent to summon him, and they brought him before them.

The King said to him, "Know that I seek honor for you, to make you the minister of my palace."

He replied and said, "I am your servant, and I will be as one of your servants."

King Solomon said to him, "If so, go and kill your wife, and bring me her head this very night, and tomorrow I will give you my daughter [as a wife], and I will make you an official over the multitude of Israel."

The man said, "I will do your will." He went to his house. His wife was pleasant and beautiful, and she had by him small children. The matter pierced his heart, and he wept and grieved. When his wife saw that his face was angered, she adjured him, and said to him, "What is with you, my lord? For I see your face is enraged!"

He said to her, "Let me be, for I have worry in my heart." Immediately, she brought before him food and drink, but he did not wish to eat.

He thought to himself, saying, "What shall I do? Shall I kill my wife, with whom I have small children?" He said to her, "Go and sleep with our children." When she lay down and fell asleep, he drew his sword to kill her, and found his youngest son sleeping between her two breasts. And another young son was sleeping with his head between her shoulders. In that very hour, Satan entered his heart to kill her. He said, "Woe unto me! What will I do if I kill her? Will these little children die [too]?" Immediately he returned his sword [to its sheath], and said [Zechariah 3:2], "*May Adonai rebuke you, Satan!*"

He returned a second time, and said, "Let me kill her, and tomorrow the King will give me his daughter [in marriage], and make me rich." Immediately he withdrew his sword over her, and saw her hair spread over the faces of the infants. Immediately, mercy entered his heart, and he said, "Even if the king gives me all of his house and all of his wealth, I will not kill my wife." Immediately he returned his sword to its sheath, and lay down with his wife until the morning.

Behold, messengers of the king came for him, and led him before [the King]. The King said to him, "What did you do? Did you fulfill what I said to you?"

He said to him, "If it is good in the eyes of the King, do not bring me into this matter. I sought to do this once and again, but my heart was not set on doing it."

Solomon said, "*I found only one man in a thousand.*"

So he left his presence, and [Solomon] left him alone for thirty days.

After thirty days, the King sent secretly to [that man's] wife, and they brought her before [the King]. The King asked her, "Is your husband good?"

She said, "Yes."

He said to her, "I have heard of all of your beauty and radiant face, and I have fallen in love with you [and want] to take you as a wife. Furthermore, let us make you sovereign over all the princesses of the kingdom, and will dress you in gold from your head to your feet."

And she said to him, "Yes. All that you desire, I will do."

He said to her, "There is only one problem: I am not able to do anything, because you have a husband."

She said, "How will we do this?"

He said to her, "Kill your husband, and afterwards I will marry you as my wife."

She said to him, "Thus I will do."

Solomon said to himself, "If this one indeed intends to kill her husband, shall we create a remedy so he doesn't die?" What did he do? He gave her a tin sword,[272] and when she saw how that sword shone [like silver], he said, "With this sword, kill him. For the moment you place it on his neck, he will be cut to pieces."

The woman returned with the sword to her house and to her husband. Her husband came and she stood before him; she embraced him and kissed him, and said to him, "Sit, my lord, the crown of my head." When he heard this, he greatly rejoiced, and he sat with no evil thought in his heart. Immediately, she brought the table and they ate and drank.[273]

Her husband said to her, "My wife, what is your business this evening?"

She said to him, "We would seek to be happy with you, and to see you drunk this evening."

---

272   Numbers 31:22, NJPS translates בדיל/*badil* as "tin". So too in Ezekiel 18:22, which lists בדיל/
        badil as a lesser metal, a "dross". The wisdom here is that Solomon fools the woman into
        thinking this is a powerful sword of silver when it is merely a dull blade.

273   Often, and potentially here, "the table" is a rabbinic euphemism for sexual intercourse.
        See BT Ḥagigah 5b, as well as commentary in Daniel Boyarin, *Carnal Israel: Reading Sex in
        Talmudic Culture*, (Berkeley University of California), 1993, pp. 123 ff.

He laughed before her, light-hearted,[274] and he drank and became drunk until he sank into slumber. Once she saw this, she girded her loins, drew the sword that the King had given her, and began to cut his skin. Immediately he awakened from his sleep, and saw—behold!—his wife was standing over him to kill him.

He said to her, "Tell me the matter, and who gave you this sword, and how did this episode come to be? And if you do not tell me, I will cut your flesh limb-by-limb."

She said to him, "Such and such is the matter: King Solomon said to me...."

He said to her, "Do not fear."

When he arose early in the morning and—behold!—the messengers of the King came for them, immediately he went with his wife to the King, and the Sanhedrin was seated before him. When the King saw them, he laughed. The king said to them, "Please, tell me how this episode came about."

They said, "Such and such happened: I awoke and found my wife standing over me to kill me. If the sword had been able to sever [my skin], I would already be dead. I took mercy on her, but she did not take mercy upon me."[275]

Solomon said, "I knew that there was no mercy in women. Therefore, I gave her a tin sword." When the Sanhedrin heard this, they said, "What the King said is true: *I found only one man in a thousand, and the one I found among so many was never a woman.*

Parable IV: The Three Brothers

An episode of three brothers who went to study Torah with King Solomon. Solomon said to them, "Rise up and serve me, and I will teach you wisdom." Then he appointed them to be ministers over his royal attendants.[276] They stayed there for thirteen years.

At the end of thirteen years, they said to each other, "What have we done? We have forsaken our houses and everything that is ours! Behold! Thirteen years we came to study Torah, but we served [Solomon] and didn't learn anything. Let us get permission and let us return to our wives."[277]

---

274   Cf. Esther 5:9, where Haman departs from the palace light-hearted and happy, only to find frustration at Mordecai's purported impudence.

275   Clearly, the husband now understands the nature of the test through which the King put him and his wife.

276   For פרגוד/*pargod* as "royal attendants" [Trnsf. from "curtain"], see Jastrow, 1214.

277   As here, the Hebrew word for house is a widely used rabbinic euphemism for a Wife. See, *Ruth Rabbah* 2:8.

One day they came before Solomon and said to him, "Our Lord: Behold, for thirteen years we left our wives, grant us permission to go and see our households."

Immediately, the King summoned the Minister of his Treasury to bring before him three hundred gold coins. He said to them, "Choose for yourselves one of two things: either I will teach each of you three pieces of wisdom, or I will give to each one of you a hundred gold coins." Immediately, they took counsel with each other, took the money, received permission, and went on their own way.

When they reached a distance of four miles from the city, the youngest spoke up and said to his brothers, "What have we done? For gold coins did we come, or to study Torah? If you take my counsel, come and let us return the money and let us study wisdom from King Solomon."

His brothers said to him, "If you want to return the money to study three words of wisdom, go! But we will not return to buy words with money."

Immediately, the younger one returned to Solomon, and said to him, "My Lord! I did not come here for the gold. Please take the gold and teach me wisdom."[278]

Immediately, he began to teach him. He said to him, "My son:

> When you go on the way, be careful that when the pillar of dawn arises, you be prepared to go; in the evening, make camp while it is yet day. Behold, this is one.
> When you see that the river is full, do not enter there; rather wait until it ebbs and returns to its place. Behold, this is two.
> Never reveal a secret to a woman, even to your wife. Behold, this is three."

Immediately he received permission [to leave], mounted his horse, and ran after his brothers. When he reached them, they said to him, "What did you learn?"

He said to them, "What I learned, I learned."

He continued to go, together with his brothers, for nine hours. They reached a certain place[279] that was pleasant for their camping. The youngest spoke up,

---

278   Here, the youngest brother imitates the biblical Solomon of 1 Kings by choosing wisdom over wealth. See also *Midrash Mishlei* 1:1, which celebrates the biblical choice made by Solomon.

279   An allusion to Genesis 28:11.

"Behold! The place is good to spend the night: there is water and wood, and grass to pasture the horses. If you wish, let us spend the night here, and when the pillar of dawn rises—if God decrees life for us—let us depart in peace."

His brothers said to him, "What a fool! At the moment you took the money and bought those words, we recognized there was no wisdom in you! We are able to continue on for eight more miles, and you say we should spend the night here?"

"Do as you wish, but I will not move from here." They went on their way, and he remained and began to cut wood, lit a fire, and made a kind of hut for himself and the animals. He let the horse graze until nightfall, and gave them barley. He ate, as did his animals, and he lay down that night securely. His brothers walked until nightfall, and were not able to find pasture for their animals, and neither wood nor fire. And a great snow fell upon them so that they died of excessive cold. But that same young man was not hurt by the snow because of the hut and the fire and the food and the drink. And when the pillar of dawn arose he got himself ready, mounted his horse, retook the road, followed after his brothers, and found them dead. When he saw them, he fell on them weeping. He took their money, buried them, and went on his way.

The sun came out, melted the snow, and filled the river up to its banks so that he was not able to cross. Immediately, he alighted from his horse and waited until the river ebbed. And when there was a path on the riverbank, he looked on the same side and saw there Solomon's servants who were bringing two animals laden with gold. They said to him, "Why do you not cross the river?"

He said, "Because it is overflowing."

But they began to cross, and when they came into the midst of the river, they drowned and died. The young man waited until the river ebbed, and he crossed, took their money, and went to his home in peace. When his brother's wives saw him, they asked about their husbands. He said to them, "They stayed to study wisdom."

He then began to purchase fields and vineyards, to build palaces, and to acquire livestock and goods. His wife asked him, "My Lord: tell me from where you got this money!"

Immediately, he became angry with her, dealt her a vigorous blow, and said, "What is it to you to ask this?" [It was] not until she coaxed him time and time again that he told her everything.[280]

One time, he was provoking his wife and began to yell. She said, "It is not enough for you that you killed your two brothers, that you would [also] want to kill me?" When the wives of his brothers heard about their death, immediately

---

280   Cf. Delilah in Judges 16.

they went and lodged a complaint about [their brother-in-law] to the King. Immediately the King commanded for him to be brought before him, and commanded his execution.

When they brought him out for execution, he said to them, "Please let me be that I might speak before the King." Immediately they led him to the King, he prostrated himself, and said, "My Lord! I am one of three brothers that stood before you for thirteen years to study wisdom. And I am the youngest, who returned the gold to learn wisdom from you. The wisdom you taught me is correct."

Immediately, the King recognized the truth, and said, "Do not fear, the money that you took from your brothers and from my servants belongs to you for the wisdom you acquired saved you from death and from the hand of this very woman. Go and be happy with your wife." At that moment, Solomon said [Proverbs 16:6, 8:19]: *How much better to acquire wisdom than gold, [gold] and fine gold.*[281]

Parable v: The Vessels of Gold

An episode of a certain man from the time of King Saul who had a very beautiful and comely wife who was [also] exceptionally wealthy. That man was exceedingly older than she, and his time came to die. And because the wife was comely, the Minister of the City set his eyes on her. He wanted to take her through force,[282] but she didn't want [him] on any account, and an endless fear entered her heart. She took all of her money and put it in jugs, stopped them up with honey, and entrusted them—in front of witnesses—to one man whom she knew and who loved her husband, and then fled the city. After some time, that minster died, and the woman returned to her house.

And the man who had had the pledge in his keeping prepared an engagement feast for his son, and needed honey for [the feast]. He went and found those jugs with honey, and took from the honey that same small amount that was in the mouth of the jugs. At the end of the matter, he found that all the jugs were filled with gold. Immediately, he took the money and filled the jugs with honey.

When the woman returned to her house, she went to the man, and said to him, "Give me the pledge that I left in your hands."

---

281   This is a conflation of two verses, one that ends a stich with "gold" and the other that begins a stitch with "gold". Proverbs 16:16 names wisdom explicitly, and Proverbs 8 is written with Wisdom speaking in the first person.

282   The phrase "through force" is the Hebrew ביד רמה/*b'yad rama*, a biblical phrase found at Exodus 14:8.

He said to her, "Go and bring me the witnesses in whose presence you gave me the honey, and then take what is yours." She went and brought the witnesses and he brought out all the jugs and gave them to her in the presence of the aforementioned witnesses. When she went to her house she found that all the jugs were filled with honey. She began to scream and weep. She went to the judge of the city to lodge a complaint against him.[283] The judge said to her, "Do you have witnesses?"

She said, "No."

He said to her, "My daughter, what may I do for you? Go and ask the king that he might judge on your behalf."

She went to King Saul, and he sent her to the Sanhedrin. They said to her, "Do you have witnesses that you entrusted money to this man?"

She said to him, "I do not have witnesses because I did this thing furtively because of my fear of the minister."

They said to her, "My daughter, we do not have the right to make a judgment except with witnesses. For we are not able to make judgments regarding judgments of the heart."

She left their presence disappointed. She began to return to her home, and encountered David, King of Israel.[284] He was then a small boy, a shepherd of the flock, and he was with other youths. Immediately, she cried out and said, "My son, I lodged [a complaint], but they would not render a judgment for me with a man who tricked me. Listen to my words, and render judgment on my account in your mercy."

He said to her, "Go to the King and ask that he grant me permission, and I will bring your judgment to light."

She returned to the king and said, "My Lord! I found one boy who, according to his word, knows how to bring my judgment to light."

He said to her, "Go and bring him before me," and the King summoned him. Saul said to him, "Is it true that you are able to bring this judgment to light?" He said, "If you give me permission, [I place] my confidence in my Maker."

---

283   The entire case here seems an inversion of a legend from *Leviticus Rabbah* 27:1. There, an African King settles the matter of a carob tree that had been purchased while neither seller nor purchaser knew it contained a great treasure. His wisdom in deciding the case is mocked by the visiting Alexander of Macedon, who explains he would have executed both men and taken the treasure for himself.

284   Here, as in the first episode, we see a younger not-yet-king whose wisdom exceeds the reigning monarch. In the first episode, it was Solomon who was wiser than David; here it is David who outsmarts Saul. Likely, this episode as well should be read as Solomon outsmarting David.

[Saul] said to her, "Go with him."

[David] said to her, "Bring out the vessels[285] that you left in pledge with that man." She brought out the vessels. He said to her, "Do you recognize these as the vessels you left in pledge with that man?"

She said to him, "Yes, my lord. Also ask that man, and he will admit that they are the vessels."

David said to her, "Go and bring me different empty vessels." She went, brought them to him, and emptied out the honey into these [new] vessels. He took these vessels, and broke the [old ones] in public. He searched and found in one place among the shards of the vessels two gold coins that were stuck on sides of the vessels. Immediately David spoke up and said to the keeper of the pledge, "Go and return the pledge to the woman."

Immediately, when Saul and all Israel heard this, they were greatly astonished by the matter. They knew the Holy Spirit rested upon him.

Parable VI: The Man with Two Heads

An episode that occurred during the time of Solomon, King of Israel. One day, Ashmedai, King of the demons, entered and said to him, "Are you the one about whom it is written, [I Kings 5:11]: [*Solomon*] *was wiser than all humanity?*"

Solomon said to him, "Thus the Holy One assured me."

Ashmedai said to him, "If you wish, I will show you something that you have never seen."

He said, "Yes."

Immediately, he extended his hand to the opposite end of the world, and he brought forth a man who had two heads and four eyes.[286] Immediately, Solomon was astonished and frightened, and he said, "Bring him in to my chamber."

He sent and summoned Benaiah, son of Jehoiada, and said to him, "What would you say: Are there human beings[287] under our feet?"[288]

---

285 Previously, כדים/*kadim*/jugs. Here, כלים/*kelim*/vessels.

286 This tale of the man with two heads is found in the *Tosafot* to BT *Menaḥot* 37a.

287 The Hebrew for "human beings" is בני אדם/*bnai Adam*, literally, "children of Adam". Importantly, the parallel example that is brought to prove this creature's humanity is literally a son of the biblical Adam.

288 In keeping with Eisenstein's footnote 3 *ad loc*, the intent of the question is whether or not there are human beings who live on the far side of the earth, directly opposite from where Solomon and Benaiah are standing.

He said, "As you live, my Lord the King, I only know because I have heard it from Ahitophel, intimate[289] of your father, that we have humans under our feet."

[Solomon] said, "If I were to show one to you, what would you say?"

[Benaiah] said, "How are you able to show [me]? From the depths of the earth it is a five hundred years' walk! And between each and every land it is also a five hundred years' walk!"

Immediately, [Solomon] sent and they brought [the two-headed man] to him. When [Benaiah] saw him, he fell on his face and said, "Blessed is the One who kept me alive and sustained me to this season!"

He said to him, "Whose son are you?"

He responded, "I am of the sons of Adam of the generation of Cain."

He said to him, "Where do you all live?"

He responded, "In the opposite end of the world."

He said to him, "Do you have the sun and the moon?"

He responded, "Yes, and we also plow and harvest, and own flocks and beasts."

He said to him, "From which direction does the sun rise?"

He responded, "In the West, and it sets in the East."

He said to him, "Do you pray?"

He responded, "Yes."

He said to him, "And what is your prayer?"

He responded [Psalm 104:24], "*How great is Your handiwork, Adonai; all You fashioned in wisdom. [The world is filled with your creations.]*"[290]

He said to him, "If you desire, we will return you to your place."

He responded to them, "Do me the favor of returning me to my place."

Immediately, the King summoned Ashmedai and said to him, "Return him to his place."

Ashmedai responded, "I will never be able to return him to his place."

When he realized this, [the two-headed man] married a woman, and fathered seven sons with her, six of them looking like the mother, and one of them looking like the father, who had two heads. And [the two-headed man] plowed and reaped and became rich, the greatest of the wealthy in the world.

---

289 אלוף/*aluf* is not used in the Bible to describe Ahitophel. Here we translate in keeping with NJPS to Micah 7:5.

290 In rabbinic tradition, this verse is the prayer pronounced over "unclean" items. In BT *Ḥullin* 126b, R. Aqiba recites this verse in appreciation of insects and crawling creatures. At BT *Avodah Zara* 20a, R. Shimon b. Gamliel pronounces these words over a beautiful heathen woman he espies at the bath house.

After some time this man died and left his inheritance to his sons. Six of them said, "We are seven in dividing the wealth of our father," but the one that had two heads said, "We are eight, and it is incumbent on me to take two portions of the inheritance."

They all went to Solomon and said to him, "Our Lord the King! We are seven, and our brother who has two heads says that we are eight and wants to apportion our father's inheritance into eight parts, and he wants to take two parts."

When Solomon heard this, the matter was baffling to him, and he immediately called the Sanhedrin and asked them, "What do you say regarding this matter?"

They said, "If we say he is one, [we fear] lest he is two," and they fell silent.

Solomon said to them, "Come the morning and I will render judgment."

At midnight he entered the Temple and stood in prayer before God, and said, "Sovereign of the Universe, When you revealed yourself to me at Gibeon, you asked, [I Kings 3:5] *'Ask, what I shall grant you'.*[291] I asked of you neither silver nor gold, but wisdom in order to judge the children of Adam justly."

The Holy One said to him, "I will give you wisdom in the morning."

In the morning,[292] he sent and gathered the entire Sanhedrin, and Solomon said to them, "Bring before me that man with two heads." They immediately brought him before Solomon, and he said to them, "See, if this head senses what I do to the other [head], they are one [man]. And if not, they are two [men]." Solomon said, "Bring hot water, vintage wine and silken garments." They brought hot water and placed it before him, and he sprinkled the hot water and vintage wine [on one head].

[The two-headed man] said "My Lord, the King! We are dying! We are dying! We are one and not two!"

[Solomon replied,] "But didn't you say to me [previously,] 'We are two'?"

When Israel saw the judgment of the King, they were astonished, and all trembled in fear before him. Therefore it is said [I Kings 5:11]: [*Solomon*] *was wiser than all* [*the children of*] *Adam.*

---

291   I Kings 3 contains the full exchange at Gibeon between God and Solomon in which God grants Solomon's request and bestows upon him wisdom unique in human history.

292   This parallels the I Kings 3 narrative, in which Solomon awakes in the morning from his dream and thereupon judges the famous case of the two prostitutes.

Conclusions: King Solomon

These parables are not precisely that: more than morality tales, they are opportunities to present the brilliance of Solomon's intellect in a properly shining spotlight. Like the King who stars in them, these stories reach the reader more through the delight of cunning guile than through the power of emotional resonance: they are much more *Sherlock Holmes* than *One Hundred Years of Solitude*, more *Indiana Jones* than *Casablanca*. Especially given their questionable ethical comments, they seem likely to have been popular fictions of their day. Thus, King Solomon steps outside his role as noble and perfect ruler of Jerusalem to play the paradigmatic wise man of incredibly clever stories. Given the limited role of Solomon in each of these tales, the most we may conclude about the King from these stories is that they shine light on his well-attested attribute of wisdom.

Conclusions: Literary Expansions

Classical Midrash cites a biblical text in order to expound upon it; vastly different Rabbinic works such as the *Mekhilta* and *Leviticus Rabbah* follow the format of quoting words of Torah and then offering commentary. Sometimes, in the extended literary form known as the proem, a biblical citation from the Writings will serve as the initial exegetical lemma, and the exercise will culminate in an arrival at an interpretation of a passage from Torah.[293] But here in the *Parables of King Solomon*, the author employs Scripture in a completely different fashion: words of Torah hardly appear at the outset of the tales;[294] in fact, they come and serve as epigrammatic morals to each story. There appears to be little or no literary connection between these biblical epigrams and the tales that precede them. Certainly, we see no evidence of any interpretation or explication of these verses in any fashion that would lead us to qualify this literature as Midrash in the Rabbinic sense of the term. In fact, if any parallels to Classical Midrash exist, they would be to *Leviticus Rabbah*, whose chapters often catalogue tales around themes—such as inebriation or proper speech—elicited by a scriptural passage.[295] Yet even this link is tenuous, as

---

293 Excellent examples of such may be seen in *Pesiqta deRav Kahana* 1 and *Lamentations Rabbah*, 1:24.

294 The sole exception being when Ashmedai—King of the Demons!—quotes Chronicles to challenge Solomon's power.

295 *Leviticus Rabbah,* Chapters 12 and 16, respectively.

in *The Parables of King Solomon*, the stories are far more expansive than any Rabbinic counterparts, and the scriptural citations lesser in number and in narrative importance.

A good example of the distance between *The Parables of King Solomon* and Rabbinic Midrash may be seen in its interpretation of *Qohelet* 7:26:

> [26]Now, I find woman more bitter than death; she is all traps, her hands are fetters and her heart is snares. He who is pleasing to God escapes her, and he who is displeasing is caught by her.

The Rabbinic Midrash *Qohelet Rabbah* treats this verse as follows: it cites its first phrase, "I find woman more bitter than death," and then offers this explanation: Our Rabbis said [this is] because she demands things from his hand that he cannot stand, and in the end he will die a bitter death.[296] While this follows the classic forms of Midrash, it is not an entirely helpful explication of the passage. In contrast, what we see in *The Parables of King Solomon* is a much more full exegesis of the biblical verse, even if it is only cited briefly [and perhaps in part] at the end of the tale. For in the tale of the wayward wife and the brigand, we see that a woman is all traps, and that she literally snares her husband. Furthermore, the husband—a devoted student of God—lives at the end of the story, while those whose action might displease God—the cheating wife and the brigand—both meet death. This could argue that our "interpretation" of Qohelet 7:26 in *The Parables* is a far fuller interpretation than the one offered by the Rabbis. However, frustrating such a tantalizing possibility is that the printed *Parables* text does not even quote Qohelet 7:26; it only cites a few words from a few verses later. Hence we see that while interpretation of a sort is clearly happening in *The Parables of King Solomon*, it is of a far different kind from Classical Rabbinic Midrash.

There is one other major marker of Medieval Midrash present in *The Parables*, and it is not a pretty one: we encounter here a misogyny that far exceeds the bounds of traditional biblical and Rabbinic sexism. In *The Parables*, women are not only second-class citizens as they are throughout much of previous Jewish literature; unfortunately, here the female becomes the object of scorn. Yasif, in his work on the *Parables*, notes that this misogyny is characteristic of the Medieval period, especially in the Muslim world. That notion is buttressed by Halberthal, who noted how the Medieval Maimonides took an inherited sexism from the Rabbis and turned it into something even more sinister:

296   *Qohelet Rabbah*, 7:26.

Maimonides inherited from Talmudic *halakhah* various discriminatory rules toward women such as disqualifying them from serving as witnesses or from attaining public office. The problematic attitude toward women was aggravated in Maimonides' writing because of the impact of the Aristotelian picture and contemporary Islamic practice on his thought and ruling. He repeatedly attributed to women an inferior intellectual standing, a lack of stable and strong character.[297]

The author of *The Parables of King Solomon* seems to have been swayed by the same influences that led Maimonides down the road towards this most problematic attitude towards women.

The Parables of King Solomon, then, mark the expansion of Medieval Midrash in novel ways. As have other texts, *The Parables* shows the influence of surrounding cultures; here, unfortunately, that influence is primarily seen not through literary creativity but rather an ugly, commonplace misogyny. Furthermore, *The Parables* seem to represent a rather remote representation to the biblical text: one tale, The Vessels of Gold, cites no Scriptural passage, and the remainder use them—at best—as an appended moralistic epigram. Lastly, as we have experienced but not remarked, these *Parables of King Solomon* have very little to do with King Solomon himself. Whether or not Yasif is correct that Solomon serves as unifying force for this novella of medieval creation, we certainly see that these tales are not really about the man in the title. Moralizing appears in a few isolated instances, but mostly these are intriguing stories that demand attention and engage the reader as a potential solver of puzzles. Instead of telling us much about King Solomon, *The Parables of King Solomon* shares fanciful, farcical tales that entertain and delight the audience.

---

297   Moshe Halberthal, *Maimonides*, [Princeton: Princeton University Press], 2014, 35.

The Form of the Throne of King Solomon, Peace be upon Him

Textual History

The Form of the Throne of King Solomon seems to appear first in Jellinek publications of *Beit HaMidrasch*. There are clearly parallels to *Midrash Abba Gurion* and much material from the *Targum* literature to Esther, yet this version seems particular to Jellinek.

Literary Introduction

The text of the midrash, *The Form of the Throne of King Solomon, Peace be upon Him*, is enclosed within a larger literary inclusio. At the opening, the people of Israel protest to God against King Ahasuerus: *How can it be that this wicked one will sit upon it (i.e., Solomon's throne)?* At the end, we understand Ahasuerus' thwarted desire to sit on Solomon's throne, and his settling to sit on a mere replica. In between, we learn he is compelled to import craftspeople from Sidon and Alexandria whose initial effort to fashion a replica of Solomon's throne ends in failure. Their second attempt results in the production of a lovely throne [Esther 1:2] but—alas!—not one that measures up to: *The Form of the Throne of King Solomon.*

Between the two literary poles of desire and reality, the midrash unfolds the historic fate of King Solomon's throne and its spectacular construction. A see-saw of historic events details the afterlives of the fabled royal seat: Shishak took it to Egypt; Sennacherib the Assyrian overthrew the Egyptian monarch and captured it; in the days of King Josiah, Pharaoh brought it back to Egypt; Nebuchadnezzar of Babylon hauled it to Riblah; and Darius the Mede transported it to Elam. Those who took possession of the throne did not fare well. Nebuchadnezzar and Darius the Mede were struck and maimed by the moving parts of this ingeniously constructed throne and Pharaoh Neco's name is midrashically linked to the Hebrew root, *nkh-to strike, smite* and he is forever-after called, Pharaoh the Gimp.

The enchantments of the throne are phantasmagoric. There are numerous sets of steps; dazzling inlaid floors of precious stones and metals; golden doves, silver crocodiles, and fearsome lions; animal and avian automata are at every turn to guide the true king to the throne. The lions had moral precepts from the Torah inscribed on their paws, to remind the king of his duty to be a just monarch.[298] Imposters found these devices treacherous impediments that would wound and maim them. The purpose of these enchantments and awe-inspiring mechanisms of the fabled throne was to chasten witnesses and urge them to testify truthfully. Ultimately, the throne serves to exalt the stature of Torah's law, and aggrandizes the Solomon who serves as its eponym.

The Text with Annotation

Our Sages of blessed memory said:[299]

At the time Ahasuerus sat on the throne of his kingdom, he sought to sit on the Throne that Solomon fashioned through the great skill and intelligence of The Holy One. Israel said before The Holy One, "Sovereign of the Universe, in the place where King Solomon sat and judged Israel—as it says [1 Chronicles 29:23]: *Then Solomon sat on the Throne of Adonai to rule,* over Israel—How can it be that this wicked one will sit upon it? Do this for the sake of Your Name, and do not let the Throne of your Glory be debased!"

Our Sages of blessed memory asked, "How is it that the Throne of Gold was found in Media?"

Our Sages of blessed memory answered:[300]

After the death of Solomon, Shishak, King of Egypt, went up against the Land of Israel and took Solomon's Throne in exchange for the *ketubah* of his daughter, and he brought it down to Egypt, as it is written [11 Chronicles 12:2]: *In the fifth year [of King Rehoboam] King Shishak of Egypt marched against Jerusalem.*

And after that, Sennacherib went up against [Egypt] and brought back the Throne from the land of Egypt and brought it back to the Land of Israel, because he was seeking to wage war with them. In that same campaign Sennacherib fell to the hand of Israel, and they took his money as booty and returned the

---

298   Cf. Exodus 23:3; Deuteronomy 16:19.

299   Midrash *Abba Gurion* begins with the citation of the verse from Esther: *At that moment, as he sat.* As mentioned in our introduction, there are many parallels between the "throne" sections of that midrash and our work; we will highlight the significant differences. Midrash *Abba Gurion,* as found in Jellinek, *Beit HaMidrasch,* 1:1.

300   *Abba Gurion,* in place of this rabbinical rhetorical device, has the following:
[Jeremiah 14:21] [*Do not spurn us, for the sake of Your Name,*] *Do not dishonor the Throne of Your Glory, [Remember: do not violate Your covenant with us.*] And how did the throne come into his [Ahasuerus'] hands?

Throne to its place. Then Hezekiah sat upon it, and partook of the Glory, and was exalted and successful in his reign, as it is written [II Chronicles 32:30]: *Hezekiah prospered in all that he did.* Hezekiah saw that the Throne had six steps.[301]

Why did Solomon see to fashion the Throne with six steps? [Each of these steps] represents the six men who will descend from David and these are they: Hezekiah, Josiah, Daniel and his associates (Hananiah, Mishael, and Azariah). And through the Holy Spirit he fashioned that Throne representing the six Kings of Judah who would sit upon it, and these are they: Solomon, Rehoboam, Hezekiah, Manasseh, Ammon, and Josiah.

In the days of Josiah, Pharaoh, King of Egypt, came up and waged war against Josiah, and took the Throne from Jerusalem and brought it to Egypt and sought to sit upon it, but he did not understand its enchantment[302] or how

---

301   *Abba Gurion* here inserts a comparison of Solomon and Hezekiah:

Concerning Solomon it is written [II Chronicles 9:23]: *All the kings of the earth came to pay homage to Solomon.* And concerning Hezekiah it is written [II Chronicles 32:23]: *Many brought tribute to Adonai to Jerusalem, and gifts to King Hezekiah of Judah.* Concerning Solomon it is written [II Chronicles 9:23]: *All the kings of the earth came to pay homage to Solomon.* And concerning Hezekiah it is written [II Kings 20:12]: *At that time, Merodach sent [... scrolls and tribute].*

Following this comparison of the two Kings who sat on the Throne, *Abba Gurion* links the two sections together by putting the here anonymous question in the mouth of Hezekiah:

And when Hezekiah saw the throne, he said, "Why did my father Solomon see fit to make six steps to the throne?"

302   Here we follow the text of *Abba Gurion*, which at times reads *menagnon* in place of *minhago* (its custom), and in other instances employs the phrase, מנהגו של מינגנון/*minhago shel minagnon/the custom of the enchantment. Manganon* might be derived from a Greek homonym, "charm, potion" or "art, contrivance" [Jastrow, 796]. "Enchantment" as an alternative Hebrew reading is backed by a variety of manuscripts to Midrash *Abba Gurion.* Buber's textual revision there is further bolstered by *Pesikta deRav Kahana* 26:1 [which Buber himself cites in his notes], a pericope that contains a more full presentation of this passage:

"[In meditating upon the death of Aaron's two sons], R. Simeon bar R. Abin began his discourse with the verse [Ecclesiastes 9:2]: *All things come alike to all: like things befall the righteous and the wicked.* The words *like things befall the righteous* apply to Noah, of whom it is said [Genesis 6:9]: *Noah was a righteous man in his genera-tion.* Concerning what befell him, R. Phinehas [in the name of] R. Johanan, citing R. Eleazar ben R. Jose the Galilean, said: When Noah went forth from the ark, a lion sprang upon him and mutilated him, so that he was not ritually fit to bring offer-ings, and in his stead his son Shem had to bring offerings. The words *like things befall... the wicked* apply to Pharaoh Necoh. When he sought to sit on Solomon's

to sit on it. And so the lion struck him on his thigh, and he became a cripple, and thus he was known as Pharaoh who-was-struck,[303] and this is translated as "Pharaoh the Gimp".[304]

When Nebuchadnezzar went up against Egypt, he found the Throne there, and took it and transported it to Babylon, and sought to ascend it, and to sit and to judge Zedekiah in Riblah.[305] Israel said before the Holy One, "Sovereign of the Universe, this text has been fulfilled against us [Deuteronomy 32:31]: *Our enemies are our judges.* But Nebuchadnezzar did not know the Throne's enchantment. He ascended to sit on it, and the lion struck him on his left side and he fell off of it [the throne], and suffered from it until the day of his death. Concerning him it is written [Isaiah 14:12]: *How are you fallen from the heavens, Shining one, son of dawn.* And did this wicked one, the son of a wicked one, from the seed of Nimrod the wicked, rise up to the heavens? But rather, when he wanted to sit on Solomon's Throne, which was given to him from the heavens, he fell out of the Throne, therefore it says, *How you are fallen from the heavens.*[306]

When Darius the Mede ruled and destroyed Babylon, he took the throne and transported it to Elam, which is in Medea, thus it is written [Jeremiah 49:38]: *I set my throne in Elam.* But despite all this, no man ever sat upon it.

When Ahasuerus reigned, he sent to bring skilled men to build a throne in its form, but they were not able. Rather, he made for himself another throne, and he sat upon it, as it is written [Esther 1:2]: *In those days, when Ahasuereus sat on the throne of his kingdom.*

How did King Solomon make the Throne? With the skill that the Holy One gave him. It was inlaid with precious gems and pearls, the likes of which no

---

throne, he did not know its workings, so that a part of its mechanism, made in the semblance of a lion, sprang up and mutilated him. Thus the one died a cripple, and the other died a cripple: *like things befall the righteous and the wicked (ibid.).*" [*Pesikta de-Rav Kahana,* tr. William G. Braude and Kapstein, Israel, J., (Philadelphia: JPS), 1975, 526.]

303   This pun on Pharaoh's name is explained beautifully by Braude and Kapstein, "Thus the epithet *necoh* in Pharaoh's name is associated with נכה/*nkh*/struck," [ibid.].

304   See *Targum Onkelos,* ad loc.

305   Both Jellinek and Eisenstein present a problematic text here. For בבבל/*b'bavel*/ *in Babylon,* we read, לבבל/*l'bavel*/*to Babylon.* We argue that the word, בבלה/*bavela*/*to Babylon,* should be emended to read, לרבלה/*l'rivlah* [as we find in Midrash *Abba Gurion*], which involves only the insertion of the letter ר/*resh,* and reflects the biblical reading in II Kings 25:6.

306   We follow Eisenstein, who here only includes the first stitch of the Isaiah citation. The analogy here is that Nebuchadnezzar never fell from the heavens, but instead fell off the chair that was a gift from the heavens.

other king or regent were able to create. It had six steps, and from the six steps one would ascend it. And twelve lions were upon it, and on each and every step there were two lions. How? When the king sought to ascend to the first step, the lions would raise their paws upwards, and there was writing inscribed on their paws. And he wouldn't go up to the second step until he read the texts that were inscribed. And what was on them? When the King turned his face to his right, he would see the text that was inscribed on the paw of the lion on the right. And what was written on it? [Deuteronomy 16:19]: *Do not show favor in judgment.* When he turned his face to his left, written there was [ibid.]: *Do not take a bribe.* And this was the case with all the lions: similar verses of judgment were written upon them, i.e., [Exodus 23:3] *Do not favor the poor in his dispute.*

And each and every step was inlaid with precious gems and pearls, and among them were precious white stones inlaid,[307] and precious white crystals. Date trees and silk embroidery beautified the throne, and ivory peacocks were positioned facing the eagles' wings. Two pillars of marble were on the heads of the lions, and two stones of gold were on either side of the Throne, and they were filled with all types of spices.[308] Two golden cathedras[309] were on either side of the throne, one for Gad the Prophet, and one for Nathan the Prophet. [There were] seventy gold cathedras for the seventy elders to sit in. On each and every cathedra there were two lions and two eagles, and they were positioned one opposite the other, and they were standing on their feet.

When the king ascended the throne, he placed his foot on the first step, the mechanism [inside the Throne] would turn, and the lion would extend its right paw, and the eagle its left wing, and the king would lean upon them [and ascend to the second step].[310] On the second step, the mechanism would turn and the eagle would extend its right wing and the lion extend its left paw, and the king would lean upon them and ascend to the third step. And thus it was for all of them. And when he ascended all the steps, a silver crocodile[311] would engage the mechanism of the Throne and retract[312] [the protective enchantment] for

---

307   We arrive at "inlaid", in the sense of being surrounded, for מכורכמות/*mecurcamot*, from כרכום/*curcom*/*besieged*, i.e. *encircling.* Jastrow, 669.

308   Perhaps these "stones" were aromatic censors, in keeping with *Abba Gurion*: two hollowed gold lions were on either side of the throne, and they were filled with aromatic spices.

309   This English word is derived from the Greek *kathedra*, which is the loan word used in our Hebrew text.

310   We read in these additions from *Abba Gurion.*

311   In *Abba Gurion*, a silver peacock.

312   This is in the sense of temporarily removing the enchantment to allow the king to ascend, in keeping with, "to move to and back", Jastrow, 545.

the king, and they would seat him on the Throne, and immediately the eagles would spread their wings, and they would ascend by means of the mechanism of the Throne, and interlace their wings above his head. Then a gold dove, positioned between the pillars, opened the Ark, took a scroll of the Torah and set it upon his knees, to fulfill what was said [Deuteronomy 17:19]: *It shall be with him that he might read it all the days of his life.* The lion on the left would extend its paw, take the crown, and place it upon the head of the King, while those who stood there said, "May the House of David reign forever."

On each and every step there was an impure animal with a pure animal:[313] on the first step an ox facing a lion; second, a wolf facing a lamb; third, a leopard facing a goat; fourth, a bear facing a deer; fifth, an eagle facing a bird. He would ascend between them, to make known that he sets peace among them, because he sits between the two sets. And when he is on each and every step, he reads one verse. On the first step [Psalm 19:8]: *The Torah of Adonai is pure [restoring the soul].* On the second [ibid.]: *The testimony of Adonai is true [making wise the simple].* On the third [ibid. 9]: *The precepts of Adonai are just [rejoicing the heart].* On the fourth [ibid.]: *The commandment of Adonai is pure [bringing light to the eyes].* On the fifth [ibid. 10]: *Reverence for Adonai is pure [enduring forever].* On the sixth [ibid.]: *The judgements of Adonai are true [altogether just].* And only then would Solomon sit on the throne.

And when the High Priest and the elders would come to King Solomon and ask of any matter of law between a man and his fellow, they would sit on his right and left, and he would decide the law with them. When they brought witnesses to testify before the king, the golden mechanism would turn, the lions would roar, the eagles would spread their wings, and the peacocks tweeted.[314] Why all this? In order to grab hold of the hearts of the witnesses, so that they would testify the truth.

And the same with Nebuchadnezzar: when he sought to sit upon it, he was broken as we described.[315]

---

313   This seems to be a secondary, or perhaps even tertiary (given the above association of the six steps with six descendants of David), tradition about the nature and design of the six steps. Both the design and ascension ceremony described in this paragraph seem difficult to harmonize with the previous description.

314   Here, there appears to be an inconsistency in the text. Above we had a crocodile on the throne, where Jellinek had "peacock". Our text in this paragraph reads "peacock", and the crocodile disappears.

315   This line, which is missing in *Abba Gurion*, appears to be a rather indelicate and awkward transition back to the previous subject about the history of Solomon's Throne. Perhaps this transition referring to Nebuchadnezzar's being "broken" refers back to his suffering all the days of his life, a comment that is also not in *Abba Gurion*.

Ahasuerus saw the same Throne, and desired to sit upon it more than Nebuchadnezzar and Darius and Pharaoh, but he was not able to sit upon it. So he brought craftsmen from Sidon and Alexandria to fashion one throne in its form, but they were not able. But they fashioned for him another lovely throne, and he sat upon it, as it is written said [Esther 1:2]: *In those days, when King Ahasuerus sat on the throne of his kingdom that was in Susa the capital.* For three years they worked on the throne that the craftsmen from Sidon and Alexandria fashioned for him, and in the third year he sat on *that* throne, as it is written [Esther 1:3]: *in the third year of his reign.*

Conclusions: King Solomon

This narrative of *The Form of the Throne of King Solomon, may peace be upon him,* is rooted in the rich folk tradition about Solomon the sage-king. It contrasts his proverbial wisdom and penchant for justice with the arbitrary and capricious rule of King Ahasuerus who bethought himself worthy to sit on Solomon's throne. The text does not develop the character of Solomon but illuminates a specific aspect of his authority. It emphasizes his virtue as a righteous judge. The importance of this aspect of Solomon's leadership pervades the narrative. This midrash draws on *Midrash Abba Gurion,* which is clearly a Purim text. Its opening words:

Abba Gurion, man of Sidon, said five things:
When false judges multiply, false witnesses multiply;
When informers multiply, falsely confiscated property multiplies.
When the impudent increase, the honor of humanity is taken away . . .[316]

Our text begins with the nearly-divine King Solomon, and then leads immediately to Ahasuerus who epitomizes the unscrupulous, mercurial and lubricious monarch. The juxtaposition of Ahasuerus and Solomon drives home the underlying teaching of the midrash: Solomon is a righteous king who should be celebrated for his adherence to the just laws of Torah.

---

316   *Abba Gurion,* opening epigram.

Conclusions: Literary Expansions

The Form and the Throne of King Solomon is a peculiar text. It is clearly connected to material from the Targum literature, has parallels in other later
Midrashim such as *Pesiqta deRav Kahana* and *Midrash Abba Gurion*, yet has
a focus and identity all of its own. In some ways it follows on the heels of
Classical Midrash, as witnessed by its compilation and subsequent explication
of Scriptural passages connected to The Throne. Furthermore, the entire narrative focus of the text—that the near-Divine Solomon has no equal among
other earthly rulers—hinges on a literal-yet-midrashic reading of I Chronicles'
claim that Solomon, "Sat on the throne of Adonai." However, *The Form of the
Throne* distances itself from earlier Midrash in part by applying the traditional
modes of Midrash to non-biblical assertions. The first instance of this is the
"exegesis" of the six steps that lead to the throne: one proposition maintains
it is for the six most pious descendants of David; a second proffers the steps
represent the six Kings of Judah who sat on the throne to which they led. A
similar instance of biblical proof being brought to bolster a markedly *non*-
biblical claim may be seen in six verses of Psalm 19 put in Solomon's mouth
as he ascended the same six steps. Perhaps the height of the distance between
an assertion of *The Form of the Throne* and the Scriptural passage to which it
is linked may be found at the end of the fantastical passage in which eagles
position themselves over a seated Solomon as a dove places a Torah Scroll on
his lap: all this, according to our text, leads up to and fulfills the verse from
Deuteronomy: [The Torah] shall be with him that he might read it all the days
of his life.

Connecting Solomon's Throne, through King Ahasuerus, to the holiday of
Purim perhaps helps us understand the thematic importance of this work. The
Jews in medieval time lived among and between different cultures; the Jewish
community was often—as in the days of Ahasuerus—subject to the whims of
foreign rulers and kings. It is not surprising that cosmopolitan Medieval Jews
connected with Purim's theme that the Jewish community, despite necessary
obeisance to foreign authority, is distinct, wise, and particularly special to God.
Just as in biblical times, none could compare to Solomon nor sit on his Throne,
so too, for a Medieval audience, does this Midrash argue for a Jewish excep-
tionalism. Especially given the vicissitudes of Jewish life in the Middle Ages,
such a legend might have at times been a needed tonic. This tale of the superi-
ority of Solomon to other earthly rulers clearly would have resonated with the
Medieval Jewish audience so aware of the many Kings and Kingdoms in which
Jews lived.

The Form of the Throne of King Solomon is connected in some ways to Classical Midrash, and in other ways it is overshadowed by parallel texts. *Midrash Abba Gurion* relates this history as only part of its biblical exegesis; *The Throne and Hippodrome of King Solomon*, which we will examine next, has in many ways a more complete description of Solomon's royal appurtenances. The novelty of *The Form of the Throne* may be found in its taut explication of the history of The Throne, its application of Midrashic exegesis to non-Biblical texts, and the comfort it seeks to grant a cosmopolitan Jewish community that was prone to experience powerlessness.

The Throne and Hippodrome of King Solomon

Textual History

The Throne and Hippodrome of King Solomon: Jellinek informs us it is housed in codicil 222 of the Royal Library in Munich, and was first published by Perles in *Graetz's Monthly Bulletin*, 1872. In 1962, Evelyne Ville-Patlagean argued that the text was produced in tenth century Byzantium; Boustan argues this is more likely the date of redaction than the date of composition.[317] The first full textual history was presented by Perles in his initial publication:

> The throne of Solomon has become the subject of various legendary descriptions and interpretations: in Targum Sheni and Midrash to the Book of Esther, dispersed in the remaining Midrashim in a comprehensive description in various works as in the Image of the Throne of King Solomon: i.e., Gabirol's, Choice of Pearls. ed. Venice 1546, Israel Isserlein's, Commentaries, ed. Riva, 1562, The *Kol Bo*, (paragraph 119) edited and copied again in Jellinek's, *Beit haMidrasch* II, pp. 83–86. The Hebrew Codex 222 contains a description (in folio 50a–56b) of Solomon's Throne, which repeats with a few more or less significant variations the beginning of the text in *Targum Sheni* to Esther 1, 2. (The Staatsbibliothek in Munich contains a collection of various midrash-like pieces). However, the Codex presents a self-contained description that is better known in its characteristics and elaborations and at its end mentions a description of Solomon's Hippodrome.[318]

To date, Perles' history remains the best scholarly analysis of sources. Thus we include an English translation of his original introduction as an Appendix.

Literary Introduction

The constellation of minor midrashim in our study narrates the life, reign, wisdom, and folklore concerning King Solomon. They often intermix history and

---

317 Boustan, 170–171.

318 *The Throne and Hippodrome of King Solomon*, Perets ben Barukh Asher Perles, in Monatsschrift für Geschichte und Wissenschaft des Judenthums (MGWJ), Breslau, 1872. [See Appendix for full translation.].

fable, truth and fiction to accomplish their aim. These artful storytelling techniques expand the biblical scope of the life of King Solomon, adapting him to the needs of later generations. No single midrash in this compendium intermingles literary, fabulous and historic genres more deftly than *The Throne and Hippodrome of King Solomon*. This midrash has two discrete sections, a longer Throne episode and a briefer Hippodrome account.

Scholars have known for a long time that thematic elements of the Throne tale draw from earlier Hebrew and Aramaic sources.[319] That material however, was transformed and adapted for the Jewish audience living under Byzantine rule. The imaginative description, the splendor of the creatures, and the intricate engineering of the Throne cast a captivating literary spell. Everything fits together with classical biblical and early midrashic depictions of Solomon. In this way, the midrash seems like a seamless continuity of earlier Solomon *aggadot*, but, in fact, it also reflects the influence of Christian-Byzantine notions of royal power.[320]

The briefer Hippodrome Account describes the racetrack that King Solomon must have built. Andrew Sharf claims, "The dimensions of its track are close to that of the hippodrome in Constantinople."[321] The early rabbis deplored the Roman circuses as places that glorified the Roman culture of death. Additionally, they promoted debauchery, idolatry, and the gladiatorial spectacles that denied the sanctity of each human life. The Hippodrome Account is unique in that it, "models the proceedings and rituals of the Hippodrome of Solomon's Jerusalem on those of medieval Constantinople, with its intertwined political and cosmological symbolism."[322] In this fashion does our unique midrash combine the commitments of Jewish culture with the trappings of Byzantine royalty to create the icon of Solomon as cosmopolitan King.

The Text with Annotation

Our Sages said: Solomon ruled over the supernal and earthly beings, as it is written [1 Chronicles 29:23]: *Solomon sat on the Throne of Adonai.*

Rabbi Yoḥanan said: Is it possible he sat on Adonai's throne? Rather, the Holy One sat him, and caused him to rule over the supernal and earthly beings.

---

319   See Jellinek, Vol. 5, XVII; *The Encyclopaedia Judaica*, Volume 16, Column 1571; Boustan, "Israelite Kingship" 171.

320   Ibid., 169.

321   Sharf, *Byzantine Jewry*, 28–29.

322   Boustan, 171.

[God] made him a throne among the earthly in the form of the Throne of Glory among the supernals. Just as the supernal Throne had the form of four beasts— a human being, a lion, an ox and an eagle—[323]so too Solomon's throne had the form of a human being, a lion, an ox, and an eagle.

Rabbi Ḥiyya taught: According to the Throne of Glory, Solomon fashioned his throne through the Holy Spirit. The image of the wheel and the cherubs behind the throne, and the image of the beasts and the wheels stood before the throne. Sixty warriors were stationed there, and on each one's head were the sixty letters of the Priestly Benediction.[324]

Rabbi Eliezer said: it was all inlaid also with precious gems and pearls—like the essence of the sky in its purity—and also animals, beasts and birds, reinforced the throne: an impure one facing a pure one, a lion opposite an ox.

Rabbi Eliezer said: the form of the lion was rampant, his two paws were raised opposite the horns of the bull, and the horns of the bull went out to meet him like two plaited webs.[325]

Rabbi Yoḥanan said: King Solomon positioned one [animal] on the right of the throne and one on the left: a lamb on the right, and a wolf on the left; a deer on the right and a bear on the left; a red deer on the right and a elephant on the left; a wild ox on the right and a griffin[326] on the left; and at the end of all of them he positioned a human being facing a demon. Over them he positioned a

---

323   The imagery here is informed by the opening chapters of Ezekiel.

324   Numbers 6:24–26.

325   The word קונטריות is difficult. Tracing the meaning of the term we found the following explanations:

    1.   Alexander Kohut served as editor of: Nathan filio Jechielles', *Aruch completum Lexicon, Targumicis, Talmudicis et Midraschicis*, originally published between 1878–1903. We used the edition printed in (Jerusalem: L'Maqor Book Publishers), No Date. On page 135a of volume 7, in the entry, קונטרון, he translates with the German, *Geflochtenes* meaning, *plaited rope*.

    2.   Samuel Krauss in his, *Griechische und Lateinsche Lehnwörter im Talmud, Midrasch und Targum*, originally published in 1899, suggests, *Wagenkorb von Rohrgeflecht*, meaning, *reed, wagon basket*. We used the following edition, (Hildesheim: Georg Verlagsbuchhandlung), 1964, 513.

    3.   Jastrow, 1335, in the entry, קינטרה/קונטרה—*knot, knotted web, sieves, transverse lacing (of a web)*.

    4.   Michael Sokoloff in his, *A Dictionary of Jewish Palestinian Aramaic of the Byzantine Period*, [Ramat Gan: Bar Ilan University Press], 1990, 482 translates, *weaving* but adds a cautionary "(unclear)".

326   Cf. M. Seligsohn in *JE*, "Solomon," vol. XI, 442.

fabulous bird[327] facing an eagle; he placed a dove, and facing it he set a hawk, and inside it was a tablet engraved with the ensign of the snake.[328]

Rabbi Yoḥanan asked: How did King Solomon ascend and sit upon the throne? He grabbed the ox by its horns, and it passed [Solomon] towards the lion,[329] and would warn him, saying, "Be careful with King Solomon, so that nothing bad happens to him." The lion passed him to the ram, the ram passed him to the leopard, the leopard to the lamb, the lamb to the wolf, the wolf to the deer, the deer to the bear, the bear to the red deer, the red deer to the elephant, the elephant to the wild ox, the wild ox to the griffin, and the griffin to the human being. They would say to [the man] in a loud voice, "Behold we have sent[330] you the King—intact—and you shall be witness on our behalf." The man passed him to the demon, and the demon took him, picked him up, and led him [in flight] between the earth and the heavens. Afterwards, he brought him to his place, and seated him on a golden cathedra, all of it inlaid with precious gems and pearls. Then the demon would ascend to the firmament and bring the pavement of sapphire,[331] and set it under his feet.

R. Yoḥanan's students asked him, "Was the demon so powerful that he could ascend to the firmament?" He responded to them, "Didn't we teach you eight things said about demons? Four are like the heavenly ministers, and four are like human beings: they eat and drink like human beings, they have intercourse like human beings, they are fruitful and multiply like human beings, and they die like human beings. And the four like the heavenly ministers: they have wings like the heavenly ministers, see-but-are-not-seen like the heavenly ministers, they stride from one end of the earth to the other like the heavenly ministers, and they know what is in the supernal and earthly [realms] like the heavenly ministers.

At that moment, a golden dove brought the king a scroll of a copy of the Torah,[332] rested it on his knees, and read from it, in order to fulfill what was said [Deuteronomy 17:18]: *let him read in it all his life.*

---

327   So Jastrow, 393. Cf. BT *Baba Batra* 73b, which tells a mythic story of a bird and then names it *Ziz* [with reference to Psalm 50:11].

328   Cf. Numbers 21:9.

329   Interestingly, the list of animals here differs from R. Yoḥanan listed in the previous *baraita*.

330   We follow Eisenstein's version of the story here. Eisenstein read *shalaḥnu*; Jellinek read *shalamnu*, which is meaningless in this context.

331   Cf. the theophany at Exodus 24:10.

332   Cf. Deuteronomy 17:18, which states that the ruling King of Israel shall have a copy of the Torah with him when seated on his throne.

R. Eliezer said: These are the animals and beasts that were engraved on the Throne: half of them were horned animals, and half of them were hooved.[333] The Holy One only engraved these on Solomon's Throne to make of them an example to Israel for the distant future: that in the distant future these and those would live side by side, as it is written [Isaiah 11:6–7]: *the wolf shall dwell with the lamb, the leopard lie down with the kid... the cow and the bear shall graze.*

R. Yoḥanan said: All of them would raise their voice, and the entire world would tremble: the ox lows, the lion roars, the ram neighs,[334] the leopard shrieks,[335] the lamb bleats, the wolf howls, the deer bells, the bear growls, the donkey brays, the elephant moans, the wild ox bellows, the griffin chirps, the human being exalts, and the demon sings. A fabulous bird would cry out, and his voice ascended to the heavens. The eagle screams like the sound [Psalm 29:3] *of the mighty waters,* the dove coos, the hawk screeches, and its sound awakens all those sleeping in Jerusalem. The snake[336] [had] in its mouth a choice vine,[337] and the sick people of Jerusalem were cured by its very sound.

R. Eliezer says: this is the snake that Moses made in the desert,[338] and this is the snake that King Hezekiah of Judah shattered.[339]

R. Yoḥanan's students asked him, "Was King Hezekiah of Judah worthy of shattering the snake that Moses made in the desert for Israel, as an ensign through which to be healed? As it is written [11 Kings 18:4]: *He shattered the bronze snake.* He said to them, "He only shattered it because in those days Israel placed its faith in it, and did not seek mercy from the Holy One. Therefore,

---

333 For "hooved" we read *talafot* in place of *tarafot*, the latter of which has no clear meaning. In both texts, six miscellaneous words appear after this word. Both Jellinek and Eisenstein print here a mark (?) questioning their presence. We believe these were likely someone's hand-written notes on a manuscript margin and erroneously incorporated into the printed text. They bear no meaning on the present text and seem to us to be indecipherable as well.

334 Cf. Jeremiah 5:8, 50:11.

335 Cf. Zephaniah 1:14.

336 The snake here seems at first to be out of place, as this passage seems to be focusing on birds. However, just as the hawk's voice serves to effect the lives of Jerusalem's inhabitants, so too does the presence of this snake effect the infirm of that city. As the subsequent teaching of R. Eliezer will expand, the presence of this snake is a way of connecting Solomon [subtly] with idolatry.

337 Likely a medicinal vine in this context.

338 Numbers 21:9.

339 11 Kings 18:1 ff. This chapter tells the story of how the ensign of the snake was worshipped as the idol, Nechushtan.

[Hezekiah] shattered it in order that they would seek mercy from God, as it is written [Deuteronomy 32:29]: *I have wounded and I will heal."*

R. Eliezer asked: How did King Solomon sit upon the throne? He would take the Torah, and look into it, and begin to judge Israel. At that moment, the lion would proclaim:[340] [Deuteronomy 1:17] *You shall show no partiality in judgment,*[341] [Exodus 23:3] *you shall show no deference to a poor man in his dispute.* The ram would respond [Deuteronomy 1:17]: *For judgment belongs to God.* The leopard would respond angrily [Deuteronomy 16:20]: *Justice, justice shall you pursue.* The lamb would raise his voice and say [Deuteronomy 16:18]: *they shall render judgment for the people with due justice.* The wolf would cry out regarding the matter of oaths, [Exodus 22:8]: *about all charges of misappropriation.* The deer would call out regarding the matter of truth, [Deuteronomy 16:18]: *they shall render judgment for the people with due justice,* at all times. The bear raised his voice, [quoting Deuteronomy 1:16]: *you shall judge with due justice.* The red deer trembled and said [Exodus 23:6]: *you shall not subvert the rights [of the poor] in judgment.* The elephant would warn, [quoting from] the song of Moses, [Deuteronomy 31:21]: *He executed God's justice, God's judgments for Israel.* The wild ox would cry out [Exodus 21:1]: *These are the laws.* The griffin would say [Deuteronomy 1:16], *"Decide justly between a man and his* neighbor.[342] And you, King, judge between every man and his neighbor." And at the end, all of them were standing, man and demon, as one, together [Deuteronomy 16:18]: *You shall appoint judges and officials.* And you, King, has God the Judge set to rule and to judge for Israel, God's people. Judge justly, and decide in truth, so that God will increase your peace and the peace of Israel. For the world is only established on three matters: on judgment, on truth, and on peace.[343]

Our Rabbis taught: There were three paths on which Solomon ascended to the Throne. On each and every path there were six steps, and on each and every step there were twelve little steps, and by a mechanism he would rise to the Throne. On each and every path there were grilles and pedestals,[344] and over each and every vault[345] twelve lions would stand, each facing the

---

340   This is the same verb as "read", and, importantly, the lion is reading Torah.
341   Here, as above, we are reading out *shor yehader b'diburo*, which is a likely corruption [and repetition] of the words that follow.
342   Deuteronomy reads, "his brother".
343   M. *Avot* 1:18.
344   See, Jastrow, 176, which references, 162.
345   The word in the text is *kuf-mem-alef-resh-alef*. Krauss, vol. 2, 550, refers us to the entry [p. 551] for *kuf-mem-resh-vav-tet-alef*, which he translates as "vault" or "dome".

other, as it is written [1 Kings 10:20, 19]: *twelve lions, two lions stood beside* the Throne.[346]

Rabbi Eliezer said: the spaces between the stone all had rock-crystal decorations,[347] and date palm trees draped in silk cloth.

Rabbi Yoḥanan's students asked him, "Why were there date palm trees and silk cloths?"

He said to them, "The trees were taller than the throne, and were attached to the vault, and cords of linen and purple were suspended from its top. On the trees were linen cloths with a whole variety of colorful images embroidered on them. When the wind entered and blew upon them, they would cover the entire Throne and surroundings of the Throne, [as far as] one hundred cubits. They had the appearance of the blast and blaze of lightning, and torches of fire, and like the appearance of the rainbow. Bells of gold were tied to their openings, and the wind would blow upon them and they would ring.

Rabbi Ḥiyya taught: 70,000 seats of gold surrounded the Throne, and there sat the Sages and their students, along with Priests, Levites, and the elect of Israel. There were 70 seats in the foyer of the Throne, and there sat the 70 elders. There were two seats opposite him: one for Gad the Seer, and one for Nathan the Prophet. There was one throne to the right for Bathsheba his mother, so she might hear his wisdom, as it written [1 Kings 2:19]: *He had a throne placed for the Queen Mother.* And it is written [1 Kings 10:19]: *And two stood beside the arms.*[348] What was at the side of its arms? These two lions that were placed one on his right and one on his left. [When] the King came to sit, he would extend his hand,[349] and the lion on his left would take the laurel and rest it on the king's head, [while] the lion on the right would place the golden scepter in the king's hand.[350] Then a silver crocodile ran [in] by means of a mechanism, and bowed down to the king. The eagles spread their wings. [When The King] came to make a decision, the lions would open their mouths opposite him, and from the lions came sparks of fire, and they would open their mouths and gnash their teeth, and they would raise their paws facing the king in the foyer of the gate. The king would be terrified in making his decision, lest he not

---

346 Here the biblical citation seems corrupted: the first stitch comes from verse 20, and the second from verse 19; furthermore, the mention of the Throne is not in these verses at all, but is in the topic sentence at 1 Kings 12:18.

347 Jastrow, 1414, citing the original Greek.

348 This citation only serves as a prooftext that two thrones stood on either side of the Throne because it omits the subject "Lions" [which we saw above].

349 Cf. Esther 5:2.

350 Cf. Esther 5:2.

rule according to reason. And he would look at Gad the Seer and Nathan the Prophet, who would decide the law by means of prophesy, and [then] the King would agree with them in their wisdom. [The King] would announce [the ruling] to the 70 elders, and the elders to the elect of Israel, and the elect of Israel to the representatives of the courts-of-law: they would lead the accused man either to life or to death. And why all this? [Because] two are better than one. Concerning this, Solomon said in his wisdom [Ecclesiastes 4:9]: *the two are better than the one.* And it is written [Ecclesiastes 4:12]: *If one attacks,* this one is King Solomon, [*the two can stand up to him*] these two are Nathan and Gad, *the threefold cord [is not easily broken]* this is the three of them [together].³⁵¹

They asked Rabbi Yoḥanan, "Why did the lions and beasts cry out before him?"

He said to them, "In those days, there were four types of capital punishment meted out by the courts-of-law, so that no man died without cause." The king rendered the judgment, and the lions would lick the soles of the feet of the King, and the Holy Spirit would chime and say, "Blessed be King Solomon!" And those standing would respond as one and say, "Long live the House of King David!"

And twelve lions [1 Kings 10:20].³⁵² These are the twelve prefects who would feed the King and his household, each of them for a full month,³⁵³ as it is written [1 Kings 4:7ff]: *Solomon had twelve prefects.* And each one of them had eighteen thousand chiefs,³⁵⁴ and each and every chief [was responsible for] a thousand, and the [chiefs of the] thousands [were responsible for] a hundred, and the [chiefs of the] hundreds [were responsible for] fifty, and [chiefs of the] fifty [were responsible for] ten, and all would [share the responsibility to] sustain the King and his household in every way, and nothing was lacking from each and every one [of these prefects] during his month.³⁵⁵ The daily

---

351   This reading is an interesting resolution to a difficulty in Ecclesiastes 9:9–12, which explains consistently how two are better than one, but ends with the teaching about the threefold cord. R. Ḥiyya here resolves that difficulty by uniting the one and the two into the threefold cord.

352   Our mss. has *baqar*/cattle, in place of lions. However, here the Midrash seems to be picking up on the earlier strand of the twelve lions mentioned in connection with the Throne. Alternatively, 1 Kings 7:25 speaks about twelve oxen that supported the tank in the portico of the Temple. But that text also reads differently from what we have in the mss. and we would need to correct the text in either case.

353   This is an imprecise version of 1 Kings 4:7.

354   The following is a re-working of Exodus 18:21–25, with Solomon here playing the combined roles of Jethro and Moses.

355   Here in parallel with 1 Kings 5:7.

food on the table was 30 kors of semolina, sixty kors of flour, ten sturdy oxen, fattened—that had been fed dough[356] [Leviticus 2:5, 7:10] *mixed in with oil*, and made to drink milk—twenty oxen stall-fed on grass and grain, one hundred fattened sheep, one hundred deer, thirty rams, twenty roebucks, and kids, fowl, fish and all varieties of delicacies [Psalm 40:14, Job 5:9,9:10] *without end*, as it is written [1 Kings 5:2]: *Solomon's daily provisions consisted of 30 kors of semolina, and 30 kors of [ordinary] flour, 10 fattened oxen, 20 pasture fed oxen, and 100 sheep and goats, besides deer and gazelles, roebucks and fatted geese.*

And what were *barburim avusim*?[357]

R. Elazar says: they even raised pheasants.

R. Yoḥanan says: fattened fowl.

It is written [Number 6:3]: *a cart for every two chieftains [and an ox for each one]*. These are the carts: the two chieftains each would bring a painted chariot on two wheels for four horses [to draw], in order to create a hippodrome for the king; and *an ox for each one*, this is the son of the chieftain who would drive the chariot.

R. Yoḥanan asked R. Zeira, "How many hippodromes were there for the king every year?"

He replied, "Twelve, corresponding to the twelve prefects, and each one would stage one in his month, thus it says [1 Kings 5:7] *he lacked for nothing.*"

He replied, "And weren't there thirteen?"[358]

He replied, "[In the thirteenth month], one wouldn't stage them with horses, but rather young men would run the hippodrome. These same young men: they cut the juncture of the tendons of their knees,[359] and there was neither horse nor beast that could outrun them.

And from what tribe were they?

R. Yossi says: from Naftali, as it is written [Genesis 49:21]: *Naftali sent its swift deer.*

---

356   *Issah*, in Even-Shoshan, dough that includes a leavening agent. Avraham Even-Shoshan, *Milon HeḤadash*, [Makor: Jerusalem], 2003.

357   Above translated as "fatted geese", but could also be rendered as "stall-fed geese", but geese aren't kept in stalls.

358   The Lunar calendar, in a leap year, adds a month.

359   Here we are not translating *dvgmt*. See Ḥullin 4:6 on the juncture of the knee. See also, JE, Vol. XI, 442, "the calves of whose legs were removed, rendering the runners so swift that no horse could compete with them".

R. Yoḥanan says: from the tribe of Gad, as it is written [1 Chron 12:9]: *Of the Gadites there withdrew to follow David to the wilderness stronghold valiant men, fighters fit for battle, armed with shield and spear; they had the appearance of lions and were as swift as gazelles upon the mountains.*

How many were there? Ten thousand young men, and these were the King's youths who were sustained from the King's table.

In *Tevet* they would run these races, and concerning them Scripture says [1 Kings 14:28, 11 Chron. 12:11]: *Whenever the King went into the House of Adonai, the runners would hoist them up and return them to the armory of the runners.*[360] And what were they carrying? Shields of gold.

What was the length of the hippodrome? Three parsangs by three parsangs, and in the middle there were two pillars and cages. Every kind of wild beast and bird were set in them, and the horses and the runners would run around them eight times in a day.

The disciples of R. Zeira asked, "On what day did they hold the hippodrome?"

R. Zeira answered, "At the end of the month."

R. Yossi said, "At the beginning of the month."

R. Abayye said, "On the second of the month."

R. Yoḥanan said, "On the third of the month."

For on these days the king would flood the cisterns: at the end of the month he would do this for the Sages and their students, for the priests and the Levites; on the first of the month he would do this for all Israel who lived in Jerusalem; on the second of the month he would do this for all who came from large cities and villages and all the nations; and on the third of the month [and thenceforth] they would not hold hippodromes.

His disciples asked, "From what place was the cistern fed?"

He replied, "It is written [11 Chron 3:16]: *At the front of the House he made two columns, 35 cubits high; the capitals on top of them were five cubits high.* And what were *the capitals*? These were the two lions on one pillar, and two golden lions on the second pillar. From two lions would flow fragrant aromas, and from [the other] two lions would come the smell of spices, to fulfill what is written [Song of Songs 1:3]: *Your ointments yield a sweet fragrance.* And from whence would they flow? From the Garden of Eden, to make an example to Israel for future times, that they are destined to see all this with their eyes, as it is written [Song of Songs 1:3]: *therefore do maidens ['alamot] love you;* do not read "maidens/'*alamot*" but rather "worlds/'*olamot*". His disciples were astonished, so R. Yoḥanan said to them, "Why are you astonished?" [They replied,] "That in the future the least of Israel will be greater than Solomon during his

---

360   NJPS translates "*raẓim*"/"runners, as guards.

reign! And just as during Solomon's time aromas would flow from the two lions, and the smell of spices from two lions, but in the future the streams of the Tigris and Euphrates[361] will be filled with *afarsimon*,[362] spices, wine, milk, honey and all varieties of sweet things set aside for the righteous. Lest you say [the same holds] for the wicked—heaven forefend!—they will not see these streams, as it is written [Job 20:17]: *Let them not enjoy the streams, the rivers of honey, the brooks of cream.*

R. Yoḥanan said, "Four companies[363] of charioteers were in the King's hippodrome, and on each one were four thousand men. Every company had lattices made, and pillars reinforced with iron, copper, and gold. On each pillar were seven more[364] with one higher than the others, and four tiers with one higher than the others. There were one hundred men on every tier. And for each company there were two doors of pine wood,[365] and set in them were all varieties of gold, precious stones, pearls, cherubs, and rising columns[366] set in gold: their brilliance would shine far beyond Jerusalem. Before each company the pipe and flute were joyfully played above, and others would strike the pipe on beat."

R. Yossi said, "They were divided into four groups. The King and his servants, the Sages and disciples, the priests and the Levites all wore blue; all Israel wore white; those from cities and towns and other places wore red; and the nations of the earth who came from afar to bring tribute to the King wore green."

---

361 Both Jellinek and Eisenstein indicate that the text here is corrupt. We read "streams" with both of them, but prefer Euphrates to Eisenstein's suggestion of Jordan, because the printed version reads "*k'ch'r'd'l* which is closer to Euphrates [*ch'd'q'l* Genesis 2:14] than it is to Jordan.

362 This is a plant grown in the Ein Gedi region, which is where the oil that bears its name was produced, and should not be identified with the persimmon today; likely balsam. See BT *Shabbat* 62b, which describes the aroma of this oil as being so powerful that it releases the power of the evil inclination.

363 Krauss, 204.

364 Perles in his prelude to "The Throne and Hippodrome of King Solomon" [See appendix] makes two suggestions concerning the problematic word, טמי:

1) This word should be read, בימי or בומי /βημα, the place where the spectators sat; or.

2) It represents "a misspelling of טרמי, referring to the seven goal-posts (μετα-τερμα)." Dr. Yoram Bitton made a simpler and more convincing textual correction. He thinks that the "מ" of טמי, should be read as a "פ" making the word, טפי, the Aramaic equivalent of the Hebrew, עוד/'od/more. See Jastrow, 546.

365 Jastrow, 1598.

366 *Timorim*, cf. BT Yoma 62b.

His disciples asked, "Why these four kinds of clothes?"

He replied, "Corresponding to four seasons: from Tishrei through Tevet the seas are like blue; from Tevet to Nisan the snow falls and thus they are dressed in white; from Nisan to Tammuz the sea is good to sail, so they wear green; from Tammuz to Tishrei the fruits are pretty and red, and therefore they wear red clothes."

Thus ends the matter of Solomon. Praise to God, Creator of the world, Amen.[367]

Conclusions: King Solomon

The Midrash, The *Throne and Hippodrome of King Solomon*, invites us into the Jewish realm of Byzantine Constantinople. We see in it the complex intersection of earlier midrash with earthly political and supernal power. It is reflected in the Throne Account by its spectacular engineering, which however, never loses sight of the Throne's ultimate purpose—to be the seat from which the monarch judges justly. The Hippodrome Account bubbles with the froth of earthly fame and power. In this iteration, the circus is stripped of its ancient associations with death and frivolity. It gives Solomon the public space to bask in his fame and power, while enjoying the skillfulness of the charioteers. Solomon's participation in the circus events gave the Jews of Byzantium a passport to participation in this important social, political and public arena of Byzantine life. Thus does our midrash not only aggrandize the wealth and magnificence of Solomon, but also the Jewish community that called him King.

Conclusions: Literary Expansions

There is so much on which to comment in *The Throne and Hippodrome of King Solomon*: the Talmudic framing, the borrowing of Byzantine motifs, and the attribution to King Solomon a Romanesque royal retinue that was frowned upon by the Rabbis of the Classical Midrash. This last aspect particularly caught the attention of Perles, for whom it served as a central cipher to understanding *The Throne and Hippodrome*. He claims:

---

367   שבח לאל בורא עולם אמן. According to Dr. Yoram Bitton, the sequence is wrong in the *roshei tevot* at the end of the whole work. It should read ש, ל, ב, ע, א, ב, and ל in the printed version have been transposed.

The Aggadist who attributes a hippodrome to Solomon in order to glorify him took his motif not from Jewish sources but formed the view based on the surrounding governing system. Public games are necessarily associated with the court of powerful regents. This circumstance already indicates that the Aggadist lived in Byzantine surroundings and based his stories on Byzantine sources. This is reinforced by the phrasing of his description leading to the evidence that he emulated the style of a prototype and seemingly relocated the famous Hippodrome in Constantinople and its appurtenances to Jerusalem in the time of Solomon, making a daring leap over countries and centuries.[368]

As we saw above, Sharf and Boustan follow Perles' lead and arrive at the same conclusion: *The Throne and Hippodrome of King Solomon* bears the direct influence of the actual appurtenances of the Byzantine Emperor who reigned in Constantinople. This appropriation of foreign motifs of power would be akin, today, to attributing to Solomon a private airplane named "Air Force One". The author of this work depicted the great Jewish king as both equal of a prototype for the Emperor who ruled in his day.

This literary focus on the present is artfully disguised by the literary trappings of the past. To an untrained eye, *The Throne and Hippodrome of King Solomon* could be identified as missing pages of a Talmudic debate, primarily between Rabbis Yoḥanan and Eliezer, about the nature and form of Solomon's Throne. The entire piece begins with an interpretive question: did, as Chronicles claims, Solomon really sit on God's own throne? The narrative continues to evaluate that question, and talmudically to pursue side issues related to Solomon's throne. Biblical texts are cited throughout, and sometimes explicated in keeping with Rabbinic Midrash.[369] However, the debate contained in *The Throne and Hippodrome of King Solomon* is found in no collection of the Rabbinic Period. It is pseudepigrapha *par excellence*.

Perhaps it is the rather anti-Rabbinic message of *The Throne and Hippodrome* that led its author to cloak it in such Rabbinic trappings: the author might have hopes this truly novel idea about the proper exercise of royal power might have found favor in the Jewish community if it seemed endorsed by the same Rabbis who elsewhere seemed to condemn Hippodromes and other royal exercises. Outside of all our Medieval Midrashim regarding King Solomon save perhaps *Midrash Al Yithallel*, *The*

---

368 Perles, *The Throne and Hippodrome*. See his article [in Appendix] for a full explication of the Byzantine realia behind the descriptions of our text.

369 Note especially the usage of *Al Tiqra ... ela ...* on the Hebrew word, '*olamot*, "worlds".

Throne and Hippodrome of King Solomon most appears like a classic text of the Rabbinic period. However, its Byzantine roots and cosmopolitan outlook betray any such creation. It seems clear that, by the advent of *The Throne and Hippodrome of King Solomon*, Medieval Jewish authors saw it fit to use the tools and trappings of classical Midrash to fashion new narratives that spoke to the realities of their present day.

Conclusions

Solomon the King

Just as King Solomon wandered from his throne in *An Episode concerning King Solomon*, so too did it take some wandering for us to encounter the fullness of the teaching of these Solomonic midrashim. Originally we set out to translate the entirety of *Midrash Abba Gurion*;[370] but the translation of *Midrash Al Yithallel* led us to believe there might be something more fruitful found in an analysis of all the Medieval Midrashim connected to this King. While some of this material had previously been translated piecemeal—a few paragraphs in the *Jewish Encyclopedia*, some scattered references in *The Legends of the Jews*, and unsourced translations in *The Folktales of the Jews*—we are happy here to offer full, annotated, and analyzed translations of this Solomon material all in one place. Looking back over our completed work, we believe we have made a contribution to a wider understanding of Solomon's multi-faceted character.

Especially while working through some of the more complicated mechanisms of the Throne material, or poring over passages of demonic esoterica, we wondered what potential contribution the publication of this work might make *beyond* its availability to a wider English-speaking audience. In preparing these notes and essays, we have discovered that we ourselves now understand the complexity of King Solomon in ways we never had before. Often overshadowed by his messianic father, both in biblical and rabbinic literature, Solomon plays a secondary role in the Jewish imagination. We believe that the core of Solomon's character *is* dichotomy: he is part pure prince of Chronicles, and also the tainted, human monarch of Kings. Delving deep into the Solomon midrashim has allowed us to appreciate fully what Solomon represented to Jewish audiences for thousands of years; we hope that now our colleagues and readers will likewise have a better handle in grasping Solomon in all his complexity.

One further note here applies to those who love literature, and those who cherish our Jewish approach to storytelling. The authors of these fascinating fantasies were unafraid in their approach: they relied heavily upon previous traditions regarding Solomon, his friends, foes, possessions, and personality; they also engaged freely with the literary traditions of their neighbors in creating masterful works that transcended cultural boundaries. The authors bor-

---

370   We were ignorant of the fact that Binyamin Elbaum was concurrently preparing a thesis focused on that work. We look forward to reading that publication.

© KONINKLIJKE BRILL NV, LEIDEN, 2017 | DOI 10.1163/9789004331334_012

rowed forms, and re-fashioned them in ways that, in our opinion, makes them uniquely Jewish. In doing so, they demonstrate the religious benefit of a wide-ranging and serious engagement with the non-Jewish world around us. For those of us who love *The Plague* or *Lolita* as much as the *Pentateuch* or *Leviticus Rabbah*, we may take encouragement from our literary-religious forbears who were so compellingly creative in making our old stories new.

Conclusions: Medieval Midrash

Solomon the Wise: Answering Sage Questions

This study, in many ways, began in a classroom of seminary students studying what we now call Medieval Midrash. The questions—often unanswerable—raised in that room have guided our entire work. While we have learned a great deal about this genre of Jewish Literature, we are aware that there are still limiting horizons to our full understanding of every aspect of Medieval Midrash. However, we are finally in a position to be able to answer, at least in part, the classic journalistic questions raised in the *Introduction* about this field: **What** exactly is Medieval Midrash? **When** were these works of art written? From **where** did these tales originate? **How** did this new literary form emerge? **Who** wrote Medieval Midrash, and **why** would anyone create these tales? Having moved from the classroom through the library to this current volume, we hope to be able to answer these very questions.

What: The Canon of Minor Midrashim

While the texts themselves date from an earlier time, the canon of Minor Midrashim was a product of *Wissenchaft des Judentums*. We have traced from Zunz to Eisenstein the historical arc of those scientific cataloguers of texts and traditions who found many manuscripts and effectively created the extant canon of this genre. Medieval Midrash exists as a field of study because of the groundbreaking work of luminous scholars, collectors, editors and publishers, beginning with Leopold Zunz (1794–1886), moving from Moritz Steinschneider (1816–1907) to Adolph Jellinek (1821–1893), then Solomon Buber (1827–1906), next Chaim M. Horowitz (1855–1905), then Solomon Aaron Wertheimer (1866–1935), on to Eleazer Grünhut (1850–1913), and concluding with Judah David Eisenstein (1854–1956), whose encyclopedic *Oẓar Midrashim*, published in New York in 1915, caps the canon we call Medieval Midrash.

In short, what we know as Medieval Midrash is found between the covers of books like *Beit HaMidrasch* and *Oẓar Midrashim*. These include hundreds of legends, parables, and other narrative pieces. Of course, the canon of Medieval Midrash is hardly closed: it is entirely possible a new generation of scholars and collectors will uncover a manuscript—or better, a trove—of texts in either the ignored-and-dusty recesses of some library or an as-yet-unknown genizah.

© KONINKLIJKE BRILL NV, LEIDEN, 2017 | DOI 10.1163/9789004331334_013

For such newly-discovered works to be considered Medieval Midrash, they will need to conform to the criteria below.

When: The Dating of Medieval Midrashim

While Medieval Midrash were collected and published in the *Wissenschaft* period, their very appellation teaches they come from a different period of time. Just as the dawn of the Jewish Enlightenment marks the *terminus ad quem* for Minor Midrashim, we learned, correspondingly, that the closing of the classical Rabbinic period marks the *terminus post quem* for this literature. We witnessed in particular with *Midrash Al-Yithallel* how classical midrashic modes were both continued and commingled with innovative literary techniques. More importantly for purposes of dating, we saw how certain texts contain explicit evidence regarding their composition: *The Throne and Hippodrome of King Solomon* relies upon *realia* from the imperial center of Byzantium and *The Episode of the Ant* demonstrates knowledge of the Quran. These and many other clues testify that the works of Medieval Midrash were written well after the classical Rabbinic Period.

While the works of Medieval Midrash are influenced by the Sages of the Talmud, the stories and legends they contain clearly belong to a later period of Jewish Literature. Indeed, many of these texts we now call Medieval Midrash did not themselves aspire to that appellation: for works like *The Parables of King Solomon* and *The Form of the Throne of King Solomon* were first labeled as "Midrash" by scholars like Jellinek and Eisenstein. However, the fact that these literary works were created after the close of the Talmud and before they were anthologized during the Enlightenment that marks these works, later identified as Midrash, clearly come from the Jewish Medieval period. As noted, this is a broad, but realistic definition about the dating of Medieval Midrash.

Where: The Geography and Culture of Medieval Midrashim

There were many centers of Jewish growth and creativity during the Medieval period: apparently, this new form of Medieval Midrash thrived in all of them. We saw how certain works, such as *The Throne and the Hippodrome of King Solomon*, were remarkably influenced by the culture and practices of the Byzantine Empire. Likewise we witnessed how the early Islamic culture impacted pieces such as *The Episode of the Ant*. Furthermore, we explored how the role Medieval Jews often played as the middlemen between cultures allowed their communities to be exposed to stories from Italy to India. Especially because the Jewish connection to trade afforded travel among competing empires over centuries, it seems as if the works of Medieval Midrash were at the very least influenced by, and likely created in, the many countries of the Medieval world where Jews resided.

How: Literary Expansions of Medieval Midrashim

We have seen that Medieval Midrash, created in the many countries in which Jews lived from the close of the Rabbinic Period to the dawn of the Enlightenment, were gathered by *Wissenschaft* scholars into the collections we know today. We are confident in our responses to the *where, when* and *what* of Medieval Midrash, even if those answers are not always as precise as we might hope. As we move to analyze the question of how this new literary genre came into being, we can be in some ways more specific and in others less certain. Clearly, only an individual author is in a position to address affirmatively how a particular piece of work came into being; describing the manner in which Medieval Midrashim were created is an imperfect effort of inference and deduction. However, because we know the details of the building blocks of this literature—from cultural *realia* to inherited folklore—the conclusions we draw about *how* Medieval Midrashim came into being are based on a high degree of specificity and focus.

An Episode of King Solomon represents the blending of many narrative traditions. We discover the roots of its characters Asmodeus and the Shamir in Classical Rabbinic works: the *Babylonian Talmud* and *Tosefta*, respectively. We see that the motif of Solomon's exile comes from the Quran, and know that legends of rings discovered in the bellies of fish are as old as folktales themselves. *An Episode* came into being based upon these many literary forebears: given the cosmopolitan setting of the Medieval Jewish community, there were many who would have been exposed to the various legends of the Rabbinic, Roman, Byzantine, and Muslim worlds. A Jewish storyteller—using the techniques of traditional midrash and enhancing them with more worldly narrative arts—created a new telling of Solomon's story, and thereby participated in the creation of a new category: Medieval Midrash.

Here it is helpful to return to Rouen. Monet's studies were carried through multiple canvasses of the Cathedral itself; Lichtenstein's *Rouen Cathedral Set V* owes an obvious, unmistakable debt to that series, even though—as a series—it has a different form and purpose. Likewise, there is little doubt that Classical Rabbinic Midrash shed a formidable light on the creation of the narrative retellings of subsequent generations, which took new forms in the canon of Medieval Midrash. Early Medieval works, such as *Midrash Al-Yithallel*, are framed as homiletic interpretations of scripture. Later works, such as *The Throne and Hippodrome of King Solomon*, imitate the back-and-forth of the Talmudic page, complete with pseudepigraphal attributions to famed scholars of yore. Even the lusty narrative of *The Parables of King Solomon* are filled with Scriptural citations, sometimes as throwaway asides. Just as the LACMA exhibit "Monet/Lichtenstein: Rouen Cathedrals" united distinct works that share a common core, so too did the scholars of the Enlightenment rightfully house these Medieval works in volumes titled, בית מדרש—House of Midrash.

Medieval Midrash, however, moves far from the classical field of biblical exegesis. Monet depicted the outlines of the Cathedral to study the interplay of light and architecture, while Lichtenstein framed only a portion of the façade in Ben-Day dots to assert his position on mass production. Likewise, while all texts called "Midrash" share moral and pedagogical concerns, this Medieval form, in comparison with Rabbinic predecessors, seems to be far more focused on the telling of a story than on the particulars of Jewish practice. For all the moralizing—some of it specious or misogynistic—of Medieval Midrash, its narratives concentrate more on edifying associations with Jewish characters than on any details of leading a traditional religious life. In style and substance, this emergent genre differed from its predecessors as much as it inherited from them. Medieval Midrash certainly grew out of the deep wells of Rabbinic interpretation, but was forged in a literary cauldron that blended together Midrash, folklore, narrative, and even other religious traditions. Out of the fertile cosmopolitan culture of which many mercantile Jews were at the center sprung this new literary innovation we call Medieval Midrash.[371]

---

371 Famed Zionist Vladimir Jabotinsky, in a very different context, defended the historical importance of this mercantile community. His 1930 article "Shall the Jewish Middle Man Be Spared?" is described by its editor as follows:

"The noted Zionist poet, linguist and traveller discusses the fate of the Jewish middleman and defends him as an important factor in our economic life without whom we would be poorer. Mr. Jabotinsky skillfully shows what the world would be without the middleman, who is so often a Jew." Vladimir Jabotinsky, "Shall the Jewish Middle Man be Spared?" *The Canadian Jewish Chronicle*, Montreal, July 18, 1930, cover page. We are grateful to Dan Meridor of Jerusalem for bringing this essay to our attention.

Who and Why: Suppositions and Speculations about Medieval Midrashim

Our close study of the Solomon Midrashim has led us to a broader, more expansive understanding of the origins of Medieval Midrash. We can now safely assert the following about the library of Medieval Midrash:

1) It is substantially different in style and purpose from Classical Rabbinic Midrash.

2) It gives explicit, internal, historic evidence of the various epochs of its composition–specifically, eras long after the close of the canon of Classical Rabbinic Midrash.

3) It clearly postdates the composition of Classical Midrash and is *not* part of the canon of Classical Rabbinic Midrash, although the authors of the Medieval Midrashim were keenly aware of the contents of that literature.

4) It reflects the cultural and social desiderata of the many lands and continents in which Jews lived during the Middle Ages.

We can build a bridge from what we have learned about Medieval Midrash to the speculation regarding two opaque matters: who might have authored such works and why they were created in the first place. These initial suppositions are just that: honest attempts to begin to answer questions that time has thus far made elusive. However, given that these works so clearly reflect the cultural situations of Jews scattered throughout the empires of the Medieval Period, we feel there are definite lessons to be drawn from how that collective experience led to the literature to which that community gave birth.

It seems that the stories, fabula, and fables of Medieval Midrash were written for—and likely by—the assimilated, mercantile, cosmopolitan class of the Jewish community. Just as the texts themselves know the cultures of many countries, so too is it likely that their authors were familiar with the terrain of many lands. We saw with the travels of the *Panchatantra* how Jewish merchants were keys to the transmission of culture from East to West. It seems logical that these Jewish seafarers, travelers, and traders were not only exporting tales from one Empire to another, but also importing them into Jewish culture as well. Whether the *Alphabet of Ben Sira* borrows academic burlesques or *The Episode of the Ant* clearly quotes the Quran, we see consistently in Medieval Midrash how foreign cultures weave their ways into these Jewish works. That literary synthesis can only occur after contact between cultures has been made. And it would have been the Jewish merchant class, freely traveling between Empires, inclined to learn (and subsequently copy) from people of other faiths, who were the most likely candidates to create this cultural amalgamation.

It is impossible that the Jews who created Medieval Midrash were sequestered behind ghetto walls. We know this in part from the heavy influence of foreign cultures over this entire literary enterprise. But we learn this as well from the lessons many of the midrashim are trying to teach. Specifically, we see with the tales of Solomon that biblical verisimilitude is of little to no import; instead, these authors appear to be people who want a King to represent what currently passed for the better character and the dreams of their community. Jewish societies of the Middle Ages were not on an equal footing with their peers in either Empire: they lacked Caliph or King to serve as an internal paragon of values, or an external sign of their communal worth. These stories of Solomon's wisdom thus helped level the playing field with Muslim and Christian contemporaries in two ways: the Midrashim provided a Regal representative of the wisdom for which Jews wanted to be known, and the stories also allowed the Jewish community to tell itself tales every bit as compelling, intricate, and delightful as those indigenous to their neighbors.

It is also telling that few, if any, of the Medieval Midrashim, are occupied with matters of traditional Jewish practice. A loose kind of moralizing, sometimes in direct conflict with normative Jewish values, is the closest we come in most of these works to anything of a religious nature. Here *The Parables of King Solomon* are especially illuminating: the first parable shows Solomon as wise because he figured out a magical path around traditional Jewish testamentary law; the second tells of bondage, lust and filicide with nary a constructive moral (unless one counts some general aphorisms about the infidelity of women); the third and fourth only mention a biblical verse at the very conclusion, while the fifth has no Scriptural citation at all; the sixth, which some argue is not original to the text, leans more heavily on biblical vocabulary but in the end only serves to prove the remarkable wisdom of Solomon. These are major departures from the themes of the classic Midrashim of the Rabbinic Period.

This different focus, which we should expand to include the assumed audience for such stories, reveals something important about the creators of Medieval Midrash: this was not the intellectual elite of the Jewish House of Study. A helpful distinction here is found through the Roman Matrona featured throughout Rabbinic Literature. The Matrona was a recurring character, assumed to be non-Jewish, who asked questions of Rabbis, tested their patience, and ultimately came to see the wisdom of the Jewish point of view.[372] This following excerpt from *Genesis Rabbah* illustrates precisely the narrative function of the Matrona:

> Rabbi Judah son of Rabbi Simon expounded [Psalm 68:7]: *God makes individuals dwell in a house.* A Matrona questioned Rabbi Yose bar Ḥalafta. She said to him, "In how many days did the Holy Blessed One create the world?"
>
> He answered, "In six days."
>
> She then said, "Then what has God been doing since that time?"
>
> He answered, "God sits and makes matches, man to woman and woman to man."
>
> She said to him, "If that is difficult," she gibed, "I too can do the same." She went and matched her slaves, giving this man to that woman, this woman to that man and so on. Sometime after, those who were wed went and beat one another: this woman saying, "I do not want this man," while this man protested, "I do not want that woman."
>
> Straightway [the Matrona] summoned Rabbi Yose bar Ḥalafta and admitted to him, "There is no God like your God! It is true: your Torah is indeed beautiful and praiseworthy, and you spoke the truth!"
>
> He replied to her, "If [making matches] is easy in your eyes, it is difficult before the Holy Blessed One as the dividing of the Red Sea." What is the proof? *God makes individuals dwell in a house.*

In many stories related in *Genesis Rabbah* and *Leviticus Rabbah*, the Matrona is mostly a foil featured by the Rabbis to make a point for their students within the walls of the House of Study. The emphasis of the Matrona tradition is that Rabbis have better answers to compelling questions than their cosmopolitan, intellectually-oriented Roman neighbors. However, these midrashim about the Matrona merely capture snippets of conversations; the homilies themselves were never delivered to Romans at all. Instead, they are the stories Sages tell themselves—and their disciples—about their interaction with the wider

---

372 Translation from *Midrash Rabbah, Genesis II*, 68:4, Rabbi Dr. H. Freedman, Tr., (London and Bournemouth: Soncino Press), 1951, 617–618, with minor changes by the authors. The same may be said of certain traditions of Rabbis encountering Christians, Epicureans, Generals, Gnostics, Idolators, Philosophers, Roman Emperors, and Samaritans. See the encounter between Rabbi Gamaliel and a Philosopher in *Genesis Rabbah* 1:9; Rabbi Me'ir and a Samaritan in *Genesis Rabbah* 4:4; Judah the Prince and Antoninus in *Genesis Rabbah* 11:4 as examples of such encounters.

world. While the stories depict a cosmopolitan community, the audience is clearly, exclusively, committed Jews.

Conversely, it seems as if the Matrona—or at least that kind of person, either a Jew not rabbinically trained or a non-Jew unconvinced of Jewish wisdom—is not the foil of, but rather the audience for, Medieval Midrash. Many of the stories we encountered in the Solomon tradition would entertain a wide audience, Jew and non-Jew alike. The only people perhaps not delighted by such tales would be the scholarly Rabbi class of the House of Study: these often lurid, barely moral tales are a far cry from the halakhic and theologic focus of the major Medieval seats of Jewish learning. Medieval Midrash does not seem aimed at a core audience of believing Jews who fully subscribe to the program of Talmud. These tales instead seem to seek a wider audience of Jew and non-Jew alike.

Medieval Midrash contains creative literature geared for wide cultural consumption. Classical Midrash incorporates Rabbis' reports to their disciples describing their dialogues with non-Jewish neighbors; in lieu of actual conversation, we discover a rabbinic framing of cross-cultural dialogue that affirms the worldview of the House of Study. It is clear that what we encounter in Medieval Midrash is not the internal reporting of how the scholarly class interacted with the wider world; more likely we read how the worldly class shared Jewish themes and characters with their cosmopolitan companions.

Of course, to ask who wrote Medieval Midrash in general is more difficult to answer than even who authored a particular piece of this textual tradition. While certainty on this matter is elusive, we do seem to find sure footing in asserting that the creators of this canon were, in the main, Jews of or influenced by the cosmopolitan mercantile class. Likewise, while contemporary literary theory has taught of the futility of attempting to ferret out authorial intent,[373] we nonetheless can deduce a few potential reasons that spurred the establishment of Medieval Midrash. The first of these, it seems, is the desire to assert cultural hegemony over powerful stories: tales of the Jewish King Solomon belonged more properly to the Jewish community where he originated than to the Christian and Muslim cultures that appropriated him as their own; thus the best stories of Solomon from every culture were re-framed as Jewish tales. Secondly, Jews wanted to participate in the flourishing Medieval culture of the narrative arts: Just as Maimonides wanted to create Jewish theology in the footsteps of Averroes and other contemporary philosophers, so too did the anonymous creators of our Medieval Midrash want to fashion elaborate

---

373   See, notably, Hix, H.L., *Morte d'Author: An Autopsy*, (Philadelphia: Temple University Press) 1990.

epics along the lines of *Arabian Nights* and other powerful pieces of storytelling. Lastly, it does seem as if the Jewish community of the Middle Ages took rightful pride in their inherited masterworks, the *Tanakh* and the Talmudic literature. In sharing the stories that dominated their own cultural milieu, they wanted to incorporate the best of their Jewish literary past in fashioning their literature of their present day.

Pride in Jewish literature, the drive to create contemporary works of meaning, and the desire to cast shared stories in a Jewish light are but three of many suppositions we could make about *why* Medieval Midrash emerged as a new field of literary endeavor. Inasmuch as we can never know precisely *who* authored these texts, so too can we never truly encounter the reasons for their creation. However, the tales themselves do provide enough evidence for us to make some reasonable, initial speculations about the most opaque origins of this material. We happily leave the conversation to future scholars to continue.

Solomon the Wise: Answering Continuing Questions

We do not hope that the study of Medieval Midrash ends here. In fact, our hope is precisely the opposite: that this initial foray into understanding these remarkable texts will spur future interest and scholarship, whether it agrees with our premises or seeks to disprove our conclusions. The beginnings of this book were borne of the frustration of not being able to find answers to even the most basic questions about the inspiring material found within the pages of *Beit HaMidrasch* and *Oẓar Midrashim*. While we stand by our work, we are fully aware that our answers are provisional, and hope that subsequent generations continue the search to improve our knowledge of Medieval Midrashim.

In addition to continued academic endeavor, the entire field of Medieval Midrash could be overturned from other directions. We could discover another genizah, another great cache of knowledge on a parallel with the trove discovered in recent centuries in Cairo. Intrepid visitors to remote libraries could uncover more texts that would not only widen the canon of Medieval Midrash, but expand our knowledge of genre as well. Scientific dating could reveal key secrets from important manuscripts kept in Cambridge, Oxford, or Hamburg. Other unforeseen details could emerge. We hope they will. Just as medieval Jews used the figure of Solomon to spread enlightenment in their day, so too do we hope that these Medieval Midrashim about Solomon inspire a new generation to bring more information about the remarkable field of Medieval Midrash to light.

Appendix A: "The Throne and Hippodrome of King Solomon"

Perets ben Baruch Asher Perles, Breslau, 1872

Translated from the German by Dr. Gabriel E. Padawer

Prelude

The following is a translation of Perles' introduction to his printing of the Munich manuscript of the titular Midrash, originally written in German. We include the introduction, as well as a few salient footnotes from his critical commentary, as full background
to the Byzantine underpinnings of The Throne and Hippodrome of King Solomon.

"The Throne and Hippodrome of King Solomon"

The throne of Solomon has become the subject of various legendary descriptions and
interpretations: in *Targum Sheni* and Midrash to the Book of Esther, dispersed in the
remaining Midrashim in a comprehensive description in various works as in the Image
of the Throne of King Solomon: i.e., Gabirol's *Choice of Pearls*. ed. Venice 1546, Israel
Isserlein', *Commentaries*, ed. Riva, 1562, The *Kol Bo*, (paragraph 119) edited and copied again in Jellinek's, *Beit haMidrasch* II, pp. 83–86. The Hebrew Codex 22 contains
a description (in folio 50a-56b) of Solomon's Throne, which repeats with a few more
or less significant variations the beginning of the text in *Targum Sheni* to Esther 1,2.
(The Staatsbibliothek in Munich contains a collection of various midrash-like pieces).
However, the Codex presents a self-contained description that is better known in its
characteristics and elaborations and at its end mentions a description of Solomon's
Hippodrome. That description is highly interesting for the history of the Midrash. It
is sufficiently known that the legendary elaboration of Solomon's Throne appears
again in Oriental and Byzantian authors, (see, Sachs, *Beiträge* I, 70–74), however, it
is difficult to determine whether these foreign descriptions are derived from Jewish
sources or the reverse. Concerning the Hippodrome, that is legendarily associated with
Solomon there can be no doubt about the derivation of the story. The Talmud is well-
known to be adamantly against the Visit to the Stadium and Hippodrome (Mishnah
Avodah Zara 1:7; Tosefta *Avoda Zara* II; . . . y. *Avoda Zara* I. "One who sits in a stadium
is a murderer (spiller of blood). God of the world, when He sees that the Theatre and
the Hippodrome flourish while the Temple lies in ruins (citation from y. *Berachot* IX

© KONINKLIJKE BRILL NV, LEIDEN, 2017 | DOI 10.1163/9789004331334_014

halacha 3; *Exodus Rabbah*. The Aggadist who attributes a hippodrome to Solomon in order to glorify him took his motif not from Jewish sources[374] but formed the view based on the surrounding governing system. Public games are necessarily associated with the court of a powerful ruler. This circumstance already indicates that the Aggadist lived in Byzantine surroundings and based his stories on Byzantine sources. This is reinforced by the phrasing of his description leading to the evidence that he emulated the style of a prototype and seemingly relocated the famous Hippodrome in Constantinople and its appurtenances to Jerusalem in the time of Solomon, making a daring leap over countries and centuries.

Let us compare the detail given in our midrash, *'Arba'a Dimotiot ha'you b'apridomin shel melech*, in the king's hippodrome there were four "*dimotiot*". The latter word should be read as "*dimosiot*" and these are the well-known, four factions or "*demoi*" of the charioteers of the circus. Byzantine writers could not tell enough about the wild carryings on of these charioteers.

> Rabbi Yose said: There were four factions: The kings and his servants, the wise and their disciples, the Priests and Levites who were dressed in sky blue (*techelet*) and all the remaining Israelites wearing white, the spectators streaming from the towns and villages, wearing red, and the heathens coming from distant lands to bring tribute and presents to the king wore green clothing.[375] The four factions of the circus were named after the four colors of the clothing worn by the charioteers, The Blues, (*Veneti, benetoi, xuaneoi*), The Whites (*albati*), The Reds (*russati*), and The Greens (*prasini*).

The pupils of Rabbi Yosi asked him, "Why these four colors of clothing?" He replied, "Corresponding to the four seasons. From Tishri to Tevet (Autumn), the days appear to be blue from Tevet until Nisan (Winter) snow falls, therefore, they dress themselves in white. From Nisan until Tammuz (Spring) the period is favorable for sea-faring, therefore, they dress themselves in green; From Tammuz until Tishri the fruit is red and ripe. So they dress themselves in red garments. These interpretations are so much in the spirit of the Aggada that it is unlikely that anyone would think that they were derived from foreign circles. Nevertheless, a close pursuit of the sources indicates that the decidedly late Jewish midrash is entirely derived from much older Byzantine interpretation. From very early times, the circus, with its appurtenances, the number

---

374   You might conceivably think of I Kings 5:6–8; II Chronicles 9. However, the Jews themselves went along with the lifestyle of the hippodrome despite the fact that they suffered under the partisanship of the factions. Malalas specifically recalls Jewish charioteers in the circus (see Graetz, *Hist. of the Jews*, v., 23,25).

375   The Hebrew text is shown later [in the printing of the manuscript].

of races and the finish-lines, the colors worn by the charioteers, etc., were the subject of symbolic interpretation. The statesman Cassiodorus who lived in the courts of Odoaker and Theodoric (end of 5th beginning 6th CE) provided a complete symbolic (meaning) of the circus:

> The circus represents the change of the seasons[376] the revolution of the sun and the moon and the resulting partition of time into months weeks and days. (Cassiodorus' explanation was contained in his *Collected Correspondence* that was highly valuable for the history of his period- *Variae Epistolae* III, 51).

The four colors of the factions represent the four seasons.; the Green the blossoming spring, the Blue the cloud covered winter sky, the Red the fiery summer, and the White the rime-coated autumn. Twelve indicators and the seven goalposts correspond to the twelve months and the seven days of the week. The twenty-four laps of six chariots [correspond to] the twenty-four hours of the day and night. The two-and four-in-hand chariots are allegories for the circuit of the months and the sun. The chariot wheels indicate the boundaries of orient and occident, the moat surrounding the circus (*Euripus*) is an image for the current of the ocean, and the towering obelisks point to the heaven. So it came about that the mysteries of nature were represented in the many-colored variety of the games. To describe all the details of the Roman circus, which can be completely related back to specific origins would be an arduous task.

According to an excerpt from a handwritten Greek collected history as related by Nicolaus Alemannus in his notes to *Procopius Historia Arcana* c. VII (P. 333 of the Orelli edition) the colors of the circus are symbolized in the following way:

> Oenomaus was the first to mention the colors of the circus which he represented the battle of the earth and the sea. Lots were drawn. He who drew the lot to play the role of earth in this battle put on a green clothes, the one representing the sea, however, wore blue garments. Oenomaus staged this battle on the 24th of March (the time of the spring equinox). When the green color won everyone hoped for the fertility of the earth; but when the blue won all hoped for a trouble free sea voyage, hence landlubbers wished for a victory of the greens, the sailors, the blues.

According to others, the blue color was dedicated to the sky and the sea (Winter), green stood for the earth and the flowers (spring), red for fire and Mars (Summer), and white for autumn, see Orelli, ibid. In the *Chronography* of Joannes Mallalas (ed. Bonn,

---

376   Compare Corippus 1, 17 cited by Ducange Constantinopolis christiana, I., 102; Jpse ingens *Circus*, plenus seu circulus anni.

p. 173–176) discusses the matter in greater detail: It was Romulus who introduced the circus games to honor the sun and the four elements; earth, water (sea), fire, and air. Oenomaus, king of Pisa, staged a race on the 25th of March to represent the battle between the earth and the sea. Oenomaus and his opponent drew lots [to determine] for which of them they would fight. The one representing the sea wore a blue garment corresponding to the blue color of the ocean, his antagonist a green garment. The sailors and the island dwellers prayed for the victory of the blue color fearing poor fish catches, storms, and shipwrecks in the case of defeat. In contrast, the land dwellers wished victory for the green color to be freed from poor harvest and famine. . . . The circus was built in the form of the universe and intended to represent heaven, earth, and sea. The twelve gates represent the twelve signs of the zodiac, which determine the earth, the sea, and the course of human life (*ton parodikon tou biou dromon*), compare below the Midrash to Psalm 16: 11, *You make me know the path of life*; the surface in the circus intended for the race (*plema*, area) is metaphoric for the earth, the moat (*Euripus*) for the sea, turning poles on both ends for the orient and the occident, the seven [perhaps, *lanes*, German obscure] for the circuit of the heavenly bodies, and the four-in-hand for the four elements, which are also indicated by the four colors of the factions: the earth by the green, the sea by the blue, fire by the red, and air by the white color. The white faction is associated with the green because air moistens and encompasses the earth while the red is associated with blue because water quenches fire. Compare also *Bulengerus de Circo* 37b from *Corippus* 1. 1. Justin.

According to these citations there can be no doubt that the later Aggadist did not independently create the interpretation of the circus but borrowed them from Byzantian legends.

According to our Midrash, Solomon staged twelve races every year presided over by one of the twelve state officials named in 1 Kings 4:19. The racecourse measured three square parsangs in length and one parsang in width exactly like the Circus Maximus [which was] three stadia long and one wide. (Plin. *Hist. Nat.* l. 36, Jul. Caes. *Bulengeri de Circo Romano ludisque circensibus liber*, Paris, p. 14b). The circuit of the races from the barrier to the goal and back repeated eight times according to the Midrash, but seven times according to Graeco-Roman reports. The races were held in the month of Tevet. The Byzantine sources concerning the timing of the races are divided. According to the notice related above they were held on the 24th of March. According to another version cited by Ducange Constantinopolis Cristiana 1., 102 they were performed on the founding day of Constantinople, the 11th of May. However, Benjamin of Tudela who expressed several words of wonder about the Hippodrome in Constantinople, averred explicitly that the races were held annually at Christmas, thus in agreement with the month of Tevet per the Midrash.[377]

---

377   The specific ordinance of the Theodosian Codex xv, Title v (de spectacculis, 425 CE) forbidding circus races on Sunday, Christmas, Easter, and other major festivals of the church

Further details will be discussed in several places in the following midrash.

Selected Notes from Perles' Critical Commentary

from Page 15 of transcription of Munich MSS, note 2:

דייקסומין=δεξαμενηa cistern or a pond. In the Yelammdenu דכסמבי
shown in *Pesiqta d'Rav Kahana*, Breslau edition, p. 96.

דכסמבי—from which place did the cistern/pond flow. Spartiamus and
Lampridini report that the emperor Heliogabalus had the moats [*euripus*] of the
circus filled with wine and ordered the performance of races on them [*navales
Circenses*]. In the hippodrome of Constantinople there was a well, φιαλη, named
Phiala that had three iron snakes spouting water, wine, and milk from their open
maws. According to our Midrash, spices and fragrances streamed from the maws
of four gilded lions. *Targum Sheni* also reports "lions flowing spices". This appears
to be a switch with the four gilded horses in the hippodrome of Constantinople,
which Theodosian of Chios caused to be produced. These were later brought to
Venice where they still may be seen above the main gate to St. Mark's church.
Rabbinic literature states in several places that flowing wine and oil was provided for the people during festive occasions; Tosefta *Shabbat* 7; b. *Berachot* 50b;
Semahot, Chapter 8; *Pesiqta Rabbati*, Chapter 37.

---

were disregarded in later times (Latin citation). Of particular interest in the above-cited
passage is that whosoever attends these public games on the forbidden holidays ... (Latin
citation concludes this fragmentary German sentences). Gothofredus concludes from this
passage that the performance of the games on Christian holidays is forbidden not only
for Christians but also for Jews and Pagans. It appears to me, however, a better interpretation is that it is a rhetorical turn of the phrase, meaning that Christians who are guilty
of such a profanation of the holidays, revert back to Judaism or to Paganism.—Libanius
(4th Century CE) *de Kalendis Januarii* avers emphatically that races were held in the circus on the third of January, that is in agreement with the month of Tevet in our midrash.
On the third of January the circus chariots were hitched to their horses, a great contest
for victory was held, and much activity occurred in the circus. Similarly, Constantine's
old calendar records the 3rd, 4th, and 5th of January to be race-days; [Latin citation]
[Gotofredus', comment to the Theodosian Code, XV, Title X, *de equis curulibus* 1]. This
agrees with ours Midrash, which reports the schedule of the circus games: End or the
beginning of the month and the second and third day of the month.
Hebrew: On what days did they hold the Hippodrome? Rabbi Ze'ara said, "At the end of
the month." Rabbi Yosi said: "On the first day (בראש) of the month." Abaye said: "On the
second of the month." Rabbi Yohannan said: "On the third of the month."

What does the Holy One of Blessing do for the Mashiach? He makes seven *hupot* of precious stones and pearls and each and (from) every *huppa* flows (literally draws) from its midst four streams of wine and of honey and of milk, and of pure persimmon.

from Page 16 of transcription of Munich MSS, note 1:

The two words לפרות and פרות obscure, probably corrupted. The image is clear: in the life to come, balsam and other aromas will stream for the pious as from a rapidly flowing brook. Compare *Vayiqra Rabba*, chapter 31:
The orb of the sun never sets until it resembles a stream of blood.

from Page 16 of transcription of Munich MSS, note 2:

Probably טרמי should be read: בימי or בומי/βημα. What is described here is the *gradus factionum* of which the δημοι, (that is) the supporters of the contenders and the Cancelli on which the spectators sat. Perhaps טמי could also be a misspelling of טרמי and refers to the seven goal-posts (meta; τερμα).

from Page 17 of transcription of Munich MSS, note 1:

The Midrash evidentially introduced characteristics of the famous palace of Blachernas in Constantinople, which was described by Benjamin of Tudela [Born Navarre 1130, died Castille 1173; set out on his famous travels sometime between 1159–1163 and returned in 1172] as the preeminent wonder next to the Hippodrome; Ducange Constantinople Christ. 131, [writing at the same time as Benjamin of Tudela] cites a contemporary chronicle which similarly describes this palace.

from Page 17 of transcription of Munich MSS, note 2:

See above. A different kind of color symbolism is given in the Midrash to Zechariah 6:1ff; where Chrystosmos in his talk about the circus similarly makes its connection to the Circus Games. He challenges his listeners not to board the chariot of the circus but instead the chariot guided by Elijah [II Kings 2:11] and to hitch up the myriads of God's carriages of the psalmists [Psalm 68:18] in the battle against the contrariness of life—I will take the opportunity to talk about a few places in the Talmud and Midrash on which a knowledge of the activities in the circus shed clearer light. This analogy is derived from the racecourse: *Lifne riqqud lifne 'asah k'dimos hevei mequddeset.*

Rashi reads, כדימוס which he interprets as *binyan*-buildings. This reading and explanation does not make good sense. [The] *Aruk* preserves כדרומוס the preferred reading contained in the preceding, *shchon lifne riqqud lifne* which thereby gains a coherent reading: the man will offer marriage to the woman if she will play (an instrument) dance, or have a foot-race with him as in the circus (δρομος). In any case Rashi's way of reading כדימוס could be retained if one takes דימוס as, δημοι, as factions of the circus: (play an instrument), dance before me, and do as Demen used to do. It is well-known that women participated in the races. The passion for the circus games was so great that even Vestal Virgins attended.

A frequently discussed but still not sufficiently elucidated passage is found in *Midrash to Psalms*, Psalm 16.

The passage appears abbreviated and with several variation in the *Pesiqta Rabbati*, ed. Buber 180a, *Vayiqra Rabba*, chapter 30, *Tanhuma Emor* and *Yalqut* Psalm 16. Boehmer in (*Keren Chemed*, VII, 29) and Sachs (Commentary II, 152) have shown correctly that... should be read as: two הנדיוסין, and whoever reaches the goal and is awarded the palm (βαιον) is the victor. That allegory is derived from the race course and, although the etymology of this Hebrew word, הנדיוסין is not yet fully explained, its meaning refers to the persons that have connection to the circus. So far, all attempts to construe the meaning of that word, for example: derived from, הנדסה, the art of mensuration; or the persons who measure the race course, εν δηιοισι; or men who live in enmity (de Lara), or derived from the Greek ενδρομεω, have resulted in failure. I have removed every difficulty by emending the הנדיוסין to הנכיוסין. Although סאכיוסין is not found otherwise in Rabbinic Literature, it is a vernacular in the Syriac as הניכוסא that is ηνιοχος , the charioteer of the circus. The way of life (ארח-חיים Psalm 16:11) is compared with a race course (see above, a similar conception of Malalas). In the interval between new year's day, which is the judgment day of the world and the Day of Atonement, there will be a race between Israel and the other people to be the first to attain the goal of coming close to God. They are represented by two charioteers that race in the circus and one of whom will take home the palm. On the Day of Atonement the Israelites put on white garments as a sign of the cleansing of sin, but an allusion to the colors of the circus. The Israelites are the Whites, form the faction of the Whites. But soon they appear with the lulav the palm, in the house of God on the festival of Sukkot. Thus they demonstrate that they are the victors in the contest and carry the sign of their victory towers in their hands. (-בימינך-נצח).

Concerning בית-ריסא, in Persian acp-ris, (race course) see my *Etymological Studies*, p. 56.—Yet another word for charioteer, besides הנביוסין = הנריוסין has been misunderstood in Rabbinic Literature. That word is אקטור, in *Mekhilta* and *Targum Yerushalmi* to Exodus 14:5: אקטורין agitators, the charioteers told Pharaoh that the Israelites have fled. The most common name for the charioteer in the circus, besides *auriga, agitator,* often appearing *Cod. Theodos. De Scenicis,* compare *Duchange glossary mediae Latin. Agitator.*—The circus has had various descriptors . There was καμπος, *flexus* (See, *Bulengerus de Circo,* p.11b), *Hesychius:* καμπος ιπποδρομος Σιχελοις. That word also appears several times in the Mishnah and the Midrashim: *Kelim* 23:2, *Kelim* 24:1, "the king ordered that to punish someone he must race in the circus," *Vayiqra Rabbah,* chapter 31; *Deuteronomy Rabbah,* chapter 2; *Pesiqta Rabbati* chapter 21, ed. Breslau, p. 48b (and also compare *Pesiqta,* Bamberg 82b, note 52).

According to the Midrash *Vayqra Rabba,* chapter 19, *Yalqut* II Kings: 24 linked to Ezekiel 19:9, Nebuchadnezzar took king Jehoiakim with him through all the cities of Palestine in a triumphal march and made him take part in chariot races in the hippodrome and in the public animal bating. Commentators misunderstood the word פרדימוס thinking it meant Latin *prodomus* (Musafia) or even a donkey made of wood and that was the interpretation of (*Math-Kehunna*). According to Buxtorf it is a *vox peregrine, cujus origo adhuc quaerenda.* The Munich manuscript of *Vayiqra Rabba* (Codex Hebrew 117) read ברדימוס and ברידימוס. It should be read as פדרומוס, which is hippodrome. This emendation is confirmed by the passage in the *Yalqut,* which repeats twice that Nebuchadnezzar sat in the racecourses of Antioch. Such an emendation is fitting in its context and is self-explanatory.

Appendix B: "Shall the Jewish Middle Man be Spared?"

Vladimir Jabotinsky, July 18, 1930
The Canadian Jewish Chronicle, front page

Editor's Preface

The noted Zionist poet, linguist and traveller discussed the fate of the Jewish middleman and defends him as an important factor in our economic life without whom we would be poorer. Mr. Jabotinsky skillfully shows what the world would be without the middleman, who is so often a Jew.

"Shall The Jewish Middle Man Be Spared?"

They want to bury him—the trader. Not only factually—which I, his fanatical adherent, can still excuse on economic grounds—but also morally. Why do people make an ideology of every simple thing? One can say in very short and convincing terms: Since a healthy economic organism cannot stand more than ten or twelve per cent of traders, one should find for the Jews other means of earning a living. But this is not sufficient—for apparently this alone does not yet stir the necessary enthusiasm. To create enthusiasm, especially among us Jews—that is, among the sons and grandsons of generations of tradesmen—one must besides construct ideologic "reasons". This is naturally not difficult, on the contrary, it is very easy. Anyone who has ever read in a book or in a newspaper on the subject, can declaim the poem by heart: The tradesman is unproductive; he is a middleman who robs both the producer and the consumer; a parasite, a superfluous social figure who has played no creative part in world history—in short, he is "trefe" from every standpoint.

This is a bad, dangerous and stupid ideology. It is bad because we Jews have already been a nation of traders—until fifty years ago this was our chief characteristic in world economy, and it does not sound right when we ourselves condemn our old mold of activity. It is dangerous because a Jew is an impressionist and takes all this very seriously, especially the young modern and educated Jew: He begins to be ashamed of his father's business, even when it goes very well (that is, when life shows that this trader at least is not "superfluous"), and the end is that intelligent forces which are needed in trade are not utilized, and we lose important economic positions.

© KONINKLIJKE BRILL NV, LEIDEN, 2017 | DOI 10.1163/9789004331334_015

It is difficult to take one or another branch of human activity and to say: This is the most important machine which brings to life all other forms of culture. Collective life is very complicated and decentralized—a real analogy between it and a true organism—like the human body, where centre is the heart—cannot be found. If you separate one factor from the whole complexity and say: This is the heart, the foot, and all other things are branches of creativeness and activity which stem from this, such a statement then has only a rhetoric value. But even if we should adopt this theory, then it is really trade which promotes all branches of creativeness, which fulfills the role of a motor or of a heart more than all the other factors.

Here the fact that only a small percentage of people can make a living from trade, not more than a tenth of those who can make a living from agriculture and industry, is unimportant. A heart too is small, certainly not even one-tenth the size of the human body. The main thing is not the size, but the role. Here we have first trade in all its phases and then "production" in its various forms. Which of the two conditions and determines the other—which is the father and which is the child? The answer lies in the very question. A beginning, a minimum, of production must, quite independently of trade, be present, even on Robinson Crusoe's island, for the great reason which Mendele Moicher Sforim calls "the habit of eating". But even the smallest progress in production, from that moment when man brought with him from the chase more skins than he needed for himself or his family, or cultivated more land than he needed for his maintenance—this first development of production only had a value because the man simultaneously discovered the art of exchange.

We all know that. But we seldom think of the role which the trader plays in our lives and how we would look without him.

In an English primer for school children one can find statistics giving the number of countries that had to be called upon to prepare the breakfast of the child. Nearly twenty countries of the five continents of the world. Other children, Jewish, for example, are perhaps not as well catered to at their breakfasts, but in a geographic sense the difference is not so great. Coffee comes from Brazil, tea from Ceylon or China, bread perhaps from the Argentine, and so on. The poorest among us wears clothing and shoes, which are produced in from ten to twelve countries. While a man spends an ordinary day of his life in France, he washes with soap, cleans his teeth with a tooth brush and paste, writes a letter with a steel pen, which he dips in ink, on a sheet of paper, smokes a cigarette, incidentally lighting a match, rides on an autobus (or the autobus rides over him and crushes him with its tires), in short, during a normal day he has made use of nature and of human effort throughout the world. And the house in which we live, the floor upon which we walk, this is very Parisian air which I breathe, and which is filled with gasoline smells and cool smoke—for all this we have to thank the trader, who has converted this globe into a small place. Should we abolish him, Paris, London, and New York would become villages and everything that we call culture would vanish as dust.

It is not a reciprocal influence. One should not say that the growth of production stimulates the development of trade in the same manner as trade stimulates production. One cannot compare it. Naturally if a Paris fashionable tailor is creating a new style, the ready-made clothes shop will have something more to sell. But this is a small matter in comparison with the fact that the whole origin and the whole development of production (taking out of consideration the patriarchal family life of the time of the Biblical flood) is from beginning to end the result of the work of the trader. Since without him no factory would be able to obtain the machines needed and raw materials which it needs to produce the first pair of shoes. And without traders there would in general be no possibility of existence for any factory, for any institution, which works for a world of merchants.

And not only material culture is a child of trade: Spiritual culture, too, with the exception perhaps of religion, was brought about and developed only by it. What would have happened to astronomy (to say nothing of geography), if the merchant would not have been forced to study the path of the stars, in order to find for his ships the right pathway to cross the ocean? Who gave Columbus money for his expedition, and why? For whom have all chemists, mechanics and mathematicians worked? Even for pure poetry I make no absolute exception. Shortly before the war there appeared in Europe a book by Leon Berar, "The Semitic Origin of Homer's Odyssey." The writer shows that this immortal poem, the beginning and the foundations of epic world poetry, consists entirely of travel impressions and adventures of Phoenician seamen and pirates and is built upon that: Again merchants! As to the Iliad, we have known long ago that the whole fight between the Greeks and the Trojans was only the final act of a long conflict between two trading peoples, which expressed itself historically in the destruction of the ancient Gretan culture, whose last colonial stronghold was Troy. The real reason for the Trojan war was not the beautiful Helen, but the fact that Troy at that time played the same geographic role which the Dardanelles play today, and that it didn't allow the merchant fleet of the Greeks to enter the granaries of the Black Sea.

One should be proud of such a historic mission and not ashamed! Unproductive? Columbus accomplished more for production than all the peasants and manual laborers of his generation put together; and he was himself a merchant, and merchants sent him out for trade purposes. There is a stupid nearsightedness in this feeling of shame of the modern Jew when he is reminded that we were and are a trading people.

Historically the trader is the true fighter for progress, the first among those who bear the banner of civilization. If what is said is true, namely, that the first and greatest of all merchants was a Jew and that we still play this role today, then we should not renounce this honor. Since even the smallest village tradesman, even if he only peddles with stockings, is part of this nobility, is a member of a class whose historic achievements and whose role in the present-day world is at least equal to, if not greater than, that of the agriculturist and factory worker. People used to call medicine and law "intelligent professions" in contradistinction to trade. I do not wish here to insult anyone—don't I myself belong to such an "intelligent profession"? But it is very questionable which of the two require more thinking, which one of the two gives an intelligent man more opportunities for creative activity.

That we Jews have too many tradesman, for whom there has for a long time not been enough place in the world economy; that it would be a good and healthy thing to increase if possible the number of Jewish land and factory workers; that in Palestine we do not need more than ten per cent of traders—all this is true and indisputable. But the anti-commercial ideology, which especially for us Jews is something like a slap in the face, appears to me as a stupid and superfluous accompanying phenomenon. By the grace of God we are descended not only of a people of law-givers, prophets and conquerors, but during the past two thousand years also from a people of merchants. Today we are seeking new and wider paths for our national activities, but that doesn't mean that we must shut up our trading stalls. To do this would mean to evacuate a position. Careful!

Bibliography

Primary Sources: Biblical and Rabbinic Periods

JPS Hebrew English Tanakh, (The Traditional Hebrew Text and the New JPS Translation), second edition, (Philadelphia: Jewish Publication Society), 2003.

Braude, William G. and, Israel J. Kapstein, trs., *Pesikta de-Rav Kahana*, (Philadelphia: JPS), 1975.

Buber, Solomon, ed., *Midrash Mishle,* (Vilna: Wittwe et Gebrüder Romm), 1893.

Buber, Solomon, ed., *Midrash Tanḥuma,* 2 volumes, (New York: Hotza'at Sefer), 1946.

Buber, Shelomo, ed., *Midrash 'Aicha Rabba,* (Vilna: The Widow Rom and Sons), 1898.

Friedman, H., Rabbi Dr. and Maurice Simon, *The Soncino Midrash,* (London: The Soncino Press), 1961, 10 volumes.

Grossfeld, Bernard, *The Aramaic Bible: The Two Targums of Esther,* (Collegeville, MN: The Liturgical Press), 1991.

Ish-Shalom, Meir, ed., *Midrash Pesiqta Rabbati,* (Vilna: Kaiser), 1900.

Kittel, Rudolph, ed., *Biblia Hebraica,* (Stuttgart: Württembergische Bibelanstalt Stuttgart), 1937.

Mandelbaum, Bernard, ed., *Pesikta De-Rav Kahana,* (New York: Jewish Theological Seminary of America), 1962, 2 volumes.

Margulies, M., *Midrash Wayyikra Rabba,* (Jerusalem: Wahrman Books), 1953–60, 3 volumes.

Midrash Rabba, (Traditional Text), (Vilna: Romm), 1899, 2 folio volumes.

Shinan, Avigdor, ed., *Midrash Shemot Rabbah,* Par. 1–14, (Tel Aviv/Jerusalem), Dvir Publishing House), 1984.

Talmud Bavli, (Traditional Text), (Vilna: Romm), 1870s–1890s, 37 folio volumes.

Talmud Yerushalmi, (Traditional Text), (New York: The Palak Brothers), 1959.

Theodor, Juda and Chanokh Albeck, eds. *Bereshit Rabba,* (Jerusalem: Wahrmann Books), 1965, 3 volumes.

Visotsky, Burton, L., *The Midrash on Proverbs,* (New Haven and London: Yale University Press), 1992.

Visotsky, Burton, L., ed., *Midrash Mishle Critical Edition Based on Vatican Mss. Ebr. 44,* (New York: The Jewish Theological Seminary of America), 1990.

Primary Sources: Medieval Period

Bacharach, Naftali Hertz ben Yaaqov Elḥanan, *Emeq HaMelech,* (Amsterdam), 1648.

Brinner, William M., *Introduction and Translation, Ibn Shahin, Nissim ben Jacob, An Elegant Composition Concerning Relief and Adversity,* (New Haven and London: Yale University Press), 1977.

Buber, Salomon, ed., *Sammlung agadischer Commentare zum Buche Ester*, (Vilna: Wittwe et Gebrüder Romm), 1886.

Buber, Solomon, ed., *Aggadat Bereshit*, (Krakow: Fischer), 1903.

Buber, Solomon, ed., *Leqah Tov*, (Jerusalem: H. Vagshal), 1986.

Buber, Solomon, ed., *Midrash Shemuel*, (Krakow: Fischer), 1893.

Buber, Solomon ed., *Midrash Tehillim*, (New York, Om Publishing Co.), 1947.

Chomsky, William, ed., *Sefer HaShorashim Shel Radaq*, (Philadelphia: Dropsie College), 1933.

Davidson, Israel, tr., *Sefer Sha'ashu'im of Rabbi Joseph ben Me'ir Zabara*, (Berlin: Eshkol Publishers), 1925.

Derenbourg, Joseph, *Deux Versions Hebraique du livre de Kalilah et Dimnah*, (Paris: F. Vieweg, Librarire-Editeur), 1881.

Dishon, Judith, *The Book of Delight*, (Jerusalem, Reuben Maas, LTD.), 1985

Eisenstein, Julius, D., *Ozar Midrashim: A Library of Two Hundred Minor Midrashim*, (Eisenstein: New York), 1915.

Finkel, Avraham Yaakov, tr., *Sefer Hasidim*, Yehudah HeHaisid, (New Jersey: Aaronson), 1997.

Fisch, S., ed., *Midrash ha-Gadol, Devarim*, (Jerusalem: Mosad ha-Rav Kook), 1972.

Gaster, Moses, *The Exempla of the Rabbis*, (K'tav: New York), 1924.

Goldschmidt, Lazarus, ed., *Sepher haJaschar*, (Berlin: Rosenthal and Co.), 1923.

Grünhut, Eleazar, *Sammlung alterer Midraschim u. wissenschaftlicher Abhandlungen*, 6 fascicles, Jerusalem, 1898–1903.

Horowitz, Chaim M., *Bibliotheca Haggadica*, 2 fascicles, (Berlin: Slobotski Publishing House), 1881.

Horowitz, Chaim M., *Sammlung zehn kleiner, nach Zahlen geordneter Midraschim*, (Frankfurt am Main: Slobotski Publishing House), 1888.

Horowitz, Chaim M., *Sammlung Kleiner Midraschim*, I, (Berlin: Druck von Itzkowski), 1881.

Jellinek, Adolph, *Sammlung Kleiner Midraschim u. vermischter Abhandlungen aus der älteren jüdischen Literatur, Nach Handschriften u. Drückwerken gesammelt u. nebst Einleitungen herausgegeben, I–IV*, Leipzig, 1853–57; V, VI, Vienna, 1872, 1877.

Kohut, Alexander, ed., *Sefer 'Aruch haShalem*, (Vienna: Abraham Fanama Publisher), 1890.

Wertheimer, S. A., *Kleinere Midraschim*, (Jerusalem), 4 fascicles, (to) 1897.

Wertheimer, S. A., *Leket Midrashim*, (Jerusalem), 1903.

Wertheimer, S. A., *Ozar Midrashim*, 2 fascicles, Jerusalem 1913, 14.

General Bibliography: Books

Abrahams, Israel, *The Book of Delight and Other Papers*, (Philadelphia: The Jewish Publication Society of America), 1912.

Abrahams, Israel., *Hebrew Ethical Wills*, (Philadelphia: Jewish Publication Society), 1926.

Bamberger, Bernard, J., *Fallen Angels*, (Philadelphia: Jewish Publication Society of America,) 5712–1952.

Ben-Amos, Daniel, *Folktales of the Jews*, (Philadelphia: Jewish Publication Society of America), 2006, 3 volumes.

Ben-Sasson, H. H., ed. "The Middle Ages," in *A History of the Jewish People*, (Cambridge: Harvard University Press), 1976.

Ben Yehuda, Eliezer, *A Complete Dictionary of Ancient and Modern Hebrew*, (New York and London: Thomas Yoseloff), 1960, 17 volumes.

Bockelmann, C., *The Encyclopaedia of Islam*, New Edition, E. van Donzel, B. Levis, and Pellat, Ch., eds. (Leiden: E.J. Brill), 1978.

Bonfils, Robert, *Tra due mondi, cultura ebraica e cultura cristiana nel medioevo*, (Naples: Ligouri), 1996.

Bouston, Ra'anan, "Israelite Kingship, Christian Rome, and the Jewish Imperial Imagination: Midrashic Precursors to the Medieval 'Throne of Solomon,'" in *Jews, Christians, and the Roman Empire: The Poetics of Power in Late Antiquity*, (Philadelphia: University of Pennsylvania Press), 2013.

Bowman, Steven, *The Jews of Byzantium 1204–1453*, (Tuscaloosa: University of Alabama Press), 1985.

Boyarin, Daniel , *Carnal Israel: Reading Sex in Talmudic Culture*, (Berkeley: University of California), 1993.

Clouston, W. A., Popular Tales and Fictions, 2 vols., (London: Blackwood and Sons), 1887.

Dan, Joseph, *The Hebrew Story in the Middle Ages*, (Jerusalem: Keter Publishing House), 1974.

Dawood, N. J., tr., *The Koran*, Penguin Classics, (London: Clays LTD.), 2004.

Dohrmann, Natalie and Annette Yoshiko Reed, eds., *Jews, Christians, and the Roman Empire: The Poetics of Power in Late Antiquity*, (Philadelphia: University of Pennsylvania Press), 2013.

Dubnov, Simon, *A History of the Jews: 2, from the Roman Empire to the Early Medieval Period*, Moshe Spiegel, tr., (South Brunswick: Thomas Yoseloff), 1968.

Freidberg, Ch. B., and Baruch Freidberg, *Bet Eked Sefarim, Bibliographical Lexicon*, (Israel), 1951–1956.

Gibbon, Edward, *The History of the Decline and Fall of the Roman Empire*, with notes by Milman, Guizot, and Wenck, Smith, William, ed., (New York: Charles C. Bigelow & Co. Inc.), Vol. v, assumed date of publication 192?.

Gilbert, Martin, *In Ishmael's House: a History of Jews in Muslim Lands*, (New Haven: Yale University Press), 2010.

Ginzberg, Louis, *The Legends of the Jews*, (Philadelphia: The Jewish Publication Society of America), 1947, 7 volumes.

Halberthal, Moshe, *People of the Book: Canon, Meaning, and Authority*, (Cambridge: Harvard University Press), 1997.

Halberthal, Moshe, *Maimonides*, (Princeton: Princeton University Press), 2014.

Hameen-Antilla, Jaako, *Maqama: History of a Genre*, (Wiesbaden: Otto Harrassowitz Verlag), 2002.

Heiman, Aaron, Sefer *Torah Hakethuvah V'hamessorah* 'al Torah Nevi'im u'Chetuvim, (Jerusalem: D'vir), 1938, 3 volumes.

Herodotus, *The Histories*, (Oxford: Oxford University Press), 2008.

Hertel, Johannes, *The Panchatantra- Text of Purnabhadra-Critical Introduction and List of Variants*, (Cambridge, Massachusetts: Harvard University), 1912.

Hix, H. L., *Morte d'Author: An Autopsy*, (Philadelphia: Temple University Press), 1990.

Jacobs, Joseph, *Jewish Contributions to Civilization, An Estimate*, (Philadelphia: The Jewish Publication Society of America), 1919.

Jastrow, Marcus, *A Dictionary of the Targumim, The Talmud Bavli and Yerushalmi, and the Midrashic Literature*, (New York: Pardes Publishing House, Inc.), 1950.

Jung, Leo, *Fallen Angels in Jewish, Christian and Mohammedan Literature* [New York: K'tav Publishing Co. Inc.], 1926.

Krauss, Samuel, *Griechische und Lateinsche Lehnwörter im Talmud, Midrasch und Targum*, (Hildesheim: Georg Verlagsbuchhandlung), 1964, 2 volumes.

Lassner, Jacob, *Demonizing the Queen of Sheba*, (University of Chicago Press: Chicago), 1993.

Levy, David, *Neuhebräisches und caldäisches Wörterbuch über die Talmudim und Midraschim*, (Leipzig: Brockhaus), 1876–1889.

Lewis, Bernard, *The Jews of Islam*, (Princeton: Princeton University Press), 1984.

Marx, Alexander, *Essays in Jewish Biography*, (Philadelphia: Jewish Publication Society), 1947.

Mendes-Flohr, Paul, *The Jew in the Modern World: A Documentary History*, Second Edition, (New York: Oxford University Press), 1995.

Rosenthal, Shraga, *Ḥeleq haShe'alot v'haTeshuvot*, (Berlin: Zvi Hirsch Issakovski Press), 1898, New Edition, (Jerusalem), 1972.

Roth, Cecil and Geoffrey Wigoder, eds., *The Encyclopaedia Judaica*, (Jerusalem: Keter Publishing House), 1971–1972, 16 volumes.

Roth, Cecil, *The Jews of Italy*, (Philadelphia: Jewish Publication Society), 5706–1946.

Safrai, Shmuel, et al., eds., *The Literature of the Sages*, Second Part, (Minneapolis: Fortress Press), 2006.

Schwarzbaum, Haim, *Biblical and Extra-Biblical Legends in Islamic Folk-Literature*, (Vio: Waldorf-Hessen), 1982.

Sharf, Andrew, *Byzantine Jewry from Justinian to the Fourth Crusade*, (New York, Shocken Books, Inc.), 1971.

Shelley, Percy Bysshe, *Complete Poetical Works*, (Boston, New York: Houghton Mifflin), 1901.

Singer, Isidore, ed., *The Jewish Encyclopedia*, (New York and London: Funk and Wagnall Company), 1901–1906, 12 Volumes.

Sokoloff. Michael, *A Dictionary of Jewish Palestinian Aramaic of the Byzantine Period*, (Ramat Gan: Bar Ilan University Press), 1990.

Starr, Joshua, *The Jews in the Byzantine Empire 641–1204*, (Athens: Verlag der Byzantinisch-Neugrieschischen Jahrbücher), 1939.

Stern, David, and Mark Mirsky, *Rabbinic Fantasies*, (New Haven: Yale University Press), 1990.

Strack. Hermann L., *Introduction to the Talmud and the Midrash*, (Philadelphia: Jewish Publications Society), 1931.

Strack, Hermann L., and Stemberger, Günter, *Introduction to the Talmud and Midrash*, (Minneapolis: The Fortress Press), 1996, Second Edition.

Torijano, Pablo A., *Solomon the Esoteric King: From King to Magus, Development of a Tradition*, (Leiden: J. Brill), 2002.

Townsend, John T., "Minor Midrashim," in Berman, Lawrence, V., et. al., *Bibliographic Essays in Jewish Studies: The Study of Judaism, Vol. II*, (New York: Anti-Defamation League of B'nai Brith by KTAV Publishing Co. Inc.), 1976.

van der Toorn, Karel , Bob Becking, and Pieter W. van der Horst, *Dictionary of Deities and Demons in the Bible*, (Grand Rapids: Eerdemans), 1999.

van Donzel, E., B. Levis, and Ch. Pellat, eds. *The Encyclopaedia of Islam, New Edition* (Leiden: E.J. Brill), 1978.

Waxman, Meyer, A History of Jewish Literature, (New York: Thomas Yoseloff), 1960, 6 volumes.

Weinberger, Leon J., *Jewish Hymnography: a literary history*, (London: Vallentine Mitchell), 1998.

Yassif, Eli, *The Hebrew Folktale: History, Genre, Meaning*, Jacqeline S. Teitelbaum, tr., (Indianapolis: University of Indiana Press), 2009.

Ye'or, Bat, *The Dhimmi: Jews and Christians under Islam*, (Teaneck Fairleigh Dickinson University Press), 1985.

Zabara, Joseph ben Meir, Moses Hadas, tr., Merriam Sherwood, *Introduction, The Book of Delight by Joseph ben Meir Zabara*, (New York: Columbia University Press), 1932.

Zinberg, Israel, *The History of Jewish Literature, The Arabic Spanish Period*, Bernard Martin, tr., (Cleveland and London: The Press of Case Western Reserve University), 1972, Vol. 1.

Leopold, Zunz, *Etwas über die Rabbinische Literatur*, Gesammelte Schriften, (Berlin: Louis Goischel Verlagsbuchhandlung), 1875.

General Bibliography: Articles

De Lange, Nicholas, "Research on Byzantine Jewry: The State of the Question," in *Jewish Studies at the Central European University* IV, 2003–2005, Andras Kovacs and Miller, Michael L., eds., (Budapest), 2006, 41–51.

Drettas, G., and Arom, S., "A Journey through Romaniot Space," *Bulletin of Judaeo-Greek Studies* 27, (2000–2001), 30–33.

Elbogen, Isaac, "Destruction or Construction," *Hebrew Union College Annual* I, 1924.

Gerard, Brett, "Throne of Solomon," *Speculum*, 29:3 (1954), 477–487.

Jabotinsky, Vladimir, "Shall the Jewish Middle Man Be Spared?" *The Canadian Jewish Chronicle*, Montreal, July 18, 1930.

Perles, Perets ben Barukh Asher, *The Throne and Hippodrome of King Solomon*, in Monatsschrift für Geschichte und Wissenschaft des Judenthums (MGWJ), Breslau, 1872.

Schechter, Solomon, ed., "Midrash Ḥefez", *The Folk-Lore Journal*, 1890:1, (London: Whiting and Co.).

Soucek, Priscilla, "Solomon's Throne/Solomon's Bath: Model or Metaphor?," *Ars Orientalis*, 23, 1993,109–134.

Ta-Shma, Israel Moses, "The History and Cultural Relations between Byzantine and Ashkenazi Jewry," *Meah She'arim*, Ezra Fleischer, et al., eds., (Jerusalem: Magnes Press), 2001, 61–70.

Verstraete, Beert, "The Ring and the Fish: A Comparison of the Use of a Similar Folklore Motif in Herodotus and a Dutch-Frisian Folktale", *The Afriadian Journal of Netherlandic Studies*, 14–18.

Yasif, Eli, "The Hebrew Narrative Anthology in the Middle Ages," *Prooftexts*, 17, (1997), pp. 153–175.

Eli Yasif, "Meshalim shel Melech Shelomo," ("Parables of King Solomon"), *Jewish Studies in Hebrew Literature* (9), (1986) pp. 357–375.

Index

Printed in the United States
By Bookmasters